COMPUTER SCIENCE MADE SIMPLE

V. Anton Spraul

American College of Computer
and Information Sciences
Professor,
Director of Curriculum Development

Edited by
Roger E. Masse

Illustrations by Scott Nurkin

BOOKS

A Made Simple Book
Broadway Books
New York

Produced by The Philip Lief Group, Inc.

COMPUTER SCIENCE MADE SIMPLE

Copyright © 2005 by Broadway Books, a division of Random House, Inc.

Printed in the United States of America

Produced by The Philip Lief Group, Inc.
Managing Editors: Judy Linden, Jill Korot, Albry Montalbano.
Design: Annie Jeon.

Broadway Books titles may be purchased for business or promotional use or for special sales.
For information, please write to: Special Markets Department, Random House, Inc.
1745 Broadway, New York, NY 10019.

MADE SIMPLE BOOKS and BROADWAY BOOKS are
trademarks of Broadway Books, a division of Random House, Inc.

Visit our website at www.broadwaybooks.com.
First Broadway Books trade paperback edition published 2005.

Library of Congress Cataloging-in-Publication Data
Spraul, V. Anton.
    Computer Science made simple / V. Anton Spraul; edited by Roger E. Masse;
    illustrations by Scott Nurkin.
        p. cm.—(Made Simple)
    Includes index.
    ISBN 0-7679-1707-3
    1. Computer Science. I. Masse, Roger E. II. Title.
    III. Series: Made Simple (Broadway Books)
    QA76.S697 2005
    004—dc22   2004065044
10 9 8 7 6 5 4 3 2 1

ACKNOWLEDGMENTS

First and foremost, I want to thank to my wife, Mary Beth, for her support and for pretending not to notice the various home improvement projects that didn't get done. I also extend thanks to everyone whose work improved this book, including my chief editor, Roger Masse, and all at The Philip Lief Group, Inc. including Jill Korot, Judy Linden, and Albry Montalbano. Thanks also to Scott Nurkin for translating my ugly stick figures into the illustrations you see on these pages. Finally, thanks to ACCIS: the president, Betty Howell; the dean, Ronan O'Beirne; and all the other faculty members, staff, and students I've had the pleasure of working with over the years.

CONTENTS

Welcome to *Computer Science Made Simple*, a novice's guide to one of the most important fields today. I wrote this book with several kinds of readers in mind. For the person curious about how computers work and what the computer terms used in magazine advertisements mean, this book will provide the answers. For those considering studying computer science, this book will clarify whether the subject is truly interesting to them. For someone already working in computer science, this book will provide information about other and newer areas in the field. And for the manager who needs to communicate with his or her tech people in their own language, this book will ease the translation.

In short, whether you are a tourist in the world of computers or plan to make a living there, I know you'll find *Computer Science Made Simple* useful.

Because computer science is too large a subject to cover in a single book, I chose to include topics that are broadly relevant. When choosing between two otherwise equal topics, I picked the one I thought was the most interesting.

If "technical" subjects sometimes scare you, have no fear: This is computer science *made simple*, after all. There's no required background for reading this book, no mathematics to solve, and no uncommon terms are used except those the book defines for you. When possible, I've simplified subjects without leaving out essential details. I haven't shied away

from tricky subjects, but I've explained them in a way that I trust anyone can understand.

Computer Science Made Simple is divided into ten easily digested chapters.

Chapter 1 answers the question, "What is Computer Science?" This chapter distinguishes computer science from related fields, like information science and computer engineering. It discusses the fields and careers within the field, and concludes with the highlights in the history of computers and computer science.

Chapter 2 introduces key concepts, such as the binary system, and describes the externally visible components of a computer system. The chapter explains not just what these components do, but how they do it.

Chapter 3 deals with the operation of the hardware inside the computer case. In particular, you'll learn the techniques used to make computers faster year after year.

Chapter 4 covers software. While computer science is named for the computer, it's really the software that defines our experience with these machines. This chapter lists the different kinds of software and explains how the most important piece of software—the operating system—controls the actions of the computer.

Chapter 5 is about programming. This book doesn't teach you how to program—that would be a whole book by itself. Instead, you'll learn how programs work, how they are designed, and about various programming languages.

Chapter 6 covers networks, where computers communicate with one another across wires, cables, and optical fiber.

Chapter 7 is about a particular network: the well-known Internet. Its history is discussed, from humble beginnings to the dramatic explosion of popularity that came about with the World Wide Web. You'll learn the technologies behind the operation of the Internet and see how a web page works.

Chapter 8 covers computer graphics. The ability to visualize whole new worlds is one of the most exciting developments in the computer revolution.

Chapter 9 covers a few advanced topics that weren't large enough for their own chapters: databases, for instance, which store huge amounts of information but must be organized carefully; and artificial intelligence attempts to get computers to "think." Today, robots do jobs that humans once did.

Chapter 10 comments on how computer science affects society. For one, computers have created challenges to our privacy and to our patent and copyright laws. For another, they have also changed business, improved education, and created new entertainments.

Finally, at the back of the book you'll find a glossary of all the terms defined in the text, a references list, and an index. Often, the sources I used are appropriate for novices, but some are not, and I've tried to steer you to the best places to expand your knowledge.

Computer science has been a part of most of my life. My father sat me down in front of a teletype computer at his office when I was eleven or twelve, and I've been hooked ever since. I taught myself to program in junior high school, and in time I became a college professor who, for the last ten years, has taught the subjects covered in *Computer Science Made Simple*.

I hope that you'll enjoy reading this book as much as I enjoyed writing it, and that you'll have moments of joy, as I do when I learn something new about technology, saying under my breath, "Huh, so *that's* how that works."

V. Anton Spraul
Birmingham, Alabama

WHAT IS COMPUTER SCIENCE?

INTRODUCTION TO COMPUTING

Computers have become a ubiquitous feature of modern life. It would be difficult to get through a day without some activity involving a computer, be it composing e-mail on a computer sitting on a desk, using a computer hidden inside a cell phone, or receiving a bill generated by a computer at the power company. Computer science allows all these activities to happen.

But what is computer science? It sounds simple enough—computer science is a branch of science that studies computers. But not everyone who works with computers is a computer scientist. The use and development of computers comprises a number of overlapping disciplines.

Before these disciplines are discussed, you need to understand a few terms.

A *program* is a series of steps to accomplish a given task. In general usage, a program might refer to everyday instructions, written in English, such as instructions to change a tire or register for a college class. In computer science, however, the term "program" refers to a series of steps given to a computer.

A *computer* is an electronic device for performing logical and mathematical operations based on its programs. The term includes not only the obvious electronic devices that have a screen, keyboard, printer, and so on, but also computers that are embedded into devices like those at supermarket checkout counters or in DVD players. What makes computers interesting and powerful is that they can be given arbitrary sets of instructions to perform.

Hardware refers to all the physical devices that make up a computer system, both those inside the computer "case" and those outside the case, like monitor, keyboard, and mouse.

Software refers to the programs the computer executes. For example, the word processor Microsoft Word, or the computer game "Half-Life," is software, as is a program that enables a cell phone display so the user can select a new ring-tone. By analogy, when you play a movie in a DVD player, the movie is the software and the player is the hardware.

A *programmer* is someone who creates programs.

User refers to a person who uses a software program or computer.

Levels of Abstraction

The *level of abstraction* in computer science refers to the distance between a particular view of a situation and the concrete reality. It is a key concept, and perhaps sounds more

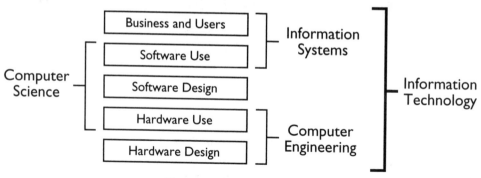

Figure 1.1—Levels of Abstraction

complicated than it is. In general, the term describes whether someone has a "big picture" view or is focused on details.

A person driving a car, for example, doesn't often think about what goes on under the hood. A mechanic does, but doesn't worry about the inside of most parts: If the part is broken, it gets replaced, not taken apart. On the other hand, a car designer must understand the engineering details of every part in the car. The driver, mechanic, and designer can view the same car at different levels of abstraction.

Figure 1.1 shows one way to divide computing into levels of abstraction.

The bottom level is hardware design. People working at this level understand how electrical properties within a computer work, and they can design new computing devices.

At the next level, hardware use, people understand how the computer works conceptually but have no concern over electrical properties or any knowledge of how to make a physical circuit.

The level above that is software design, where people create new programs for computers to execute. And then comes software use, the level at which people use existing programs to perform tasks, not create new ones. Someone

who is an expert at Microsoft Word works on this level.

The top level isn't about computing at all, but about the people and businesses that use computers. Those who understand how a business works, or how users interact with programs, operate at this level.

Major Fields in Computing

You may have heard terms like "computer engineering," "computer science," "information systems," and "information technology" and wondered if they were synonymous. They are not, but they're related through the levels of abstraction. You need to understand these terms too.

Computer engineering focuses on the bottom levels of abstraction: hardware design and use. It is an extension of electrical engineering, covering the design and analysis of computer hardware. In fact, in a university, computer engineering is most often taught in the school of engineering. While a computer engineer understands programming, most of his or her focus is on hardware, not software.

Computer science, the subject of this book, is the systematic study of computing processes. It is concerned with the middle levels of abstraction, from hardware use to software use. Computer scientists work primarily in the development of software, either at the practical level (improving the speed at which a web page performs a search) or the theoretical (exploring the limits of computers' recognition of human speech). The hope is that every subject that begins as theoretical ends as practical. To better understand software design and development, the computer scientist must understand how a computer works, even if he or she can't create one, and thus is also an experienced computer user. In a university, computer science is most often taught in the school of science and mathematics.

Covering the top levels of abstraction is *information systems*, which is the study of how computing technology is used in business. Someone schooled in information systems has knowledge of business operations and programming, but is more interested in solving a business problem with existing solutions than in trying to invent novel solutions. In a university, information systems may be taught in the same department as computer science or it may be taught in the business school.

Finally, *information technology* is a broad term that does not refer to a particular field but instead covers all the levels of abstraction. While often restricted to mean the use of technology in business (similar to information systems), in general, the term encompasses the design, development, and implementation of computer hardware and software.

PROFESSIONS IN COMPUTER SCIENCE

What, then, do computer scientists do? There are many professions for people with degrees

and with a background in computer science. Consider a few of the most common professional jobs.

Programmer

A computer scientist's natural activity is in front of a computer, writing a program, so of course it stands to reason that his or her general job title is *programmer*. While the basic concepts of programming never change, two programmers can have jobs that are very different from each other. Writing a computer game, for example, is different than writing tax-preparation software.

Two broad subcategories of programming are applications and systems. An *applications programmer* writes programs directly for users. Someone who helped create Microsoft Word is an applications programmer. A *systems programmer* writes programs that operate computers behind the scenes. For example, a systems programmer would create the software that directs traffic around the Internet.

Even within these categories, programmers have different specialized knowledge. A programmer writing software for a bank needs some knowledge of finance, while one developing software to display molecules needs some background in chemistry.

It should be noted that while "programmer" is still in use as a general term, it has fallen out of favor as a job title. This is because the work of developing software involves creating specifications and designs; that is, it's now more than just programming. In response, a new term has arisen to reflect the total process: software engineer.

Software Engineer

A *software engineer* is involved in all stages of software development, from initial meeting with prospective clients to installing updates to a program years after it was first developed. In truth, most programmers are actually software engineers since it would be difficult for anyone to do a good job of writing a program if they haven't been involved in the early stages of design.

The term "software engineer" arose not only to better reflect a total process, which includes programming, as we noted above, but also because of the growing importance of correct software in the computer industry. Computers are increasingly involved in our lives, and are often critical to what we do, so software failure could be catastrophic.

Consider a construction analogy in which a 100-story tower has been designed and tested by someone who was called a "builder." If you worked there, you'd no doubt prefer that the building were designed by a "structural engineer"—someone who rigorously tested the design in accordance with accepted principles. Similarly, an astronaut boarding a space shuttle doesn't want to rely on a computer program written by a mere "programmer" to bring the craft safely back home, but instead wants the software written by a "software engineer." Again, these activities imply that a formal, proven process was used to create the software. It gives a greater assurance that the software is free of serious defects.

Systems Analyst

A *systems analyst* makes decisions when whole systems must be introduced, upgraded, or replaced. If a chain of grocery stores determines that its current inventory control system is inadequate, for instance, a systems analyst—or team of analysts—would decide what the best solution is, taking into account all the costs involved, including purchasing new hardware, developing new software, training employees to use the new system, and so on. The best solution for the grocery store chain could involve replacing all the computers at the checkout counters or writing new software for the existing hardware.

You can see in the above example that the term "system" encompasses not only computers and software, but everything that interacts with them, including the people who use them. A good systems analyst must take the skills, needs, and wants of other employees into account when making decisions.

Note that many people with the title "systems analyst" do not analyze systems exclusively, especially in smaller organizations. They are also involved in the development of the software once the system plan has been approved. Thus, systems analysts are often software engineers as well.

System Manager

Once a new system is in place, someone must ensure that it continues to work. A person responsible for maintaining an existing computer system is a *system manager*. He or she monitors the hardware and software, and, if the needed use of the system outstrips its capacity, prioritizes requests.

The system manager also supervises day-to-day tasks with the system, such as the replacement or repair of malfunctioning equipment, and is involved in the same kind of high-level decisions as systems analysts. At some organizations, both roles may be combined into one position, which is given an omnibus title such as "information technology manager."

Network Manager

A *network* is a set of computers connected together so they can share data. A *network manager* is a kind of system manager who specializes in network operations: keeping the network operational, connecting new computers to the network as new employees are hired, upgrading the networking technology as needs change, and performing similar tasks.

This position is fraught with peril, because at many offices all work must cease when the network is "down," or nonoperational.

Researcher

A computer science researcher is involved in formal investigation of the computer science field, which is a little different than research in other sciences.

A researcher in chemistry, for example, might mix several chemicals together as an experiment, observe the results, determine the properties of the existing compound, and compare this result with the result that was expected—the hypothesis. A computer science researcher, in contrast, does not generally conduct experiments. Since it is exactly known how a computer will interpret a given instruction or set of instructions, the researcher will know, or can test, whether a given idea will work before it is actually implemented as a program. Indeed, much research can be done without using a computer at all.

Research in this field can be practical or theoretical. Practical research has a known

application already, such as an improvement for an existing process; for instance, a method to search Web pages faster or better. Theoretical research is meant to advance the discipline, without a specific practical goal in mind. Of course, today's theoretical solution may turn out to have practical ramifications tomorrow.

At one time, most research in computer science was performed at colleges and universities by faculty members whose salaries were at least partially funded by grants from government and private research organizations. Further research came from candidates for doctoral degrees whose research topics related to their faculty mentor. While academic research still takes place, an increasing amount of research is done by private companies. Because the software industry is so lucrative, market forces can often drive research faster than academic concerns. While an exceptional computer science department in a university might have an annual research budget of $5 million, Microsoft (the world's largest software company) has an annual research budget of over $5 billion.

Teacher

Like all disciplines, computer science needs people in the current generation to teach those from the next generation, to pass along the accumulated knowledge and experience of the field.

At one time, most teachers of computer science were college professors. Now, computer science is often taught in high school as well. And because the industry is advancing so fast and there's a need to teach workers who are already in the field, companies employ teachers as well. Commonly, they give seminars to keep a company's employees up-to-date with the latest technologies.

Chief Information Officer

Not many people have the title Chief Information Officer, but that this title even exists is testament to the importance of computing in the business world. A Chief Information Officer, or CIO, is at the highest level of management, involved with all the central decisions affecting the company.

This constitutes a historical change in modern companies. Before there were CIOs, computing was considered an appendage of business, rather than an integral part of it. Like a services department, it was called when something specific was needed. Now, of course, computers help guide a company's direction. Information technology can no longer be considered an afterthought, after the strategic plans have been made. The use of technology must be part of the plans themselves.

Chief Information Officers come from a variety of backgrounds, but tend to have education and experience both in computer science and business.

SUBJECT AREAS IN COMPUTER SCIENCE

Within the computer science field, computer scientists can work in many areas. Depending on the profession, some computer scientists may need to know a little about each area, while others may need deep knowledge of one or two areas.

Artificial Intelligence

Artificial intelligence can be described as programming computers to perform tasks that require intelligence if humans were performing the tasks. This is not the only definition, though, and of all the areas in computer science, this one has perhaps the most contentious boundaries.

Some researchers believe artificial intelligence must mimic the processes of the human brain; others are interested only in solving problems that seem to require intelligence, like understanding a request written in English.

Theory of Computation

The theory of computation puts limits on what can be computed. Some limits are practical. It may be shown, for instance, that a computer could solve a certain problem, but it would take hundreds of years to get the result. Other limits are absolute. Strange as it may seem, some questions have a fixed, numerical answer that cannot be computed.

Scientists in this area also compare programming solutions to specific tasks in a formal way. For example, a common computing task is *sorting*, which just means to put items in some order (like alphabetizing a list of student records by last name). Countless ways can be used to approach the sorting problem, each with advantages and disadvantages. Computational theory is used to determine which situations are most suited to a particular approach.

Human-Computer Interaction

The computer scientist working in human-computer interaction investigates how people use computers now and how people and computers can work together better in the future.

This research is similar to graphic design. A graphic designer is a specialist who knows how the colors, fonts, arrangement of text, pictures, and other elements make a book, magazine, or advertisement easier for the viewer to understand. Now that computer interfaces are increasingly graphical, the same kinds of ideas are used, except that a computer is interactive.

For example, many programs now have a "toolbar," which is a row of pictures that allow the user to select commonly used operations without navigating the entire menu of options. This kind of design innovation is a result of study in human-computer interaction.

Information Management

A *database* in general usage is any organized collection of data. In computer science, a database specifically means a collection of data that is stored in a computer-readable form. Examples include an online book catalog at the library or the account information for each person who has a VISA card.

The information management area is concerned with how databases are created, stored, accessed, shared, updated, and secured.

Computer Graphics

Computer graphics is the generation of images through computers. It includes simple text displays as well as images that appear to be in three dimensions.

An important part of computer graphics is *computer visualization*, which attempts to pictorially display data in a way that is most understandable for the user. For instance, a visualization can allow surgeons to preview a

surgical procedure before actually performing it. Other forms of visualization involve data that have no natural pictorial form. As a result, these must be displayed in a form that tells a story or makes a point. If you've seen a graph or chart generated with a computer program that seemed to have no clear meaning, you know why this area is important.

Like many areas in computer science, computer visualization is as much human psychology as machine capability. The computer visualization expert asks, "How do we as human beings process visuals?"

As computer graphics become more advanced, they terminate at a point called *virtual reality*, in which graphics and sensory feedback are all-encompassing. This can be seen, for example, a room in which every surface is covered with synchronized computer displays. It's important to note that virtual reality does not promise an experience indistinguishable from the "real world," although that may be a goal for some researchers. Rather, it is an experience in which the outside world is temporarily blocked from our senses.

Software Engineering

As previously discussed, a software engineer is involved with the entire process of a program's development, not just in programming. *Software engineering* is concerned with improving the process of making software. This means creating new processes for software engineers to follow, new techniques for project management, new methods to test software to ensure its quality, and new metrics for measuring how effective any of the other new ideas have been.

MYTHS OF COMPUTER SCIENCE

Computer Science Is All about Math

The kind and degree of math involved with computer science depends on what area one works in. Most programming involves math no more advanced than high school algebra, but some specialties require more. Someone who writes a mortgage interest calculator would need to understand financial calculations. Someone who writes a program to plot the trajectory of a satellite through space needs to understand trigonometry and calculus. Most programs, though, are built upon basic operations like addition and multiplication.

Men Are Better Suited to Computer Science than Women

Judging by the number of men and women working in the field, one could say that men as a group are more *interested* in computer science than women. But there's nothing to suggest that men are better at it. Women may have avoided computer science because of an aversion to math (which is probably caused by another myth) and because of media portrayals of computer scientists as socially awkward, pasty-faced "geeks." Computer science is a field that rewards excellence, regardless of gender or ethnicity, and all those interested should apply.

Computer Science Is for Geniuses

Genius never hurt anyone in the sciences, but having a high IQ and a knack for programming and other computer science concepts are two different things. While the people at the top of any profession usually have extraordinary abilities (that's why they're at the top), plenty of "ordinary" people have excelled in this field.

Computer Security

Much sensitive data is stored on computers, including tax records, credit card bills, bank accounts, and medical histories. And with computers increasingly interconnected, it's become easier for data to be stolen. The old adage, "A chain is only as strong as its weakest link," shows its truth here in the information age, where every computer is a link to another. So it's no surprise that *computer security* is a rapidly growing field.

Computer security involves finding ways to protect data from unauthorized access. This includes installing software to limit intrusions to a network, instructing employees on safe habits, and analyzing the aftermath of a system break-in to learn how to prevent a recurrence.

A related field is *computer forensics*, though in fact this is almost the reverse of computer security since it involves breaking through security to retrieve partially deleted files. The purpose of this "break-in" is to obtain and analyze evidence to be used in a court trial.

THE HISTORY OF COMPUTING

The presence of computers on desks in homes and businesses is a recent idea, having only flowered in the past twenty-five years, but the idea of a machine to perform computations is a surprisingly old one. In this section we'll explore a few of the highlights in the history of the computer and computer science.

The Abacus

The first efforts toward mechanical assistance aided in counting, not computation. An *abacus* is a mechanical device with beads sliding on rods, which is used as a counting device. It dates to at least the Roman Empire, and its ancestor, the counting board, was in use as far back as 500 B.C. The abacus is considered a counting device because all the computation is still done by the person using the device. The abacus did show, however, that a machine could be used to store numbers.

Jacquard's Mechanical Loom

A loom is a machine for weaving a pattern into fabric. Early loom designs were operated by hand. For each "line" in the design, certain threads were "pulled" by an experienced weaver (or a poor worker under the direction of a weaver) to get the finished pattern. As you might guess, this process was slow and tedious.

In 1801, Frenchman Joseph-Marie Jacquard invented a mechanical loom in which threads had to be pulled at each stage in a pattern that was stored in a series of *punch cards*. A punch card encodes data with holes in specific locations (Figure 1.2). In the case of weaving, every thread that could be pulled had a location on the card. If there was a hole in that location, the thread was pulled. Jacquard's loom used a series of these punch cards on a belt. The loom would weave the line dictated by the current card, then automatically advance to the next card.

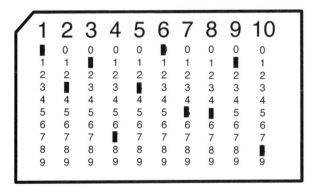

Figure 1.2—Punch Card

Jacquard's loom is not necessarily a computer, because it does no mathematical calculations, but it introduced the important idea of a programmable machine. The loom is a "universal weaver" that processes different sets of punch cards to make different woven fabrics.

Babbage's Counting Machine

Eventually someone put together a machine that could count and could execute a program, and wondered if a machine could be made to compute numbers. Charles Babbage, an English researcher, spent much of the 1800s trying to develop just such a machine.

One of Babbage's early designs was for a device he called the "Difference Engine," which produced successive terms in a mathematical series while an operator turned a crank. This may not seem a dramatic development, but at the time, mathematicians relied on tables of mathematical functions in which each value had been painstakingly calculated by hand. Thus, the Difference Engine was revolutionary.

Its success led Babbage to a more ambitious design: the Analytical Engine. Rather than being tied to a specific task like the Difference Engine, the Analytical Engine was conceived as a general-purpose computing device. Different programs would be fed to the machine using a belt of punch cards, just as in Jacquard's loom.

The Analytical Engine was never built, because Babbage ran out of money. Like many researchers today, he was dependent on government grants to continue his work. In addition, his design may not have been possible to implement using the technology of the day. He was undoubtedly a man ahead of his time.

Hollerith's Punch Cards

Under its Constitution, the U.S. government is required every ten years to count how many people reside in each state, a process known as the census. These numbers are used to determine the proportion of representatives each state receives in the House of Representatives.

Originally, this process was done entirely by hand. Census takers would fill out forms for each household, and then the results of these forms would be tabulated by state. This method was so onerous that by the late 1800s the 1880 census took more than ten years to complete, which meant that the next census was starting before the results of the previous one were known. Clearly, something had to be done.

The government created a contest to find the best solution to the problem. In 1890 it was won by a census agent named William Hollerith. In his design, each census form was encoded into a punch card. Machines called "tabulators" could rapidly process stacks of these cards.

This method was not only dramatically faster than manual tabulation, but also allowed the government to track demographics as never before, ask more questions of each citizen, and break up data along multiple categories. For example, rather than counting men who were above a certain age or were veterans, the tabulators could count the men who were in both categories, which allowed the government to better anticipate the funds that would be needed for veterans' pensions.

The system was a resounding success and led to Hollerith's founding of the Tabulating Machine Company, which, several mergers later, became International Business Machines,

or IBM, a company that would later dominate the world of computers for decades.

ABC

In the period from 1939 to 1942, John Atanasoff, a professor at Iowa State University, and Clifford Berry, a graduate student at the same school, created what is now considered the first modern computer. Their machine, which they called the Atanasoff-Berry Computer, or ABC, weighed about 700 pounds and had to be housed in the basement of the physics department. By current standards, it was a terribly slow machine, reportedly capable of only a single calculation every fifteen seconds. In contrast, a computer today can perform billions of calculations a second.

Atanasoff and Berry never completed the patent process on their work, and the machine itself was dismantled a few years after it was built, when the physics department needed its basement space back. This was unfortunate, as their pioneering work in the field was underappreciated. Credit for the first modern computer was instead bestowed on a more famous project: ENIAC.

ENIAC

Like William Hollerith's punched cards, the ENIAC story is driven by governmental need. When World War II began, the United States was woefully underprepared for military operations. The army needed to develop and test a large number of weapons in a short period of time. In particular, it had to perform a number of ballistics tests to create artillery tables—in essence, a book showing how far an artillery shell would fly from a specific gun, given wind conditions, the angle of the gun barrel, and so on.

Like the mathematical tables of Babbage's time, these artillery tables had been created by hand, but by now the army already had some devices for assisting in calculation. Called differential analyzers, they operated on mechanical principles (much like Babbage's machines), not on electronics. But something better was needed, in aid of which the army hired John Mauchly and J. Presper Eckert, computer scientists at the University of Pennsylvania. In 1946, the machine they proposed was called ENIAC, which stands for Electronic Numerical Integrator and Computer. Like the ABC, it was truly a modern computer.

The term "modern" might seem too strong if you actually saw this machine. Computers of that era relied on the *vacuum tube*, a device that resembled a lightbulb through which one electrical current can control another. This controlling aspect was used to build logical circuits, because by itself one vacuum tube doesn't do much. Indeed, ENIAC required about 19,000 vacuum tubes to do its work, filled an entire room, weighed thirty tons, and drew about 200 kilowatts (that is, 200,000 watts) of power. In comparison, a desktop computer purchased today would draw about 400 watts of power, which means ENIAC drew about 500 times more current, even though its actual ability to compute is dwarfed by the most inexpensive desktop computers of today.

What makes ENIAC so important is its reliance on electronics to solve a real-world problem. There were as few mechanical parts as possible, although some mechanics were inevitable. For example, ENIAC still used punch cards for input and output, and the parts that read and produced these cards were mechanical. The vacuum tubes were built into minicircuits that performed elementary logical functions and were built into larger circuits.

Those circuits were built into even larger circuits, a design idea that is still used today.

For decades the ENIAC was considered the first computer, but in the 1970s the judge in a patent infringement case determined that ENIAC was based on the designs of the ABC. Other claims were also made, including those of Konrad Zuse, whose work in wartime Germany wasn't known to the rest of the world for decades; and the Mark I, a computer developed around the same time at Harvard. The question of what was the first modern computer may never be settled.

Knuth's Research

To this point computers were seen as increasingly useful tools, but computer science was not considered a serious discipline, separate from mathematics. One of the leading figures who changed this was Donald Knuth.

As an undergraduate studying physics and mathematics at the Case Institute of Technology in Cleveland in the 1950s, Knuth had his first contact with the school's IBM computer. From then on, computers and programs were his obsession. He wrote programs for the IBM computer to analyze the college's basketball statistics, and published research papers while still an undergraduate. When he completed the work for his bachelor's degree, the college was so impressed with his computer work that he was awarded a master's at the same time. His most famous accomplishment is *The Art of Computer Programming*, a proposed masterwork of seven volumes, of which three are completed. It's no exaggeration to say that Donald Knuth's writings are to computer science what those of Albert Einstein are to physics.

The IBM PC

For decades after World War II, computers were shared. Though they had grown smaller since the days of ENIAC, they were still very large and expensive. As a consequence, entire universities or companies, or even groups of schools and companies, would share the use of a single, large, and—for the time—powerful computer.

The people who used this *mainframe*, as these computers were called, would often never see it. The computer was generally locked in a secure location, and users would connect to it through phone lines or other wiring. At first, all the user saw was a teletype, which is like a combination of an electric typewriter and a printer. But later, video screens were introduced, which showed green or orange text on a black background.

By the late 1970s, computer scientists realized that smaller, less powerful computers could be placed right on user's desks. "Garage" companies, so named because they were so small they might literally consist of one or two people working out of a garage, began making small computers for individuals, not whole companies. Sometimes these computers came in the form of kits.

IBM, the company that grew out of Hollerith's census tabulators, was at this time very successful making mainframes. At first, IBM was skeptical that a market even existed for smaller computers, but eventually it decided to act. In 1981 the company introduced the IBM PC. The "PC" stood for "personal computer," which is where that term for a single-user computer originates.

The price was over $1,500, which in 1980 was a lot of money, but it was still remarkably inexpensive compared to mainframes. In addition, the IBM name gave the personal computer instant legitimacy. Yet, the IBM PC did not mark a revolution in technology. The machine had been built almost entirely from off-the-shelf parts. What was revolutionary was the concept: A computer would appear on our desks at work, would come into our homes, would become an ordinary appliance like the telephone.

EXPLORATION: WHAT DOES $1,500 BUY?

Find a computer for sale for around $1,500, which was the cost of the original IBM PC. A good place to shop is Dell® (www.dell.com). Compare what you find to the features of the original home computer.

	IBM PC	Today's Computer
Processor speed (in gigahertz, or GHz)	about 0.005	_____
Main memory (RAM) (in megabytes, or MB)	about 0.02	_____
Size of disk drive (in gigabytes, or GB)	only had "floppy" drives; held less than 0.001 GB	_____
Input devices	keyboard only	_____
Output devices	screen only	_____

At the start of 1983, when *Time* magazine would normally select its "Man of the Year," for 1982, the editors instead selected "The Computer" as its "Machine of the Year." The computer had come of age.

As you will find, today's computers are not simply a little faster than the original desktops. A gymnasium full of IBM PCs would not equal the power of a single system today. You may not know what all these terms mean, but you will before you finish this book. For now, just marvel at how little $1,500 once bought (or, to be optimistic, how much $1,500 buys now).

Apple Macintosh

Although a great improvement over punch cards, some computer scientists saw limitations in a computer with only a keyboard for input and text for output. It was fine for researchers and computer experts to interact with the machine through obscure commands and oblique text messages, but if the computer was going into every home, it needed to interact with users in a different way.

In the early 1970s, researchers at Xerox developed a series of computers that communicated with the user through pictures, not just words. The culmination of their early efforts was the Xerox Star. It had "windows," a "mouse," and many other elements you would recognize today. Eventually this method of computer use—mostly visual, with little text—would be called a *graphical user interface* (or GUI), and every computer would have one. Unfortunately for the executives at Xerox, they proved better at funding interesting projects than at marketing the results.

Steve Jobs, the president of Apple Computers, toured the Xerox research facility in 1979,

having traded some Apple stock for Xerox stock. He'd been told about this new interface and wanted to see it. He left impressed, and decided that Apple's new computer, the "Apple Lisa," would be the first mass-produced computer with a graphical user interface. Many of the Xerox researchers would soon be working at Apple.

Not many Apple Lisas were sold. It was an expensive computer, costing $10,000 when it debuted in 1983. But because Jobs was convinced that the GUI was the model for the future, he tried again.

During the Super Bowl in 1984, Apple ran one of the most famous commercials in history to introduce their next computer, the Apple Macintosh. Directed by Ridley Scott, director of the movie *Blade Runner*, it depicted an Orwellian future of gray-clad workers who mindlessly pay homage to a "Big Brother" figure on a huge video screen, until an athletic woman in running clothes smashes the screen with a flying hammer. What this had to do with the Macintosh was never clear, but the commercial was widely discussed around office water coolers and was repeated on news programs. Soon everyone had heard of the "Mac."

The new computer was cheaper than the Lisa, but less powerful. As with the Lisa, it was a slow seller at first, but the company stuck with it. There was no turning back to text-based computers.

Microsoft Windows

When IBM was readying its PC for launch, they needed an *operating system*, which is the core program that allows a computer to function. This is the program that starts to run when you turn on a computer, before you touch the keyboard or the mouse. Microsoft purchased an operating system from another company and adapted it for use on the IBM PC, calling its software *MS-DOS*, for Microsoft Disk Operating System.

In 1985, Microsoft's initial fortunes were made with MS-DOS, but once Microsoft chairman Bill Gates saw the Apple Macintosh, he knew the days of MS-DOS were numbered. Microsoft developed its own GUI, a program that would run on top of MS-DOS, and called it "Windows."

Few people remember the original Windows today, or its sequel, Windows 2.0. They were crude interfaces by today's standards. They are most famous for starting a long legal battle with Apple, which claimed that the "look and feel" of Windows legally infringed on the designs of Apple computers. Microsoft, in turn, claimed that Apple had stolen the important ideas from Xerox anyway. Microsoft eventually won.

In 1990, Windows 3.0 was released, the first version that was truly popular with users and developers. In 1995, Windows 95 was re- leased, which, unlike the previous versions, was an entire operating system and interface in one, and did not require that MS-DOS be installed beforehand on the system. Soon Windows 98, Windows NT, Windows 2000, and Windows XP were developed. These products dominate the industry as of this book's first printing, and the vast majority of computers run some form of Windows.

As Microsoft became ubiquitous in the comput- ing world, a backlash developed. Critics claimed

the company's software presence on almost every computer in the world gave them an unfair competitive advantage. The company became entangled in antitrust lawsuits from rival companies and governments around the globe.

Linux

Some thought that the problem with Windows wasn't that it was nearly universal—there are advantages to everyone, as far as that's con- cerned—but that it was *proprietary*. That is, it was owned or controlled by one company, which means that no one outside of that com- pany knows exactly how the product works. In computer science, the opposite of proprietary is *open-source*. That is, no one company owns or controls the product, and anyone can look at how the product works and even make sug- gestions on how to improve it.

In 1991, Linus Torvalds, a student in Finland, made an innocent post to an e-mail group. He wrote that he was working on a free version of UNIX, an operating system that had been in use for twenty years. The Torvalds version, which came to be called Linux (Linus UNIX), was released under an agreement called the General Public License. In essence, anyone could use Linux in any way and modify it in any way, as long as any changes made were not hidden or charged for. This ensured that Linux would remain "open."

"Windows versus Linux" has become the main battleground in the larger war of "proprietary versus open-source." Adherents on both sides believe their approach will lead to more effec- tive software.

SUMMARY

A computer is any programmable electronic device. To use a computer, one must have hardware (all the physical parts of the computer itself) and software (the programs that execute on the computer). Programmers write programs, and users use them.

Computer science is the systematic study of computing processes. It is not directly involved with the design of new hardware, but rather, with the use and improvement of hardware that currently exists. Computer science is not directly concerned with business operations, but it wants to provide the tools businesses and others can use.

Computer scientists work in a variety of different jobs. Some work directly in the creation of new programs and are called programmers or software engineers. Others work in research and teaching. Still others neither program nor research, but maintain existing computer systems.

Research areas in computer science include artificial intelligence, human-computer interaction, information management, computer graphics, software engineering, and computer security.

Human beings have always sought new tools to make life easier. Early tools eased our physical labor, and later tools, like the abacus, eased our mental labors. The idea of a mechanical tool to help with computation led to Babbage's work and eventually culminated in the ABC and ENIAC, ushering in the computer age. With the release of the IBM PC, computing came into the home. Other developments led to the Apple Macintosh, Microsoft Windows, and Linux.

BASIC COMPUTER CONCEPTS

KEY TERMS

personal computer, binary, bit, byte, digital,
analog, input device, output device, storage
device, sequential access device, random
access device, hard drive, optical drive

KEY TERMINOLOGY AND CONCEPTS

Understanding key terms and some basic
concepts will help you grasp the power and
use of computers.

Classification of Computers

Computer scientists classify computers based
on their power and their use.

A *personal computer* (like the IBM PC from
Chapter 1) is designed for use by one person
at a time. This is what most of us think about
when someone says "computer," because it's
the kind of computer we are most likely to
see. The computers people use at home or
students use in school labs are personal
computers.

A *laptop* is a compact personal computer with
all the devices shrunk into one container to
make the computer easily portable. The general term *device* in computer science refers to
any hardware component. Thus, a laptop is
any computer where all the hardware is inside
a single, readily carried container.

A *workstation* is also a computer designed for
use by one person at a time, but it is connected
to a network—a set of computers connected
together to share data. At an insurance company, for example, all the employees may have
computers on their desks with the computers
connected to a network so they can share customer data. While computers intended as
workstations may be more powerful than personal computers, this is not always the case.

A *mainframe* is a powerful computer that is
shared by multiple users at one time. Each
user has a *terminal*, which in this context is
simply a keyboard and screen combination
used to access the mainframe. If the terminal
is nothing more than a screen and keyboard,
it's called a "dumb terminal" because it does
no processing of its own. However, a workstation can also be used, in which case it's called
a "smart terminal."

A *minicomputer* is any computer powerful
enough to be used by multiple people but
not powerful enough to be considered a
mainframe. This term is fading from use.

A *supercomputer* is among the fastest of current
computers. Because this classification is based
on performance, no computer can stay in this
category forever. Systems that were considered
supercomputers ten years ago are ordinary in
their abilities today.

A *server* is a computer on a network that
provides a service to other computers.

Mainframes are often used as servers, but not every server is a mainframe. Even a personal computer is powerful enough to be a server.

A *client* is a computer that uses a server for some service. An example of the client-server relationship is an automated teller machine. The ATM is a computer, but all it really knows is how much money it has left inside of it. When you request money from your account at an ATM, the ATM must consult a central computer at your bank to determine if your account has a high enough balance to grant your request and to debit your account once you have been given your money. The ATM is the client in this relationship, and the central computer at the bank is the server.

Binary

Computers are electronic machines. Essentially everything they do involves turning electrical switches off or on. It's difficult at first to imagine that everything computers are capable of grows from this basic principle. To see how, you need to understand the concept of a binary system.

Binary Basics

Binary means having two states. In the computer's case, the two states are *off* or *on*. The trick to understanding binary is seeing how a series of these "off" and "on" states can represent any data you can think of.

Suppose a young man—call him Todd—is a senior computer science student living off-campus in an apartment with his roommate, Stu. Todd's friend Marta has asked him to a movie this weekend, and Todd has promised to let her know if he can go after checking his schedule. Unfortunately, Todd knows that Stu will be on the phone all night to his long-distance girlfriend.

Todd and Marta solve this problem with an idea borrowed from Paul Revere. Todd has two windows in his bedroom with a lamp in front of each. By turning on one lamp, or the other, or both, or neither, he can set up one of four signals that Marta can see from her dorm down the hill.

If Todd had more lamps, he could send a greater variety of signals. To send any letter of the alphabet, for example, Todd would need the ability to send twenty-six different signals. This would require five lights.

Message number	Left lamp	Right lamp	Meaning
1	off	off	Can't go, too busy
2	on	off	Can go but not until Saturday night
3	off	on	Can go to Sunday matinee
4	on	on	Can go Friday night

Lamp Signal System for Movies

off	off	off	off	off	I	A
off	off	off	off	on	2	B
off	off	off	on	off	3	C
off	off	off	on	on	4	D
off	off	on	off	off	5	E
...						
on	on	off	off	off	25	Y
on	on	off	off	on	26	Z

Lamp Signal System for Letters

For Christmas, Todd buys strands of outdoor lights to hang on his apartment balcony (Figure 2.1). Each strand has five lights and he can pull lights out to turn them off. Thus, each strand can be one letter in a message using the previous letter system. If he hangs fourteen strands from his balcony, he can spell out MERRYCHRISTMAS to Marta. A few days later Todd can change the lights to spell out another message: HAVEAGOODNYEVE.

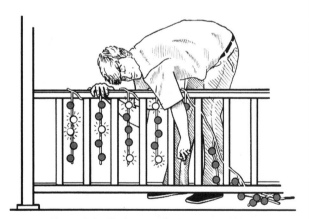

Figure 2.1—Todd and His Christmas Lights

Binary in Computer Science

If you type "Merry Christmas" into a word processing program and then erase that and type "Have a good New Year's Eve," the electrical patterns inside the computer are changing just like the lights on Todd's balcony.

In computer science, the *off* signals are written as the number 0, and the *on* signals are written as the number 1. Thus, the *E* row in the chart above is written as 00100, because the first two and last lamps are off, and the one in the middle is on. A single on/off indicator, written as a 0 or 1, is called a *bit*, which comes from the term *binary digit*.

Bits are formed into *bytes*, which are groups of eight bits. Why eight? This number of bits allows one byte to store one *character*, which is any letter, digit, or other symbol that can be displayed by typing on a keyboard. Eight bits allow 256 combinations, which is more than enough for all the lowercase letters (twenty-six), uppercase letters (another twenty-six), digits 0 through 9, and special symbols, like $, %, and the quotation marks. Even the space between words is a character. When you read that some computer devices can store as much data as a novel or an encyclopedia, that piece of information is relying on the idea of one byte equals one character. If the average word length is five characters (four letters plus the space before the next word) and a typical novel has 80,000 words, then it takes 400,000 bytes to store a novel.

Any data can be stored as binary, as long as every possible value can be matched with a whole number, which can then be turned into a binary value. Data that is already numeric, like students' test grades, inventory counts, or account balances, is easy. Textual data can be stored easily as well, as you've just seen. The process becomes tricky, though, without an obvious one-to-one correspondence between the original data and the set of binary values.

Digital Versus Analog

Consider a room with two lamps, one on the ceiling and the other on a table. The ceiling lamp is controlled by a variable dimmer switch on the wall. When this knob is rotated clockwise, the light gets brighter. When the knob is rotated counterclockwise, the light gets dimmer. The lamp on the table also has a knob, but when it turns, it clicks into distinct positions. If the lamp is off, rotating the knob clockwise one step makes a dim light, rotating it another makes a medium light, rotating it again makes it fully bright, and then rotating it once more turns the lamp off again.

The table lamp has four distinct positions and could easily be mimicked in binary. The number of positions for the ceiling lamp, though, is countless, because the dimmer switch doesn't have distinct steps. Put another way, the table lamp has no choices in between medium-bright and fully bright, while the ceiling lamp has many possibilities between any two levels of brightness.

Data with distinct values (like the table lamp) is called *discrete* data. Data with continuous values (like the ceiling lamp) is called *analog* data.

Discrete data stored in binary form is *digital*. Just think of "digital" as "numeric" and then "digital data" becomes "data stored as numbers." Digital data is stored as binary patterns, but from our level of abstraction, think of those patterns as numbers.

With a set of distinct values, a binary encoding can be easily assigned to each one. With analog data, though, the data first has to be turned into discrete data.

This process is easiest to understand when there's only one value. Consider an ordinary mercury thermometer. To read the temperature, you compare the end of the line of mercury to a scale printed on the outside of the glass. This reading is an analog measurement. The mercury line can be any length and often doesn't line up with a mark on the temperature scale.

Now consider a thermometer with a numeric display like a calculator. To display the temperature as a number, the thermometer has to convert the temperature from some kind of analog measurement to a discrete one. The process of converting an analog measurement to a number is called *quantization*.

This process loses some of the original data. Suppose you have a thermometer with a digital display hanging on your wall. It shows 72 degrees, but a minute later it changes to 73 degrees. You would not think that the temperature of the room changed one degree in an instant. Instead, the temperature was slowly rising, and at a point when it became closer to 73 than 72, the display changed. Analog data has a continuous range of values. When they are replaced by a finite set of values, some rounding off must occur. The difference between analog data and its discrete representation is *quantization error*. Thus, if the temperature is actually 72.423 and the display reads 72, the 0.423 is the quantization error. This quantization error can be reduced by having more possible digital values. If the temperature could be displayed as 72.4, for example, then the quantization error would only be 0.023.

When a signal varies continuously over time, more sacrifices must be made to produce a digital version. Consider music that is changed into "digital audio." When music plays through a speaker, the speaker's cone moves in and out as the flow of current in the wire from the stereo goes up and down. A plotted line showing how strong the current is over time would be a continuous, if jagged, line.

The music example is a more complicated situation than the one dealing with temperature. The current has not only a continuous range of values (like the temperature), but also a changing value. To convert this kind of signal into discrete form requires a process called *sampling*. In statistics, sampling is used when an entire population cannot be queried. For instance, when 10,000 voters are asked who they will vote for in the presidential election, these 10,000 people represent, stand in, for the whole country.

In computer science, sampling means taking analog measurements at intervals and then quantizing each measurement (Figure 2.2). With the music example, rather than trying to capture the entire original signal, the audio is sampled many times per second, and whatever signal strength is recorded at that point is turned into a number.

Just as with quantization, the original signal is reproduced better when more samples are allotted per second. Whenever you see digital audio mentioned, it has two numbers that indicate its quality. One is the *sample rate*, which is the number of samples taken per second. The other is the number of *bits per sample*, which indicates how large a range is given to each quantized value. As these values increase, the reproduction becomes more accurate, but the resulting digital data also takes up more space.

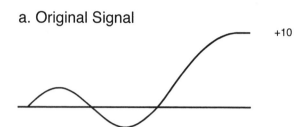

a. Original Signal

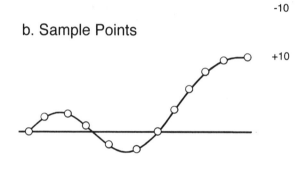

b. Sample Points

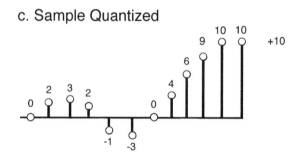

c. Sample Quantized

d. Original signal now list of numbers

0, 2, 3, 2, -1, -3, 0, 4, 6, 9, 10, 10

Figure 2.2—Sampling

IS DIGITAL BETTER?

Advertisements often tout that something is "digital." Satellite television companies, for example, offer "120 channels, all with digital-quality picture and sound!"

The truth is that digital is not always better than analog. One main advantage to digital signals, besides being the only thing a computer can work with, is perfect reproduction. Because everything is stored as a bit, the same series of bits can be reproduced elsewhere for an exact copy of the original data. A copy of a VHS tape, which is analog, is a little "fuzzier" than the original, while a copy of a DVD is the same as the original.

Beyond that, though, DVD has no inherent advantage. DVD recordings of movies tend to use high sample and bit rates and therefore look better than VHS tapes of the same movie. But a DVD that used a low sample (perhaps to fit a very long movie on a single DVD) might look worse than a well-made VHS tape of the same movie. Similarly, when audio CDs were first introduced to the market, the record companies would sometimes go back to the decades-old original tape masters and transfer them to CD without thinking about the process. This process meant that noise and hiss on the original tape, which weren't audible on analog recordings, were quite loud on the CDs. Far from sounding better, they sounded much worse than the records they replaced.

Don't assume that everything that's digital is high quality.

Powers of 2

Because we originally counted on our fingers, we humans have a system based on the number 10. That means we work naturally with numbers like 10, or 1,000, or 1,000,000. Also, that means that adding a possible digit to a number multiplies the maximum value by 10. For example, if a car has an odometer with five digits, it can display mileage up to 99,999. If we add a digit, we can display mileage up to 999,999, which is ten times as much.

Since computers use the binary system, they are naturally suited at working with numbers that are powers of 2. While adding a digit to a number allows ten times the maximum value, adding a bit to a binary number only doubles the maximum value. That means that two bits can store four values (remember Todd's lamps), three bits can store eight values, and so on. Computers thus work best with values in the series 1, 2, 4, 8, 16, 32, 64, 128, 256, 512, and so on, where each number is twice the previous number. These numbers are called "powers of 2."

As a consequence, computers are not described as having 250 or 500 megabytes of storage. Instead it's always a number like 256 or 512.

Size Terminology

Most of the world relies on the metric system, but the system hasn't caught on in the United States except in scientific fields. The following chart lists the metric sizes that come up most often in computer science.

The first column is the prefix that's placed in front of the unit, like "kilo" in "kilobyte." The second column is the abbreviation for the prefix. For example, the short form of kilobyte is "kb." Note that the capitalization is important: M means "mega" but m means "milli." The third column is the general value of that prefix, which is how it is used outside of computer science. The fourth column is the

Prefix	Abbreviation	General Value	Computer Science Value	Sample Use
Giga	G	1,000,000,000	1,073,741,824	2.6 gigahertz
Mega	M	1,000,000	1,048,576	512 megabits
Kilo	k	1,000	1,024	256 kilobytes
Milli	m	1/1000		30 milliseconds

Metric Size Designations

value commonly used in computer science, and the fifth column provides some examples. These values are not the same because of the powers of 2. A kilobyte isn't 1,000 bytes; it's 1,024 bytes, because 1,024 is a power of 2. In general, though, the difference between the two values is not important. Because 1,000,000,000 is a lot easier to remember than 1,073,741,824, one can dispense with the fourth column, except when an exact value is absolutely necessary.

SYSTEM COMPONENTS

A computer system is more than just a computer. It's a set of components that work together to make a computer usable. Suppose you purchased a computer system today. What you would get is a collection of devices closely resembling those depicted in Figure 2.3.

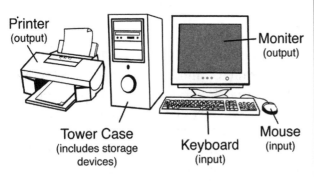

Figure 2.3—A Personal Computer System

The *case* is the box that contains the circuitry of the actual computer, along with some devices and connections for others. Some cases are wider than they are tall and are intended to sit on desktops. Others are taller than they are wide and sit on the floor. These are called *towers*.

In this chapter, stay at the "computer user" level of abstraction and don't worry too much about what you can't see inside the case. At the moment it's more important how the parts on the outside of the case interact with the other components.

The other components are divided into several categories: input devices, output devices, storage devices, and utility devices. An *input device* is used to give data to the computer. An *output device* transmits data from the computer back to the user. A *storage device* keeps data for later use.

Input Devices

Common input devices include a keyboard, mouse, scanner, digital camera, and gamepad. Learn how each device works.

Keyboard

The most common input device is a keyboard, which is like a typewriter. The earliest keyboards had only the same keys that a typewriter does, just the letters, numbers, and other printable symbols. Over time, keyboards have gained more functionality. Most have an area on the right called a numeric keypad, which puts all the number keys together to allow fast entry of numeric data. In addition, many keyboards now have additional keys for common tasks, such as playing music or opening the user's favorite program.

While keyboards have grown more complex, the technology behind them works on simple principles. Each key is just an electrical switch. The keyboard can signal which key is pressed by assigning each key a binary pattern and transmitting that pattern to the computer.

KEYBOARD AND KEYPAD DESIGN

Have you ever wondered why the keys on a typewriter or keyboard are in an order where the letters on the top row spell QWERTY? Early typewriters would easily jam when operators typed letters next to each other too quickly. As a result, the keys were laid out so that those keys often struck in succession were not next to each other. In essence, the keys are arranged to slow typists. You can purchase keyboards with other layouts, like the "Dvorak" layout, which is intended to speed typing, not slow it down.

Take a look at a computer keyboard's numeric keypad, and then look at how the number keys are laid out on a touch-tone phone. They are opposite. On a phone, the 123 row is on the top, but on a keyboard it's on the bottom. Why? The phone, like the typewriter, was designed to slow down its operator because early phone systems couldn't handle a fast dialer. The numeric keypad, however, is built for speed, which is the whole point of it being there.

Mouse

The second most common input device is the *mouse*, which is a device that moves a cursor—a small arrow or other pointing shape—on the screen as it is moved. It also has one or more buttons to allow further input. Newer designs may also have a wheel that can be rolled up and down. In most programs that display pages of text, rolling the wheel moves the text up and down in unison.

Mice track their positions in multiple ways. The most common design has a rubber-covered ball on the bottom. As the mouse is slid across the desk, the ball rolls. Inside the mouse, the ball is rubbing against two rollers. If you open the compartment at the bottom of a mouse, you will see them. One roller tracks the up-down movement of the mouse; the other tracks the left-right movement. After the mouse transmits the movement of these rollers to the computer as a binary number, the computer uses this data to determine where the mouse's cursor should appear on the screen.

This design is simple, but has some problems. First, the ball doesn't roll very well on some surfaces. The surface needs to be smooth enough so the ball doesn't "skip," but not so smooth that the ball slides without turning. Most users employ a square of specially designed material called a *mouse pad* for this reason. Second, the rolling ball tends to pick up all the dirt and lint on the desk or pad and carry it inside, where it lodges on the rollers. The mouse's tracking gets steadily worse until it is cleaned.

An improved design is the *optical mouse*, which tracks the mouse position using an optical sensor, not a rolling ball. Hundreds of times per second, the mouse takes a picture of what's beneath it, and by comparing this picture to the previous one, determines how far it has moved and in what direction. Because an optical mouse has no ball, it rarely needs to be cleaned and can be used without a mouse pad.

Scanner

A *scanner* converts printed images into computer images. Some scanners can only produce black-and-white images. Their operation is similar to a photocopier. The paper to be scanned is placed on a clear sheet of glass or plastic. A bar underneath this sheet slides from one end of the paper to the other. This bar contains a bright white light and a line of optical sensors. By checking how much the light reflects back into each sensor as the bar moves, the image can be built up as a series of "grayscale" dots. Each dot is given a number. For example, 0 could be totally white, 15 could be pitch-black, and 8 could be neutral gray. These numbers are easily encoded into binary.

Color scanners are a little more complicated but work on the same principle. Some designs have different sensors for each of the three primary colors: blue, green, and red. Other designs have only one set of sensors, but make three passes across the paper. For the first pass, a red light is turned on, which makes the red in the image turn dark. Then the next pass uses a green light, and the last pass uses a blue light. Storing a color image takes a lot more space than a gray-scale image. For each dot in the image, its level of red, green, and blue must be stored, which means that each dot is three numbers, not just one.

Digital Camera

A *digital camera* uses optical sensors to capture a photo directly in digital form. It uses the same kinds of sensors that a one-pass color scanner uses, but instead of a line, a grid is formed. The light from the scene hits the grid, and the image is recorded.

Gamepad

Personal computers are often used to play games. All video game systems (like the XBox) are just single-purpose computers, anyway. A *gamepad* is an input device specialized for controlling games. The technology behind the gamepad is simple, since it is made of a number of buttons, which are just switches.

Output Devices

Common output devices include a monitor, printer, and speaker.

Monitor

A *monitor*, the most important output device, is a computer display screen. Early monitors displayed white or a single color on a black background, but current monitors can display as many colors as the human eye can distinguish. There are two kinds of monitors: CRT and LCD.

A *CRT* is a cathode ray tube monitor, which means it works like a television. At one end of the tube is a device that produces a stream of electrons. At the other end is a screen that has been coated with substances that briefly glow different colors when struck by electrons. A device that aims the electron beam scans the screen left to right, top to bottom, and the beam is turned on or off to make some of the screen glow or not. CRT screens are inexpensive, but because the electron beam has to be shot from well behind the screen, monitors of this type tend to be very deep and thus take a lot of space on the desktop. Also, CRT screens are gently curved instead of flat, which means that the images they display appear to bend at the edges.

An *LCD* is a liquid crystal display. Liquid crystal, as the name implies, has properties of both a liquid and a solid. The important feature for its use in monitors is that it turns solid when exposed to an electrical current, and it is opaque when in the solid state but clear when in the liquid state. A two-color LCD display uses a grid of liquid crystal cells in front of a bright light source, and current is sent to the cells that should be darker. More advanced displays can vary the level of transparency to make a gray-scale image. For a color display, filters are placed over the display to divide it into red, green, and blue columns.

LCD monitors were originally designed for laptop computers, where a CRT was too big to be practical. Now, they are gaining popularity with desktop computers because they take up less space and the screens are perfectly flat.

Printer

A *printer* outputs text or images to paper. Different types of printers exist for different needs. A printer used for a term paper should be fast, while a printer for photographs must print in high-quality color.

A *dot-matrix printer* works by pressing an inked ribbon against the paper with a set of pins. The ribbon used is like that in a typewriter. As the print head moves across the paper, pins on the head fire out, pressing the ribbon against the paper to make a dot. These dots make up the image on the paper. As the print head reaches one side of the paper, the paper is advanced the height of the print head, and

the print head continues in the opposite direction. Dot-matrix printers, which are inexpensive to purchase and operate, are very fast, but the output quality is poor because it's easy to see the dots in the image. They are often used by companies for items like billing statements, which are printed in bulk.

An *ink-jet printer* works by spraying ink at the paper. It is much slower than a dot-matrix printer because it makes more passes to produce the same size image, but it has several advantages. It produces a better-looking image than a dot-matrix printer because the image is not made of distinct dots. Also, some ink-jet printers can print in color, with red, yellow, and blue inks in separate reservoirs and a separate black ink reservoir because producing black by mixing all three colors wastes a lot of ink.

Ink-jet printers are inexpensive to purchase, but their cost per page of use is higher than a dot-matrix. Also, the images they produce can smear if the paper is handled soon after printing because the ink is still wet. These are the default printers for home users and for business users who only print occasionally.

A *laser printer* works using electrostatic principles to transfer ink to the paper. It's not as complicated as it sounds. A drum inside the printer rotates past a laser beam that is scanning back and forth. The drum is made of a material that becomes electrostatically charged where it is struck by the scanning laser. Anyone who has taken clothes from a hot dryer knows that static electricity can make things stick together. That's how it is used here. The drum is sprayed with *toner*, which is a powder form of ink that has been given the opposite charge of the drum. The toner sticks where the laser hits on the drum.

A piece of paper is then rolled against the drum, transferring the toner to it. If the process stopped at this point, the image wouldn't stay on the paper long because there's only static electricity holding the toner in place. The last stage in the cycle is the *fuser*, which is a set of very hot rollers that melt the toner into the paper. If you've ever wondered what a laser printer is doing when you turn it on and a blinking light indicates it isn't ready yet, it is waiting for the fuser to reach the right temperature.

The print quality of laser printers is excellent. Although they are more expensive than ink-jet printers for an initial purchase, the cost of ink can be less because expensive toner cartridges last much longer than ink-jet cartridges. Also, because the ink is fused into the paper, rather than sprayed on wet like an ink-jet, the image doesn't smear. In addition, laser printers are fast. They are often used for business communications, where print quality counts, although prices have gone down enough that home users who want higher quality purchase them also.

While most laser printers produce black-and-white output, some can produce color. These printers work by running the paper through the whole process four times, one pass each for red, yellow, blue, and black toner. Color laser printers are very expensive.

For high-quality color printing, though, few printers can match a *dye sublimation printer*. "Sublimation" means going from a solid directly to a gas, such as a block of dry ice turning into a fog without melting into a puddle first. A dye sublimation printer works by heating a ribbon so that the solid ink inside turns into a gas and then seeps into the paper. The ribbon has strips of different color inks in it to produce the different colors and has a back-and-forth print head like a dot-matrix or ink-jet printer.

Print quality is excellent with dye sublimation printers. In many cases the result is indistinguishable from a traditional photograph. Because the ink seeps into the paper as a gas and then dries, it tends to spread out a little so that the adjacent colors mix together. In contrast, a color ink-jet printer makes little dots of different colors. If you stand away from the image, the colors mix together, but move too close and the painting becomes just a bunch of dots. Dye sublimation makes a smoothly colored image. This concept will be discussed further in Chapter 8.

However, dye sublimation printers are very expensive. They are only needed for professional quality photographic printing.

Speaker

Not all computer output is visual. Some of it is aural. Most computer systems are capable of producing sound through speakers. Computer speakers are no different in construction than those in a normal stereo system.

Computers use sound to enhance or reinforce what's happening on the monitor. For example, most e-mail programs make a little "ding" sound when a new piece of mail arrives. This sound gives the user a cue without having to interrupt the user's work. Computer games also use sound to more fully envelop the user in the game's reality.

Storage Devices

Common storage devices include a tape drive, floppy drive, hard drive, and optical drive. The purpose of a storage device is to allow the writing and reading of data organized into collections called *files*.

Tape Drive

The earliest computer storage devices were tape drives. A *tape drive* records information on tape the same way an audio or video-cassette does, by creating a pattern of magnetic impulses on it. To create this pattern, the tape is dragged over an electromagnet—called the "record head" or "write head"—which is switched on or off to produce the desired pattern. This process leads to easy schemes for storing digital data. In the simplest arrange-ment, it is turned on to create a 1 bit and off to create a 0 bit. When the magnetized tape is dragged across a "read head," it reproduces the original signal in the head. In general, the term *read/write heads*, or just *heads*, refers to the small electromagnets that produce or retrieve signals from magnetic media.

The main problem with a tape drive is that it is a *sequential access device*, which means it must be processed in order. There's no easy way to jump immediately to a specific piece of data.

The situation is analogous to the difference between a videocassette and a DVD. If you have a favorite scene in a videocassette movie you want to watch, you have to fast-forward the tape from the beginning to that scene. You'll end up starting and stopping the tape a lot, playing a second or two of the movie to see how far you've gotten.

Most DVDs, though, have a menu that allows you to jump immediately to a particular scene. A DVD player is known as a *random access device*, which means you can jump to any point without going through the previous points first. Random access is also known as

direct access, which probably makes more sense.

At one time, tape drives were used as a com-puter's primary storage device, but that is no longer the case. Now they are used primarily for creating backups. A *backup* is a copy of all the data on a computer's primary storage de-vices, or at least all the data that cannot be easily replaced. Backups are used in case the computer's primary storage devices have a cat-astrophic failure, or the computer is destroyed, such as in a fire. Backups are the perfect appli-cation for tape drives, because tapes are cheap for the amount of storage they hold and be-cause the sequential access is not an issue.

Floppy Drive

A *floppy disk* is a flexible circle of plastic that stores data magnetically (like a tape drive). Today's floppy disks are stored in rigid shells; it's the disk inside that's "floppy," not the cas-ing. The earliest floppy disks were ten inches in diameter, while current disks are three and a half inches; yet because they pack the data more densely, they store more overall.

A *floppy drive* is a device to read and write floppy disks. Like a tape drive, a floppy drive has electromagnetic "heads," but in a tape drive the head stays still and the tape is pulled past it. In a floppy drive, the disk spins but the heads move too. The heads are on an arm that hovers over the disk and can move the heads from the inside edge to the outside edge of the disk, something like the needle arm of a phonograph, except that the heads on a floppy drive do not touch the disk. A special electric engine called a "stepper motor" is used be-cause it can be instructed to rotate an exact number of times. This method allows the heads to be precisely placed.

A disk is organized into tracks, which are concentric circles that separate the data, like the lanes on a running track. Each track is divided into segments called "sectors." To read a particular sector, the disk is spun and the arm is moved to place the heads over the sector's track. Then the drive waits until the spinning of the disk has brought the desired sector under the head.

Floppy disks are an example of *removable media* (or removable storage), which refers to storage devices that can be easily taken out of the computer and taken elsewhere.

Because it can go immediately to a desired sector of data, the floppy disk is a random access device. Commonly, it has been used to back up small amounts of data and to transfer data from one computer to another. Its time may have passed, however, because storage demands have risen and networks provide easier ways to transfer data between computers. Floppy drives, which were once ubiquitous on personal computers, are no longer a standard feature.

Hard Drive

Hard drives are very similar to floppy drives. A *hard drive*, as its name implies, stores data on a rigid magnetized disk or set of disks. Hard disks pack data much more densely than floppy disks. Because a single hard drive unit may contain multiple disks, the storage capacity is much greater. Where a single floppy disk may contain several megabytes of data, a hard drive can store 100 gigabytes of data or more, which means one hard drive is equivalent to tens of thousands of floppy disks. Hard drives are also much faster at writing and retrieving data.

To achieve this higher density and performance, hard drives spin thousands of times per minute, and use a faster and more precise mechanism for controlling the arm the heads ride on. One measure of a particular hard drive's performance is *seek time*, which is the length of time needed to move the heads over a specified track. Current hard drives have seek times under ten milliseconds, or put another way, they can find a track in less than 1/100 of a second.

Although technically a "hard disk" would be a disk inside the hard drive, in common use "hard disk" and "hard drive" are used interchangeably to refer to the entire device, not a particular disk inside the device. This is probably because hard drives are sealed. The media is not only not removable, but also can't be seen without opening the drive casing. Hard drives are sealed because the data is so precisely aligned than any dust that fell on a disk could ruin the data stored there.

Hard drives are the central storage device on computers today, and their capacity seems to double every couple of years. One problem larger drives have exacerbated is *fragmentation*, which is the state where files have been split up into small pieces across the disk. When a hard drive is new, the disk is one big block of unused storage, and files can be stored contiguously on the disk, perhaps all on the same track. Over time, as files are stored and erased, they split up the leftover space into smaller and smaller chunks. Eventually individual files are too big for any one chunk and have to be split up and spread across multiple tracks. Although seek times for drives are very fast, a file can still be read much faster when it is on the same track. Having files spread all over the disk is analogous to a messy desk: Although you can find what you need eventually, you have to sift through the piles to find it.

Fragmentation is one reason why computers that have been in use for a long time seem to have slowed down from when they were bought. The closer a hard drive gets to capacity, the more fragmentation occurs. A program called a *defragmenter* carefully shuffles the file fragments around to get them all contiguous again, improving performance.

Optical Drive

An *optical drive* reads data using a laser and light sensor. Bits are represented on an optical disc by placing bumps on the surface. The laser light reflects differently off the bumps and smooth parts of the disc to produce the binary 1 and 0 signals.

The first consumer use of optical drives was not for personal computers but for music. The availability of compact discs, or CDs, enabled consumers to purchase music in digital form, rather than analog form as on vinyl records. Although the CD was eventually co-opted by the computer industry, its specifications were dictated by the music industry.

A music CD can hold about seventy-four minutes of music. This time was selected so it would hold as much as any single vinyl record. Because of the sample rate and bit rate chosen by the industry, this works out to a data capacity of about 780 megabytes.

Unlike floppy and hard disks, a CD doesn't have concentric tracks. It contains one long spiral track, just like a vinyl record. A single track is used because a music CD needs to continuously read the disc to play the music. If it had to jump from one track to another, small gaps would appear in the music play-back. The single track causes trouble when applied to computers, though, because the CD

is used as a random access device. Finding the right spot to start reading on a CD is much slower than finding a track on a floppy or hard disk. It can take about ten times as long.

If you've ever been on a merry-go-round, you know that you go faster on the edge than you do toward the middle. To counter this effect, a CD player spins the disc slower as the laser moves to the outer part of the disc. Again, this is done because the data needs to be read and turned into music at a constant rate.

An optical disc used for storing computer data is called a *CD-ROM*. A CD reader in a computer system is known as a *CD-ROM drive*. In both cases the ROM stands for *read-only memory*, which means storage data that can be read but not altered. CD-ROM drives can read and play music CDs but are mainly used to install software on CD-ROMs. *Installation* refers to a process where software is copied onto the hard drive and registration steps are taken to connect the software to the operating system, including making the new software appear in the operating system's "list of programs."

Early CD-ROM drives read data at the same speed as a music CD player, which by computer standards is very slow. Logically, this meant that reading the entire disc would take seventy-four minutes! Current CD-ROM drives can read about fifty times faster than a CD player and are able to read the outer part of the disc at about the same speed as the inner part.

While CDs and CD-ROMs are manufactured with the bumps in place, another technology allows users to make discs with their own computers. A *CD-RW drive*, or computer disc read/write drive, can read discs and create discs using specially made blanks. The blank discs are quite different from ordinary CDs. They contain a special dye that is initially clear but darkens when heated. A CD-RW contains a more powerful laser that is used to heat up the dye in different spots to make reflecting and nonreflecting areas that can be read like a regular CD. Because of the heat involved in the dye process, creating a CD in this way is known as *burning*.

Some blanks are called CD-Ws (W for write-only) and can be used only once because after the dye has darkened, there's no way to make it clear again. Other blanks are called CD-RWs (RW for read/write), which use a substance that is heated to one of two temperatures. Heated to one temperature, that spot on the CD is reflective when it cools; heated to another, it is opaque.

The *DVD*, a more recent invention, works along the same principles. A DVD is an optical disc of much greater capacity than a CD-ROM, and a *DVD drive* is a device in a computer system for reading DVDs. The name DVD originally stood for Digital Video Disc because it was developed to store movies digitally, but later the name was changed to Digital Versatile Disc because any kind of data can be stored on a DVD, just like a CD.

A basic DVD can hold about 4.7 gigabytes of data, which is about six times as much as a CD-ROM. Some DVDs have two layers of data. The bottom layer is like that on a CD-ROM, a shiny surface with smooth spots and bumps. Above that is a semitransparent layer that's more like a CD-RW, with lighter and darker spots. Having both layers allows the capacity to almost double to around 8 gigabytes. You will sometimes see a 17 gigabyte capacity listed for DVDs—for a double-sided DVD that uses two layers on each side.

Because most DVD readers can only read one side, though, the user has to eject the DVD, flip it over, and put it back in the reader. From a user's point of view having a double-sided DVD isn't better than having two single-sided DVDs.

As with CDs, blank DVDs and DVD burners are also available and work along the same principles.

DISK OR DISC?

For some reason optical media, such as CDs and DVDs, are usually referred to as discs, with a *c*, although you will sometimes see the term "optical disk." Magnetic media such as floppies and hard drives, however, are almost always referred to as disks, with a *k*. This is nothing more than a spelling difference reinforced by tradition. Both *disc* and *disk* simply indicate that the media are round.

SUMMARY

Computers come in all sizes. At one end, personal computers are used by one person. At the other end, mainframes and supercomputers are used by whole organizations.

Computers store data as bits, 0's and 1's. Inside the computer, bits are either high or low voltages. On a hard drive or floppy drive, they are spots on the media magnetized in different ways. On CDs and DVDs, they are spots that reflect light differently.

All data can be stored as bits, which is then called "digital data." Some data is inherently numeric, which is easy to make digital. Other data is analog, reflecting some continuous range of values found in the real world. Such data can be made digital, but it must be sampled and quantized first.

A computer system is more than just a computer. It contains input devices (such as a keyboard and a mouse), output devices (such as a monitor and printer), and storage devices (such as a hard drive and a CD-ROM drive).

HARDWARE

KEY TERMS

CPU, bus, main memory, RAM, booting, machine language, stored program concept, logic circuit, cache, backwards compatibility, motherboard, interfaces

COMPUTER ARCHITECTURE

Having looked at all the parts of a computer system, now open the case of the computer to see what's inside and to learn how it works.

Overview

The diagram in Figure 3.1 shows the major internal components of a computer. Each of these components is discussed in detail in this chapter, but for now look at the big picture.

At the left of the diagram is the *central processing unit* or *CPU*. This is the device that actually performs the computing tasks. In a sense, the CPU is the computer. Some people even refer to the entire computer case and everything inside of it as the CPU, but that's not accurate. CPUs are often simply called *processors*, although processors can be used outside of the "central" role of a computer.

The processor occupies a tiny amount of space inside a computer's case. A modern CPU sits inside a flat package about the size and shape of a saltine cracker. That's just the package; the actual processor inside is even smaller. Because of its small size and flat, square shape, the CPU and other packaged circuits inside computers are called *chips*.

Next to the CPU is the *main memory*, which is where the computer stores programs and data while it is on.

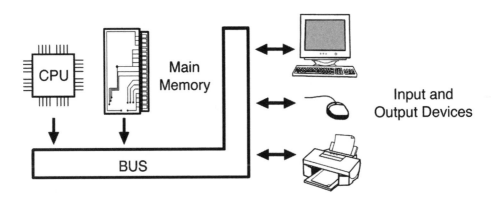

Figure 3.1—Simplified Computer Architecture

On the right of the diagram you'll see the kinds of devices discussed in Chapter 2: keyboard, mouse, monitor, printer, hard drive, CD-ROM drive, and so on. The CPU, main memory, and all the other devices are connected by an electrical path called the *bus*. Like a city bus, this bus is a shared resource, too. If you were to get on a bus at First Avenue and plan to get off at Tenth Avenue, you'd have to sit through all the stops in between. Likewise, a computer bus carries traffic to and from all the devices that are connected. Mostly this means data traveling to and from the CPU, but in some cases data travels directly from one device to another without involving the CPU.

All this activity means that the bus can get congested, which erodes performance. Because of this, computers have multiple buses, which ease the congestion. For example, because the CPU and main memory have to communicate so frequently, there's often a bus just between them.

Main Memory

Main memory consists of RAM, which is supplemented by virtual memory.

RAM

The main memory in a computer is made of *RAM*, which stands for Random Access Memory. The term "random access" means the same thing here as in the previous chapter: that the data in the memory can be accessed in any order.

RAM is made of *capacitors*, which are devices that store small electrical charges. Each capacitor stores one bit. If the capacitor is mostly charged, it's considered a 1 bit, and if it's close

to empty, it's a 0. There are two categories of RAM. *Dynamic RAM* uses capacitors that must be recharged periodically. *Static RAM* uses capacitors that hold their charge indefinitely. Static RAM is faster because it doesn't have to waste time with the periodic recharge, but dynamic RAM is much cheaper to make. Because main memories are so large, they use dynamic RAM.

RAM is divided into cells of memory called *words*, which may be a single byte (eight bits) or multiple bytes. Each word's location in RAM is specified by a unique *address*, which is just a whole number that starts from 0. For example, if a computer system has 256 megabytes of RAM, then it has 268,435,456 bytes (remember from Chapter 2 that "mega" in this context is 1,048,576, not 1,000,000). Thus, on this system the addresses range from 0 to 268,435,455. If a word on this system is two bytes, for instance, then only the even numbers in that range are legitimate addresses.

The capacitors in RAM are wired into grids. Think of a piece of graph paper with a capacitor wherever the lines cross. The lines on the graph would be wires called "control lines." Although every control line has many capacitors on it, if one vertical line and one horizontal line are selected, the lines cross in only one place. In the same way, the capacitors are wired to respond only when both of their control lines are activated.

Computer Operation

When a user requests the execution of a program, the computer brings the program from where it is stored (usually the hard drive) into main memory. Any temporary data the program needs is also stored in main memory. Storing the programs and data in main memory is necessary because storage devices like hard drives are very slow compared to the CPU. The main memory acts as a temporary "scratch pad" where the currently active program and data can be kept for quick access.

As the program executes, the CPU may need to access the devices previously discussed. For example, suppose a user opens a word processing program, such as Microsoft Word. This action brings the program into main memory. Throughout the execution of the program, data is sent to the monitor for display. Also throughout the execution, the CPU must read the instructions of the program from main memory. Suppose the user opens an existing document for editing with Word. To do so, he or she clicks the mouse on a menu item that reads "Open," then types the name of the file using the keyboard or clicks the file name from a list of Word files. Now the computer must access the hard drive again to load the file into main memory. The user edits the file, by using the keyboard and the mouse, then prints it by accessing the printer, and then saves the file, which stores it back on the hard drive.

Booting

The previous discussion assumes the operating system is already running so that the user has a way to select a program to run. But what starts the operating system? At first it seems like a chicken-and-egg problem. If the operating system is used to tell the computer what program to run next and the operating system is itself a program, what tells the computer to run anything when it's first turned on?

The process by which a computer starts and executes the operating system is called *booting*. This is short for "bootstrapping," which

means to lift oneself up by one's own bootstraps, as the expression goes, which is analogous to the seemingly impossible task the computer has when it starts.

The secret ingredient is called the *BIOS*, which stands for Basic Input/Output System. This is a set of small programs stored in ROM. Recall that *ROM*, as in CD-ROM, means read-only memory. Here it refers to memory that is accessed like RAM but is "hard-wired"; that is, it can't be changed.

When a computer's power is turned on, the BIOS acts like a drill sergeant waking up the troops. It initializes all the devices in the system and performs some self-diagnostic tests. Then it performs its most important task, which is loading the operating system.

Actually, the BIOS isn't capable of loading the operating system on its own. Instead, it retrieves a program from a special location on the primary hard drive called the *boot sector*. This short program is part of the operating system, and its job is to retrieve the rest of the operating system into memory.

When you turn on a computer, you often see a few seconds of plain-looking text, perhaps with a simple logo for the manufacturer of the computer. During this time, the BIOS is running. A few seconds later the screen displays the logo of the operating system (like "Windows XP"). That's the program from the boot sector. Finally the full operating system is loaded and you can begin running other programs.

CPU

Since the CPU is the heart of a computer, it deserves a closer look.

CPU Organization

A CPU has three essential components: an ALU, registers, and a CU, as shown in the diagram in Figure 3.2.

The *ALU*, or *arithmetic logic unit*, performs mathematical calculations and logical operations. To the ALU, all the data in a computer (which is stored as binary, as you saw in Chapter 1) is considered a number. An example of an ALU's mathematical operation is multiplying two numbers together. An example of a logical operation is comparing two numbers to determine which one is larger.

A *register* is temporary storage for data. Different CPUs have different numbers of registers. While computers store most of their active data in RAM, the ALU can only directly access the registers. Thus, having more registers is an advantage.

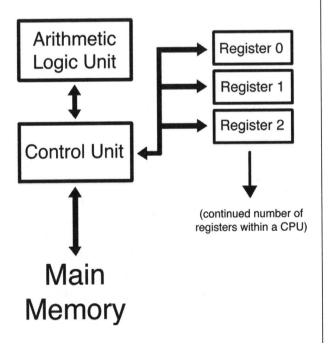

(continued number of registers within a CPU)

Figure 3.2—CPU Organization

The *CU*, or *control unit*, controls the movement of data inside the CPU. It can be thought of as the CPU's traffic cop. It determines, for example, which registers are sent to the ALU for computation.

The CU is itself controlled by the program the CPU is executing. A program is made of a series of instructions. The format of these instructions is specific to the particular model of CPU and is known as the *machine language* of the CPU. A single instruction either retrieves data from an address in RAM into a register, stores data from a register to an address in RAM, or sends values from two registers to the ALU to perform a computation or comparison.

The instructions themselves are stored in RAM along with the data. This means that to the CPU, an instruction is just another set of bits, another binary pattern. Having the programs stored in the same memory as data is known as the *stored program concept*. Because the concept was popularized in a well-known article by mathematician John von Neumann, the stored program concept was once referred to as *von Neumann architecture*. However, since this term gives the mistaken impression that von Neumann invented the concept, it is rarely used now, a situation similar to the ENIAC/ABC controversy described in Chapter 1.

Because binary patterns are hard for the human mind to follow, when computer scientists talk about a machine language, they do so at an elevated level of abstraction called *assembly language*, which is a machine language written in a human-readable form. Each assembly language instruction corresponds exactly with one machine language instruction; it's just written with words and numbers instead of a bit pattern. Here's an example of assembly instructions:

```
move      10000, register1
move      10004, register2
add       register1, register2
```

The first instruction copies the data from address 10000 in RAM to a register in the CPU. The second instruction copies data from address 10004 in RAM to another register. The third instruction adds the contents of the two registers, and the resulting sum is stored in register2.

When you read that a computer can perform about a billion instructions per second (as current CPUs can), keep in mind how small these instructions are. Simply retrieving two pieces of data and adding them together takes three machine language instructions, as shown above. Actions that seem trivial to the user, such as opening a window in the middle of the screen to say, "Are you sure you want to quit without saving your work?" require the execution of countless instructions on the CPU.

The heart of CPU operation is the fetch-execute cycle. The CPU endlessly repeats the following steps:

1. First, the next instruction is retrieved from memory.

2. Then, the control unit decodes the instruction, which means breaking apart the binary pattern of the instruction into pieces to determine how to execute the instruction.

3. Finally, the instruction is executed.

Physical Characteristics

How does a CPU actually compute? Although from our point of view the CPU is capable of

adding, multiplying, and so on, from the CPUs point of view it is not manipulating numbers, but rather, patterns of bits (on/off values) that represent numbers.

The basic bit manipulation control is called the *transistor*, which is a device that allows one flow of current to control another. Again using lamps as an example, imagine that you have a lamp with its own on/off switch plugged into a power socket and that socket is controlled by another switch on the wall. If the lamp switch is "on," you can turn the lamp on or off by using the switch on the wall. If the lamp switch is "off," it doesn't matter how the switch on the wall is set; the lamp will be off.

This arrangement produces what's called the "And operation": the lamp is on only if both switches—the wall switch "and" the lamp switch—are on. By wiring multiple transistors together in different combinations, more complicated logical operations can be performed. A particular way to connect a group of transistors is called a *logic circuit*, circuits that can be combined to form even more complicated logic circuits. As you might expect, it takes a lot of transistors to accomplish useful tasks. Simply to add two bytes representing two whole numbers together requires over 100 transistors. A modern processor contains millions of transistors.

Early computers (like the ENIAC described in Chapter 1) used vacuum tubes as transistors. Now, transistors are made of silicon and metal. A modern CPU is built in layers like a very flat wedding cake. Different layers have different patterns of metal running through them. The way the layers are put together, every line of metal in one layer that crosses over a line of metal in another layer results in a transistor with the flow of power in one line controlling the flow in the other. The design of CPUs is so complicated that it takes a powerful computer to help design them.

Cache

While all that is necessary to make a CPU are the ALU, CU, and registers, most CPUs devote a large percentage of their tiny real estate to another set of components, called the *cache*. This is fast-access memory that is used for faster retrieval than is possible from main memory. The cache would be equivalent to a file you keep on your desk, rather than putting it back in the filing cabinet, because you think you'll use it again soon.

Cache access is faster than main memory for two reasons. First, because the cache memory is inside the CPU, the data doesn't have as far to travel as data from main memory. And second, cache memory is made from faster static RAM, not dynamic RAM.

Cache is essential to the performance of current CPUs. Retrieval from main memory is too slow relative to the CPUs' clock speed. If the CPU had to wait for every piece of data to come from RAM, it would spend most of its time idling. Because early CPUs did not have caches, the speed of early computers was limited by the speed of main memory access, not the power of CPU. This weakness was called the *von Neumann bottleneck*, because it was an inevitable consequence of the von Neumann (stored program) architecture.

For cache to be effective, however, the right data has to be in the cache when the CPU needs it. Because cache can only hold a fraction of the data in main memory, the CPU has rules to determine which items in RAM are to be held in cache at any given time.

These rules are based upon the *principle of locality*, which says that when a particular address in memory is accessed, it's likely that nearby addresses will be accessed soon. Using this principle, when an address is requested and the data is not currently in cache, the CPU retrieves the requested address and all the addresses around it in a block and puts them all in cache.

Challenges of Modern CPUs

In addition to cache being essential to the performance of current CPUs, designers of modern CPUs have challenges that weren't faced in the early days of computing, as explained below.

Backwards Compatibility

Most personal computers sold today are descendants of the IBM PC and probably contain a CPU called a Pentium IV, which is a specific make of CPU produced by Intel Corporation. However, if you purchased a personal computer with an Intel CPU two years ago, it would have contained a Pentium III; and before that, a Pentium II; and before that, the original Pentium; and before that, another processor, called the 486; and before that, the 386 processor; and so on.

When Intel introduced its Pentium IV CPU, it was sold mainly to people who already owned a computer with a previous Intel CPU, but who now wanted one that was faster. They were willing to purchase a new computer, but only if their existing software would work on the new CPU. Intel, therefore, had to ensure that all programs that would execute on the previous processors would execute on the new one. This ability is known as *backwards compatibility*.

Without backwards compatibility, computer progress would be difficult because the cost of upgrading a system would be very high. While this makes the user's life much easier, it restricts the CPU designer's freedom and makes his or her job much harder. For example, the registers on early Intel CPUs contained 16 bits, or 2 bytes, while later Intel CPUs required 32 bit registers. The solution was to design the registers on later CPUs to act as both 16 bit and 32 bit registers, depending on what size data was sent to them.

Moore's Law

Back in 1965 researcher Gordon Moore wrote an article predicting that the number of transistors in a typical processor would double every two years. The unstated implication behind this prediction, which became known as Moore's Law, is that performance would also double every two years. To Moore's credit, this prediction has been proven correct over the last thirty years.

But this increase cannot continue forever. To add more transistors, either the CPU must get bigger or everything on it must get smaller. Increasing the size of the CPU is not desirable because the larger the CPU is, the more it costs to manufacture, and larger CPUs make the current flow a longer distance, which decreases performances—when the goal of adding transistors is to increase performance.

As a result, the circuits have become smaller, with narrowing circuit lines approaching 0.09 microns, or 0.0000035 inches. At this level, the slightest imperfection in materials during the processor's creation ruins it. If you read about a CPU maker's problems with "yield," this term refers to the number of processors that are usable versus the number

that have to be thrown away because of these flaws.

Soon the point will be reached where the circuit lines are only a few atoms across, but technology can go only so far in this direction.

Some researchers are working on designs based on quantum physics, where computers will store information in the quantum state of the atoms themselves. Some amazing properties of quantum mechanics, if harnessed, would allow computations to be performed must faster than with current designs.

Pipelining

The description of the basic fetch/execute cycle implies that the CPU fetches one instruction, decodes it, executes it completely, and then goes back for another. At one time this basic cycle was the norm, but eventually another scheme had to be employed to allow the execution of instructions to overlap.

Remember Todd, the college student sending messages with Christmas lights? Let's assume that Todd has had enough of Stu, his phone-hogging roommate, and decides to get an apartment of his own. He enlists a bunch of his friends to help move him into his new place.

At first the move isn't well organized. He backs a truck up to the front door of the apartment building and asks his friends to grab stuff off the truck and carry it inside. However, the building is old, with hallways and staircases so narrow that Todd's friends are running into each other as they dart from the truck to the apartment and back. They decide to take turns carrying, rather than everyone unloading at once.

The problem is, if they take turns carrying items into the apartment, the move will take all day. One person can make the round-trip only so fast. So Todd devises a method to utilize his free labor more effectively. Instead of asking any one person to carry something all the way from the truck to the apartment, he staggers them twenty feet apart along that path. Each person now only has to carry an item twenty feet, and no one crosses paths with anyone else.

In other words, instead of only one item being moved at once, as many items can be moved as there are people to move them. Although the first item off the truck doesn't get to the apartment any faster, the second item comes right behind it, and the third right behind the second, and the overall speed of the move is greatly increased.

In computer science, this idea of breaking up instructions into smaller pieces so that their execution can overlap is called *pipelining*. Just as with Todd's movers, there is a limit to how fast one instruction can be executed on a CPU. Because the logic circuits are long chains of transistors, it takes time for the power to flow from one end to the other. Using pipelining, one large circuit is broken into different stages, and once a result comes out of one stage, that stage can be used for another instruction. CPUs today divide execution into a dozen or more stages (see Figure 3.3).

But although pipelining boosts performance, it does have drawbacks. Consider Todd's situation again. Suppose, in addition to his own stuff, he's got several boxes of things that belong to his friend Marta. He intends to leave these in the truck and drive them over to her place when he's done moving. But he forgot to mention this to the friends helping him move. At some point, one of Marta's boxes arrives at the front of the line. Once Todd recognizes it, the progress of the move comes to a halt while that box is returned to the truck.

A similar problem occurs in pipelined CPUs. The CPU executes some instructions conditionally. That is, it executes an instruction comparing two numbers, and then the result of that comparison determines which of two different sets of instructions is executed next.

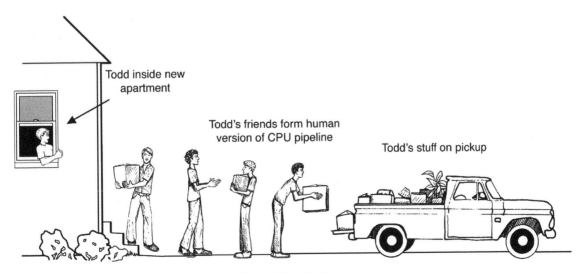

Todd inside new apartment

Todd's friends form human version of CPU pipeline

Todd's stuff on pickup

Figure 3.3—Pipelining

When a pipelined CPU reaches a comparison, it has to guess how the results will go, because the result won't be known until the comparison instruction reaches the front of the pipe. If it guesses wrong, it will have a pipeline full of partially executed instructions that must now be discarded. Then, the correct sequence of instructions is begun at the back end of the pipeline. If this happens too often, performance is degraded.

CPUs with pipelines, therefore, have sophisticated logic, called *branch prediction*, to help the CPU guess how comparisons turn out. One technique used is to track how the comparison turns out, and if the same comparison comes up again soon, the CPU guesses it will turn out the same way. But the technique means the CPU must somehow temporarily store the results of comparisons, which further complicates its design.

Heat Dissipation

If you opened the case of a computer system, you probably would not be able to see the CPU package. That's because the CPU is covered by two other devices. Immediately on top is the *heatsink*, which is just a metal block with fins that draw away heat from the CPU. Between the heatsink and the CPU there is a special paste that helps fill the gap between them completely and creates effective heat transfer. And on top of that is a small electric fan.

Why so much trouble? CPUs generate an enormous amount of heat. As they have become more complicated, all the components on a CPU have had to shrink, and that shrinkage causes more heat—similar to how water flows harder through a narrower pipe. If the heat wasn't conducted away from the CPU, the CPU would quickly melt itself. In addition

to the heatsink and fan, the CPU commonly has a thermal sensor attached. If the computer senses the CPU is about to overheat, it can shut down the system.

With some computers, even this arrangement is not enough. The hottest CPUs use a liquid-cooling system. Some work like a radiator in a car, with a pump to run a coolant past the CPU to collect the heat and then through a series of channels where the heat is released into the air. Other systems immerse the entire circuit board in a nonconductive liquid.

Multiprocessing

One way computer designers avoid these problems is to divide the work among multiple processors. *Multiprocessing* is the use of multiple CPUs in the same computer.

Originally, multiprocessing meant two separate physical CPUs, which were actually two different chips. Now, CPU designers are developing the *dual-core processor*, which combines two logically independent processors on the same chip.

The advantage of multiprocessing is that it increases the performance of a computer system without increasing the speed at which one CPU executes. The performance increases without the increase in heat.

However, multiprocessing provides only a limited benefit. One would hope that two processors would double the performance of one processor, but this is rarely the case because not all computer tasks are easily divided.

For example, if you were asked to bake ten dozen cookies for a bake sale, you could call a friend and ask him or her to make five dozen cookies, and you would make the other five dozen. Having two cooks in two kitchens would allow the cookies to be baked in half the time. But if you were asked to make a single, giant lasagna, there would no benefit in asking for help. In the same way, some computer tasks can be easily shared among multiple processors, but some cannot.

The Problem of Comparing CPUs

Different makes and models of CPU have different characteristics, but it is not easy to find the right criteria for comparing them.

CISC vs. RISC

Early CPUs had machine languages with very simple instructions. They might not even be able to multiply two numbers as a single instruction. Instead, many "add" instructions would have to be executed. Over time, as CPUs became more complicated, so did their machine languages. Single instructions were added to do the work of multiple instructions in previous CPUs. For example, to retrieve two numbers from memory and multiply them could be one instruction.

These CPUs with large numbers of more powerful instructions become known as *CISCs*, or Complex Instruction Set Computers. Having more powerful instructions would seem an advantage, and it is, but it has strong disadvantages as well. The main problem is that the logic circuits for executing an instruction must be more complicated as well, which means they take up more space on the chip. This in turn leaves less space on the chip for other things, like registers and cache, which improve the CPU's performance.

Because of these problems, CPU designers started making instructions simple again, as simple as they could make them. With the saved space, they added large register sets and caches. This meant that programs had to execute more instructions to accomplish the same tasks as CISCs, but because each instruction could execute faster, the overall performance was better. CPUs that use a small set of fast-executing instructions are called *RISCs*, or Reduced Instruction Set Computers.

The RISC idea can be said to have won for now, and most processors can be said to be more RISC-like than CISC-like. Those that retain CISC features do so mainly for backwards compatibility. Why is RISC faster? Because the design executes instructions faster, the only way for CISC to keep up is if the number of instructions per program can be dramatically reduced. This isn't possible because the most common instructions used in programs are the simplest ones. The most complicated instructions on a CISC machine—the ones that do the work of many RISC instructions—are so rarely used in actual programs that they make little difference.

Clock Speed

When a computer is advertised, a number like 2.8 GHz is often displayed prominently at the top of the feature list. This number is the *clock speed*, which is the number of CPU cycles per second. The *Hz* indicates "Hertz," which means cycles per second. The *G* means "Giga," which, as discussed in Chapter 1, means 1 billion. Thus, a 2.8 GHz processor has an internal clock that pulses nearly three billion times a second, and the actions of the CPU are triggered by those pulses.

If a CPU executed one machine language instruction per cycle, the clock speed would directly give the number of instructions per second, but because of pipelining and other complications, these numbers are never the same. The clock speed is most useful in comparing two CPUs of the same make and model. An Intel Pentium IV executing at 2.8 GHz is a little faster than the same Pentium IV executing at 2.6 GHz.

Clock speed is not reliable, however, when comparing different model CPUs. AMD, another chip maker, has a CPU called the Athlon XP. When this chip is clocked at 2.2 GHz, it executes about the same number of instructions per second as a 2.8 GHz Pentium IV.

AMD chooses not to identify their processors by clock speed because their processors would appear to the consumer as slower than they really are. Intel is planning to follow suit, because it is offering many variants of the same chip now. Having multiple Pentiums with the same clock speed available won't help consumers pick the right one for their needs. Instead, both companies will use artificial model numbers that have nothing to do with clock speed.

Benchmarking

Still, the question remains open: How does one compare one CPU's performance against another if clock speed isn't the answer? The best solution is *benchmarking*, which in computer science means running the same program on multiple computer systems and timing the results. If both computers are as identical as possible except for the different CPUs, then the difference in overall performance of the system should be attributable to the difference in processors.

Unfortunately, even benchmarking is not an absolute guide. CPUs have different strengths and weaknesses. Just because CPU A is ten percent faster than CPU B using one particular program doesn't mean it will be ten percent faster on all programs. CPU A may even be slower on other programs. Still, benchmarking is the most reliable tool for comparisons of real-world performance, especially if the benchmarks are performed using the kind of software the user is interested in running.

HARDWARE DEVICES

Now that you've seen how the computer functions, take a closer look at some of the other internal components.

Motherboard

The components inside a computer are located on a large circuit board called the *motherboard*. If you looked at a motherboard, you would see the CPU, main memory RAM, and connections for the other devices like the hard drive and CD-ROM drive. You would also see circuit traces connecting these components. These are the buses.

You would also see other chips soldered onto the board, resembling mini-CPUs. They might even have their own heatsink and fan. These other chips are device interfaces.

Graphics Card

The CPU does not directly generate the images that are displayed on the monitor. Instead, the images are produced by a specialized device called a *graphics card* or *display adapter*. These are small circuit boards that fit into a slot on the motherboard.

Because a video screen is constantly refreshed, the image displayed must be stored in RAM. Originally, graphics cards were just the RAM to hold the image and a device that constantly scanned through the RAM and converted the image stored there into the signals the monitor needed for display. Now, graphic cards are much more complicated.

Computers, especially those used for entertainment, have to generate incredibly complicated images and do so many times a second. Today, graphics cards are almost complete computers in miniature. They have their own large banks of specialized RAM, sometimes almost as much as main memory. They have their own processors, which are generally more complicated, in terms of number of transistors, than the CPUs in the same system. Because these processors get very hot, they too have heatsinks and fans. Some even draw so much power that they need a special direct connection to the computer's power supply.

Sound Card

As with video, the CPU doesn't generate sound directly. Instead, the audio you hear is produced by a *sound card*, which is a circuit board that fits into a slot on the motherboard. Because users are often less picky about sound than video, some motherboards have the sound-producing circuits directly hardwired onto the motherboard.

The heart of a sound card is a digital-to-analog converter. This converter performs the task of *modulation*, which is the opposite of sampling. It takes numbers and converts them back into continuous signals. These are the signals sent to your speakers or headphones.

DEVICE INTERFACES

Different devices have different methods of communication with the computer. A particular device's method of communication is called its *interface*. Many of the "extra" chips on a motherboard are actually translators for a certain kind of interface. It's as if the CPU only speaks English, but the hard drive and CD-ROM speak Russian, the keyboard speaks German, and the mouse speaks a dialect of Spanish.

Having different interfaces may seem an inefficient way to make a computer. Why not have everyone agree on the same language? There are two reasons why this hasn't happened. First, the interfaces are optimized to the needs of the devices that use them. A hard drive has to transmit a tremendous amount of data in a short time, but the keyboard sends only a handful of bytes to the computer every second, even for the fastest typists. Any interface fast enough for the hard drive would be serious overkill for a keyboard. Second, just like with CPUs, designers have to be aware of backwards compatibility. When someone introduces a new keyboard interface that requires users to purchase new keyboards, even though the old interface and keyboard worked fine, users will complain.

Some common interfaces used in computers today include USB, Firewire, IDE, and SCSI.

USB

USB, which stands for Universal Serial Bus, is an interface for external components, like mice, keyboards, and printers.

The word "serial" means that USB uses *serial transmission*, in which bits are sent one at a time along the same wire. In contrast, *parallel transmission* sends bits in groups, like one byte at a time, by having a wire for each bit that is sent. Parallel transmission would seem to be faster, but because it is more complicated, the overhead often outweighs the benefits.

The USB interface can transmit at a rate of 12 Mbps. *M* means "Mega," *bps* means "bits per second," and thus 12 Mbps means about 12 million bits per second, or 1.5 million bytes per second.

USB allows chaining, which means multiple devices can share the same interface. In the case of USB, up to 127 devices can chain onto one interface. That is, if a computer has one USB socket on the back of the case, up to 127 devices can communicate with the computer through that one socket. This chaining means the devices form a bus, just like the ones on the motherboard, only one that can change over time.

To allow for the physical connection of so many devices, some larger devices like printers may have both an outgoing socket (to connect to the computer) and an incoming socket (for another device to plug into and continue the chain). Because some devices, like mice, won't have any incoming sockets, users can purchase USB "hubs," which are nothing more than a set of extra incoming sockets.

One special feature of USB is that it allows *hot-swapping*, which means devices can be safely plugged or unplugged while the computer is running. The USB interface can alert the computer's operating system when a device is connected or disconnected from the system.

Firewire

Firewire is another type of high-speed serial bus. Developed by Apple, it is also known as IEEE 1394, after its official standards designation.

It's much faster than USB, transmitting data up to 400 Mbps. This speed is necessary because Firewire's intended use is connecting computers with video devices like camcorders and digital cameras, where video data is large. The speed of the interface is also good for devices like portable hard drives.

Like USB, Firewire allows hot-swapping and can chain up to sixty-three devices.

IDE

IDE, Integrated Drive Electronics, is a standard interface for connecting hard drives and optical drives. The name was chosen originally because the hard drive contains its own interface hardware, whereas previous hard drives had separate interface "cards" that had to be installed in the computer first.

IDE has been superseded by *EIDE*, or Enhanced IDE, which allows for faster data transmission and larger hard drives.

A single IDE interface on a motherboard, known as a port, can support two drives. If two drives are on the same port, one drive must be designated a "master" and the other a "slave." Usually this is done by setting switches on the drives themselves. Because many computers have more than two drives, motherboards using IDE have at least two ports.

SCSI

SCSI (pronounced "scuzzy") stands for Small Computer System Interface and is another standard interface for hard drives and optical drives. Note that drives are built for particular interfaces. A hard drive made for IDE will not work on a SCSI interface.

In general, SCSI interfaces and drives are more expensive than their IDE counterparts but perform better. SCSI interfaces can support up to seven devices.

Both SCSI and IDE use parallel transmission. If you look inside a computer case, you will probably find that the hard drives are connected to the motherboard using a ribbon cable, which, like it sounds, is flat like a ribbon. If you look closely at a ribbon cable, you will see that it is ribbed like corduroy. Each of those ribs contains a wire to allow the parallel transmission of data.

SUMMARY

Internally, a computer is a CPU, main memory, and connections to devices, all linked by a set of buses. Programs and data are stored in main memory, which is made of RAM. The CPU can access any bytes of data inside RAM using a unique numerical address.

When a computer is turned on, it goes through a process known as booting, in which the BIOS reads a small part of the operating system from the boot sector of the hard drive.

The small part of the operating system loads the rest of the operating system into memory.

The basic components of a CPU are the ALU, the CU, and registers. The CU's job is to execute instructions of a program, which involve moving data into and out of registers, and sending data to the ALU for mathematical operations and comparisons. CPUs also contain a cache, which is high-speed memory that holds a subset of RAM so it can be accessed quicker.

According to Moore's Law, CPUs get twice as complex every two years. Having more transistors means more heat, but computers have increasingly elaborate schemes for dissipating heat away from the CPU.

Different makes and models of CPU are difficult to compare. The listed clock speed for a CPU may be misleading. The best bet is to run the same programs on computers with different CPUs and record the results.

Computer components are linked together on a motherboard. In addition to the basics of CPU and RAM, the motherboard provides interfaces for all the other devices in the computer system. Each type of device uses a different interface. External devices like a mouse or a digital camera might use USB or Firewire. Storage devices commonly use the IDE or SCSI interface.

TYPES OF SOFTWARE

Software can be categorized many different
ways. One way is to divide all programs
into a few broad categories: system software,
application software, utility software, and
malicious software.

System Software

System software includes all the programs necessary to run a computer. Chief among these
programs is the operating system itself, the
most important software running on a computer. As explained in Chapter 3, the operating
system runs all the other programs. Without
the operating system, the computer is useless.

Also included under system software are
programs necessary for particular pieces
of hardware. When you purchase a printer,
for example, it often comes with a CD of
software, which must be installed for the
printer to function.

Application Software

Application software provides specific services to
the user, such as programs for word processing,

e-mail, computer games, financial management,
spreadsheets, and image manipulation.

A *word processor* allows a user to create, edit,
and format textual documents. Early word
processors were very crude—"cut" and "paste"
were once new ideas—but even then these programs were often what sold people on computers. Word processors today are so advanced
that they have more features than professional
magazine layout programs had a few years ago.

E-mail clients allow the user to receive electronic messages, compose and send messages,
and organize messages in folders. Recall from
Chapter 2 that a client is a program that interacts with a central computer called a server.
E-mail programs are called clients because
they retrieve and send mail through servers.

Computer game software allows a user to play
a game on a computer. These games can run
from very simple ("Solitaire") to incredibly
complex ("Deus Ex: Invisible War"). Many
computer games now have development
budgets like that of a Hollywood film.

Financial software tracks a user's financial
accounts or prepares finance-related paperwork, such as tax forms. Examples in this
category are Intuit's Quicken, Microsoft's
Money, and Kiplinger's TaxCut.

Spreadsheet software provides a matrix of cells,
in which each cell can be a number, a line of
text, or a calculation involving the values in

other cells. The power of a spreadsheet lies in being able to change a single value and have all the related results recalculate automatically. For example, if you create a spreadsheet that shows how much money you will have in five, ten, and fifteen years based on your current income, expenses, and return on your investments, you can change any of the input values and instantly see the results on your future earnings. Spreadsheet programs were among the first popular applications on computers. The idea of laying out calculations into cells like this had been used, on paper, for years, but of course performing the calculations by hand was tedious. A computer spreadsheet saves all that tedious work.

Image manipulation was once reserved for photography professionals. But as digital photography has grown more popular and easier to use, even amateur shutterbugs want to modify their photographs and other images. The king of image manipulation software is Adobe's Photoshop. In fact, the word "photoshop" has become a verb meaning "manipulate the image" in the same way that "Xerox" has come to mean "copy."

Utility Software

Utility software enhances a user's computer experience. Examples of utilities are virus scanners, programs that clean unneeded files off the hard drive, screen savers, and so on. One might describe these programs as extensions of system software—features the user wished were part of the operating system but aren't. In fact, many operating system features start off as utilities.

Malware

Malware, a contraction of the words "malicious software," is a new term, but it is convenient and growing in use. Malware includes all programs that users don't want on their systems. Such software includes viruses, Trojan horses, and spyware.

Viruses

A computer *virus* is a short piece of programming code that attaches itself to a legitimate program and attempts to replicate by copying itself to other programs. For example, if a virus attaches itself to your word processor every time you run it, the virus will execute first. Some viruses do nothing but replicate or display joke messages at certain times, but more malevolent viruses erase files on the hard drive. Even a virus that only replicates, however, can seriously damage the performance of a computer or prevent its proper function.

A *worm* is a type of virus that spreads not only to other programs on the computer it has infected, but also across network links. For example, some worms find the e-mail program on a computer and then e-mail themselves to every entry in the address book.

Trojan Horses

A *Trojan horse* is a program that masquerades as a legitimate piece of software but has a sinister ulterior function. For example, a program on a Web site may be advertised as a game. It will even run as a game, but when it runs, it signals back to the program's developer, who can then use the program to surreptitiously pilfer files from the user's computer.

Spyware

Spyware is hidden software that tracks user activity and reports back to the program's developer. The most common type of spyware is used by advertisers to track Web sites a user visits so that tailored advertising can be later sent to the user. Spyware is often introduced to a computer system through a Trojan horse.

AVOIDING MALWARE

Malware makes its way into a computer system because of weaknesses in system software design, user gullibility, or a combination of both. Keeping a system completely free of malware may not always be possible, but you can dramatically improve your odds by staying alert.

You can't fix problems with your computer's operating system, but you should always install any security updates as soon as they are available.

Avoiding gullibility, though, is entirely in your hands. One key is to never install any software unless you know and trust the *original* source of the software. *Original* is emphasized because if our friend Todd sends Marta a program as an e-mail attachment, Marta must decide if she trusts who wrote the program, not if she trusts Todd, who could be passing along a virus-infested program or a Trojan horse without realizing it (Figure 4.1). The e-mail may have been generated by a worm and not written by Todd at all. If you don't know what company created a program, don't install it.

Finally, don't open any e-mailed file attachment unless you know what kind of file it is. Learn to recognize the file types of the programs you work with: *doc* for Microsoft Word, for example, or *mov* for Apple's QuickTime movies. Certain file types that appear to be just data files can also contain program code and thus could contain malware. If you are unsure, don't open the file.

Figure 4.1—Know Who You're Trusting

OPERATING SYSTEMS

The computer science view of an operating system is much deeper than that of the typical user. A user only thinks about the part of the operating system that can be seen and interacted with, which is known as the *shell*. Users often refer to the shell as the desktop. If you have used a recent computer with the Windows operating system, then the shell is in fact its desktop, with the start menu and the current time displayed in the corners along with everything else you see when the computer is first turned on.

The shell is an important part of an operating system, but it's a very small part. Most of what an operating system does happens "behind the curtain." In this section, you can look behind that curtain.

Functions of an Operating System

An operating system exists for many kinds of management: process, file, memory, event, output device, security, and application and system data.

Process Management

The earliest computer systems allowed only *batch processing*, which means they executed only one program at a time. A school or company would have one computer (a mainframe), and the users would have to schedule time on it, the same way they would schedule the use of a conference room or an overhead projector.

Modern operating systems allow *multitasking*, which means several programs can be running at once. Originally this was seen as a way to avoid scheduling conflicts on a shared computer, but the capability has proven useful for personal computers as well. Multitasking has changed the way people use computers and the way they work in general. It's common for a user to have many programs open at once—an e-mail program, an instant messenger, a word processor, and a Web browser, for instance—and actively switch from one to the other as the work demands.

Even when the user is only running one program, though, the modern operating system depends on multitasking. That's because the operating system runs many *background tasks*, which are programs that receive no direct user interaction. An example of a background task is a print spooler. This program accepts print data to be printed from any application—like a word processor or e-mail program—and then slowly sends the data to the printer. The print spooler is needed because printers can only accept a certain amount of data at a time. If a word processor were responsible for directly sending data to the printer, the word processor would be busy, and thus unusable, until the print job was finished. By handing the data off to a "middleman," the user can continue working immediately after starting the print job.

The operating system is responsible for keeping all the programs and background tasks executing, which is known as *process management* because the operating system deals with "processes" instead of "programs." A single program may have several instances running at the same time, and each instance is a separate process.

For example, it's common for users to have multiple Web browser windows open at once, and many nefarious Web sites will open a second window for you—usually containing an advertisement. Each of these windows is running the same program, but different processes. Each window represents another copy of the program in memory, and to the operating system it doesn't matter that they are copies of the same program.

Because most computers have only a single CPU, only one process can actually be running at any given time. The operating system achieves multitasking through a technique called *time-slicing*. Simply put, this means that the operating system runs a process for a short period of time (a fraction of a second), then sets it aside and runs another process for a while, and so on. A program that seems to be running continuously is actually being constantly started and stopped.

The operating system must decide how long and how often to run each process before moving on to the next one. A process can be in one of several states. A *running process* is currently executing on the CPU. A *ready process* is waiting for its turn to execute on the CPU. A *blocked process* is waiting for some event to happen to make it ready. For example, if the user has requested to save a file with the same name as an existing file, the program may put up an "Are you sure you want to overwrite the existing file?" message and wait for a response from the user. Because the process cannot continue until the user has made a decision, the operating system won't waste the CPU's time on it.

The length of a time slice must be determined carefully. *Task switching*, which is the term for pausing one process and starting another, takes time. If you recall the explanation in Chapter 3 about pipelining, the pipeline must begin anew when the CPU switches to a different process. Also, all the values in the CPU's registers must be stored in main memory so that when the process gets its next time slice, it can pick up right where it left off.

In general, then, the performance of the system is improved by having as few task switches as possible, which means having long time slices. The problem is, even though long slices keep the CPU doing as much useful work as possible, they lower the perceived performance of the system. That is, the user's experience with the system suffers, because there's often a greater delay between the user's action and the program's reaction on the monitor. Thus, the operating system must carefully manage the time slices to give the best balance between overall performance and user experience.

The operating system tries to schedule the use of the CPU to give more of its time to the processes that need it. This is not easy for the operating system to arrange because there's no way to predict which programs will be the busiest. Instead, the operating system monitors the use of the CPU and assumes that past use is a predictor of future use. The processes are in a queue, like a line at a ticket window. When they get to the front, they use the CPU for a moment before they have to get back in line. If the process doesn't need all the CPU time it is offered, such as a background process, it is moved all the way to the back of the line, which means it takes a long time to get to the front again. However, a process still executing when its time slice runs out is assumed to be busy and is only sent back to a point in the middle of the line. This way, the busy processes get to the front of the CPU queue more often.

File Management

File management refers to the ability to read and modify files on storage devices and to create and delete files.

In Chapter 3 we said that storage devices like hard drives are divided into tracks and sectors, and a single file that occupies many sectors could be spread all over a disk. This fragmentation makes accessing a file tricky. Fortunately for application programmers, locating the fragments of a file are the responsibility of the operating system.

Each storage device has both a logical and physical structure. The logical structure is what the user sees. Consider a small file stored on a Windows operating system under the name *C:\MyDocuments\Myfile.txt*. Here, *Myfile.txt* is the name of the file, and *C:\MyDocuments* is the file's logical location. On a Windows system, it means that the file is on a hard drive indicated by the letter C

CHAPTER 4: **SOFTWARE** 53

and that on that drive it is stored in a folder called "My Documents."

Remember the physical structure that was discussed in Chapter 3: each file is stored across various sectors on a disk. The logical structure and physical structure are not related. Just because two files are located in the same folder, for example, does not mean they are anywhere near each other on the physical storage device.

Thus, a primary job of file management is mapping logical file locations to physical locations. To do this, the operating system maintains a directory on each storage device. The directory lists which physical locations go with which files and also keeps track of which locations on the storage device are free, that is, that are not currently used by any file. As files grow and shrink, and are created and deleted, the operating system changes the directory to reflect how the sectors are currently used. This file management allows all the application programs to deal exclusively with the logical file structure.

Note that the operating system will generally cache files. If you recall from Chapter 3, the CPU has a cache, which is a small amount of RAM that can hold recently used data close by, so if it's needed again soon, the request doesn't have to go all the way to main memory. Similarly, the operating system may hold recently accessed file data in main memory— so if it's needed again, the request doesn't have to go back to the storage device. Or, if a program has requested the first fifty bytes from a file, the operating system may go ahead and retrieve several kilobytes or more from the file in anticipation of a later request. This process is another form of caching.

SOFTWARE HOOKS

Certain utility programs must integrate themselves with the operating system to function. A good example is a program that scans files for viruses before they are used. If you are in a word processing program and ask the program to open a file, that file must pass through the virus scanner on its way from the operating system to the word processor.

To allow these kinds of utilities to function, the operating system must provide "hooks." A hook is a request for the operating system to invoke another program for a certain operation. The virus scanning program establishes a hook that says, "Whenever you are opening a file, call me first."

A few years ago many were complaining that Microsoft's dominance of the operating system market gave it an unfair advantage when it came to writing applications. One of the accusations was that because Microsoft had more intimate knowledge of the operating system, Microsoft developers could write software that relied on undocumented hooks, giving their programs abilities others could not match.

Memory Management

Another important function of the operating system is *memory management*, which is the service associated with the allocation of main memory. Essentially, the memory manager decides which main memory addresses are associated with which processes at any given time. All the processes currently running, and the operating system itself, have main memory needs that must be met.

When a program is first begun, it is given enough memory to hold some part of the program and data. Over time, the program may request additional main memory space. A request for main memory that occurs during a program's execution is known as a *dynamic memory allocation* and is a function provided by the operating system.

One problem with dynamic memory allocations is that a program must remember to deallocate the memory when it is no longer needed so the memory can be used by another program, and all programs are expected to return all dynamic memory before closing. If a program neglects to deallocate its dynamic memory when it no longer needs it, the result is a *memory leak*, a block of memory that is allocated but unused. Memory leaks degrade system performance because, in essence, the system now has less main memory.

Another complication of dynamic memory is that some memory is shared between processes. When this happens, the memory manager's job is more difficult, because it must track each use of the allocated memory. Just because one process has signaled it is done with the memory doesn't mean the memory can be deallocated. Instead, the operating system must wait until all processes have signaled.

Although today's computers have large main memories, they are often not large enough. As memory sizes have grown, the size of the average program has grown even faster. Consider that some software packages come in multiple CD-ROM sets, and a single CD-ROM can hold more data than the main memory for most computers. In addition, because of multitasking, many users are running multiple programs at once.

One way to never run out of RAM is through a technique called *virtual memory*, in which a

larger main memory is simulated through the use of storage on the hard drive. The operating system maintains a table that maps each program's simulated address with the physical addresses in main memory.

As an example of how this works, let's say that the user requests to start TypeEdit, a word processing program whose size is fifty kilobytes. The operating system retrieves the first portion of the program, say 1,000 bytes, and decides to store it in main memory starting at address 100,000,000. The operating system notes this in its virtual memory table. The program itself is unaware of where it is located in physical memory. It is written as if it was stored at location 0. The entry in the table would look something like this:

Program	Virtual Address Range	Physical Address
TypeEdit	0–999	100,000,000–100,000,999

If the program executed an instruction that said, "Store this value at location 45," the operating system, using this table, would translate that instruction to: "Store this value at location 100,000,045."

Now suppose the program needed to execute the portion of the program at locations 1,000–1,999. Because this part of the program isn't in memory, the operating system retrieves it, and stores it at 75,000. Now the table looks like this:

Program	Virtual Address Range	Physical Address
TypeEdit	0–999	100,000,000–100,000,999
TypeEdit	1,000–1,999	75,000–75,999

Thus, each currently running process has entries in this table, and this way, each process can act as if it has the entire main memory to itself, letting the operating system handle the details.

The blocks of physical memory that the operating system hands out are called *pages*. When a process requests a virtual memory range that is not currently in main memory (as TypeEdit did in the second part of the example), it's known as a *page fault*.

Pages may also need to be written to the hard drive. If a page contains nothing but program instructions, it can simply be written over by another page because the operating system can always retrieve that part of the program again. But if a page contains a program's current data, that data needs to be kept for when the program needs it again. The operating system maintains a special area on the hard drive, called the *swap file*, for the temporary storage of pages. For the best performance, this file is usually allocated as one contiguous block in the middle of the disk so that whatever other hard drive access is going on, the needed page is never far away from the read/write head's current position.

Over time, a process may gain pages or lose pages. The more active a program is, the more pages it is awarded. The goal of the virtual memory manager is to minimize the number of page faults because every page fault is a slow trip back to the hard drive. If you've ever had a large number of programs open at once and then switched from a program you've been using a lot to one you haven't used in a few minutes, you may have noticed a temporary slowdown. That's because, over time, the active program grabbed most of the pages in memory. When you switched to the inactive

program, it suddenly needed a lot of pages it hadn't needed in minutes, and this generated a large number of page faults. In extreme cases, there are so many active processes competing for main memory that the computer spends most of its time swapping pages, a phenomenon known as *thrashing*.

In general, when you see the hard drive light flash and you are not opening or saving a file, it's a good bet you're seeing the virtual memory manager at work.

Event Management

Another important function of a modern operating system is event management. In computer science, an *event* is a specific action that produces a reaction in some program. If you click the mouse in a certain spot on a program's window, for instance, the program may respond by displaying a menu. Mouse clicks and keystrokes are user-initiated events. Other events may be generated by the operating system itself. For example, a program that displays the current time in a corner of the screen might request a timer event to occur every minute so it can update its display.

It is the operating system's responsibility to route events to the appropriate programs. The programs do not directly communicate with the mouse or keyboard. Instead, the operating system collects all the events and sends messages to the programs that need them.

This separation between application programs and hardware is another example of abstraction, the concept introduced in Chapter 1. The programs are one level of abstraction removed from the mouse and keyboard. Different keyboards and mice may have different characteristics, but only the operating system needs to deal with that. It handles this with another layer of software between the operating system and devices. Software that acts as a middleman between the operating system and a device is called a *device driver*. These drivers are provided by the manufacturer of the device.

For output devices, the operating system expects input in a standard format. The job of an input device's driver is to provide the input in that format. This way, the programs that use the input devices can treat them generically, without worrying about who made them or what specific features they may have.

Output Device Management

The reverse of event management is output device management. Just as the operating system acts as middleman between programs and input devices, it also acts as a middleman between programs and the monitor or printer.

Device drivers exist for output devices too. For output devices, the operating system provides a generic set of commands that programs can use to display or print, and, on the other end, issue display or print commands in a standard format. The device drivers translate this standard output into the commands that the specific printer or graphic card expects.

Writing device drivers is a critical programming job. The graphic card's driver, for example, is probably executed more than any other program in the computer. An excellently designed piece of hardware can still produce a poor user experience if the driver is flawed or does not take advantage of all the device's strengths.

Look at the chain of actions that would occur when a user types a letter in a word processing program (Figure 4.2). The user presses the S key on the keyboard. The keyboard's device driver communicates this key press to the

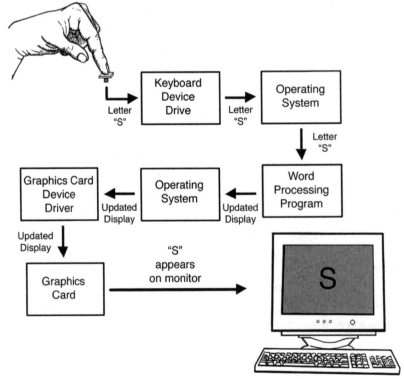

Figure 4.2—Chain of Actions

operating system. The operating system determines that the key press belongs to the word processing program and sends the key press to it. The word processor determines that an S must appear in the display at the current cursor location. Now, it must update its display. To do so, it communicates back to the operating system. The operating system communicates with the device driver for the system's graphics card. The device driver communicates with the graphics card, which generates the display for the monitor. Thus, even a simple word processor's keystroke involves the interoperation of many pieces of software.

Security

The operating system is involved in many aspects of computer security as well. Perhaps the most obvious aspect of this responsibility is *user authentication*, which just means positively identifying a user, usually through a user name and password. Some operating systems, like Windows XP, allow multiple user accounts on a single personal computer, and each user can have private folders and files that other users cannot view, modify, or delete. If a computer is connected to a network, the operating system may be required to authenticate the user before the computer can access files across that network.

The operating system also provides security in less obvious ways. As stated earlier, in a multitasking operating system, a single computer can have multiple programs running. A flawed or malicious program could alter the instructions or data of another program, corrupting the data or crashing the program. The operating system enforces rules to keep each program separate. This separation doesn't prevent a program from crashing or corrupting its own data, but it helps to prevent a single program's malfunction from creating system-wide havoc.

Application and System Data Management

Operating systems must store system data. An operating system is installed on a wide variety of computers with different configurations of hardware and software, and these configurations must be tracked. The operating system stores data detailing the kind of CPU in the system, the size of the hard drive, the kind of graphics card, the name of the device driver for each device in the system, and other hardware-related data. On a system with user accounts, all the account information and user preferences must be stored. The operating system also may offer choices of display resolution, organization of menus, whether certain user actions generate a sound, and so on.

Operating systems also store some application data. Most programs allow the user to customize the interface to some extent, by adding or removing a certain "toolbar," changing the colors used, and so on. This data is stored with the operating system also.

Current Operating Systems

Current operating systems include Windows, UNIX, Mac OS, and Palm OS.

Windows

As mentioned in Chapter 1, Microsoft's Windows series of operating systems, which currently dominate the computer industry, have a long and colorful history. Microsoft gained prominence with its first operating system, DOS ("disk operating system"), which was a text-based system. If you wanted to run a program, you typed the name of the program at the "command line" and DOS would run it for you. If you wanted to delete a file, you typed "del" and the name of the file to delete it. Although primitive by today's standards, DOS was the provided operating system for the original IBM PC, and when the latter began selling in huge numbers, it established Microsoft's position.

The first release of Windows, in 1985, can be seen as a reaction to the introduction of the Apple Macintosh the year before. The first Windows was not a whole operating system so much as just a shell that provided a graphical interface, a mouse-based way to run programs while DOS, behind the scenes, still did all the work. While this first version contained many of the features taken for granted now, it had a long way to go. For example, multiple programs could be running in separate windows, but the windows could not overlap.

Another problem with early versions of Windows was the use of *nonpreemptive multitasking*, which means the applications were responsible for giving up the CPU when their time slice was over. In contrast, most operating systems, including current versions of Windows, use *preemptive multitasking*, in which the CPU control automatically returns to the operating system after an application's time is up.

With nonpreemptive multitasking, an application is expected to "check in" with the operating system every so often, so the operating system can regain control. The problem arises when the program "crashes" or is tied up waiting for some event that isn't occurring. If the application never checks in, the operating system never gets control back, and the whole system is frozen. With preemptive multitasking, a misbehaving application won't keep the operating system from maintaining control of the computer. Other applications are allowed to continue.

Windows really took off with the release of Windows 95. This version was the first that did not need DOS to be installed on the computer first. Parallel with the development of Windows 95, however, Microsoft had developed a completely new operating system, called NT, for "new technology." Originally, NT was supposed to have been a text-based operating system like DOS, but during development, Microsoft decided it would have a graphical interface and be released under the name Windows NT.

Now, Microsoft had two diverging operating systems: Windows 95, an evolutionary development from the days of DOS, and Windows NT, a new operating system with a more modern design and all the interface features of Windows. Microsoft developed both because of backwards compatibility. Just like Intel and their CPU development, Microsoft worried about forcing everyone to switch to a completely new operating system. Although Microsoft took pains to allow older software and hardware to work with NT, the system was so different that some incompatibility was inevitable. Thus, Microsoft hedged its bets and kept the old operating system alive, reasoning that home users would use Windows 95 and business users would switch to Windows NT.

Eventually, though, the "new technology" won. Windows 95 became Windows 98 and then Windows ME ("millennium edition"). Windows NT became Windows 2000 and then Windows XP. With Windows XP, Microsoft is only producing a single operating system again. Windows XP is used by home and business users alike.

UNIX

The UNIX operating system, developed at AT&T's Bell Laboratories, has been around for over thirty years. Where operating systems like Windows tend to emphasize features that help novice users, UNIX emphasizes features that help programmers and expert users. For example, UNIX has a feature called a *pipe*, which is a mechanism for setting the output of one program as the input of another program. If Program A corrects the spelling of a text document, Program B formats a document in a three-column layout, and Program C prints a document, then a user can pass a document through A and B to C to spell-check, format, and print the document in a single command.

Though UNIX is old, it has all the features of a modern operating system, including multitasking. One of its strengths is its simplicity, which allows it to be easily modified for use on newer computers.

By itself, though, UNIX has no graphical interface; it is purely a text-based operating system. This problem is quickly remedied through the use of X-Windows, a separate graphical user interface system that runs on top of UNIX. Although UNIX and X-Windows are two different things, and X-Windows could be run on other operating systems, X-Windows can be considered the de facto interface for UNIX, except on the Macintosh.

UNIX has surged in popularity in the last few years because of Linux, an open-source version of UNIX discussed in Chapter 1.

UNIX offers users a great deal of low-level control and is therefore popular with expert users. Home users, though, have been slower to accept this operating system. Many popular programs are not available for UNIX, and it is more difficult for the typical home user to learn. Some UNIX programmers almost seem to take pride in offering obscure commands and interfaces.

Mac OS

Mac OS is the operating system for the Apple Macintosh computer; the *OS* stands for "operating system." Unlike UNIX, the Mac OS developers strove to make their operating system as painless to use as possible. Many of the features that are common to all graphical interfaces were introduced in Mac OS.

The first versions of Mac OS, simply called "System," as in "System 1.0," only supported a black-and-white display and could only run a single program at a time. However, users could switch from one program to another, giving the appearance of multitasking.

By version 8.0, the name changed to Mac OS and the operating system supported multitasking, albeit nonpreemptive multitasking.

A current version is Mac OS X, where the *X* indicates the roman number for 10. This version actually uses Unix as the base operating system, while providing a polished graphical interface (called "Aqua") that is as easy to use as Macintosh owners expect. While the Mac OS holds only a tiny percentage of the marketplace, those who use the Macintosh are a devoted bunch, almost fanatical in their appreciation of the operating system's elegance.

Palm OS

The above-mentioned operating systems are designed for use on personal or larger computers. The Palm OS operating system is for small computers. It was designed for the

Palm Pilot, one of the original personal digital assistants. A PDA, as it's called, is a handheld computer that functions as an appointment calendar, note pad, and calculator, and can perform other basic computing tasks.

Over time, PDAs and cell phones have merged, creating "smart phones" with e-mail and Web browsing capability in addition to basic PDA and cell phone features.

The Palm OS is a tiny operating system compared to the other systems, because the storage capabilities of handheld devices are so small. This small storage space is not a problem because Palm OS only needs to support a fraction of the features of the others. It doesn't need complicated file management, for example.

SUITES AND COMPONENTS

In recent years, attention has shifted away from independent application programs toward programs that work together as a team. *Interoperability* refers to the ability of different pieces of hardware and software to communicate with each other. Software interoperability is an important trend.

Suites

One way to get programs to work together is to write them together. A *suite* is a set of applications that is sold as one package, and it offers several advantages to the consumer. The price of the suite, for instance, is usually much lower than the price of the individual applications, and because the programs are produced by the same developer, they can be made to interoperate.

Consider a suite of standard office applications, which include word processing, spreadsheet, and e-mail programs. Interoperability could allow the e-mail program to use the word processor program for editing. In other words, while you were composing a new e-mail message, the e-mail program's editing window would display the word processing program.

If the programs didn't communicate in this way, then the e-mail program would need its own programming code for editing text. This capability would be redundant, and probably the e-mail program would have fewer editing features.

Similarly, the word processor might allow a spreadsheet to be displayed inside a document. When editing the spreadsheet, the user is actually using the spreadsheet program, even though the spreadsheet is inside a word processing document. Or, the word processor might allow a graph, generated from spreadsheet data, to be displayed in a document. If the user later edited the spreadsheet data, the graph would automatically be updated the next time the document was opened in the word processor.

Another advantage to a suite is that each program can have a similar interface style. Developers talk about a program's "look and feel." When a program looks and feels like another program that the user is already comfortable with, the user can learn the program more easily.

Different suites exist for different kinds of users. The most common suite, as already mentioned, is the "office" suite for use in business and home offices. It usually includes a word processor, spreadsheet, e-mail, presentation software, and sometimes other components.

Other common suites are used by web page designers. They include programs to edit web pages, organize entire Web sites, manipulate images, and so on.

Still another suite highlights graphic design and is used for the design and layout of books, magazines, advertisements, and other materials. Typical programs include a photograph manipulator, an illustration program, a document layout program, and so on. Because so much content is directed towards the Web, many graphic designer suites also include the features of a web page design suite too.

Components

Interoperability among programs from the same developer isn't simple, but interoperability between programs from different developers is even more complicated. What's needed is a standard way of communicating. Programs that conform to some standard interface to facilitate interoperability are called *components*.

There are many advantages of components to developers. For one, using components can decrease development time significantly. Consider how many programs need to let the user edit text like a word processor, such as e-mail programs, presentation software, and data entry programs. Rather than develop that functionality themselves, a programming team can purchase a component with that capability and simply plug it into their developing application.

Components can also lead to fewer software errors. If one company makes a word processor component that hundreds of other companies will use, the component is rigorously tested and so widely used that any flaws are soon uncovered and the component is repaired

and redistributed. Now, suppose that instead, 100 companies each develop their own word processing capability from the ground up. It's much more likely that some of the applications will have errors in the text editor because fewer people will have seen and tested each application.

A couple of specific implementations include COM and CORBA.

COM

Microsoft's solution for interoperability is called *COM*, which stands for Component Object Model, and it allows the building of applications using components from different developers. In this context, an "object" is just a program that exists to provide a service to applications.

COM works well, but because it is backed by Microsoft, it is viewed as a Windows-centric technology, even though Microsoft makes COM technology work under other operating systems as well. Some developers are nervous about conforming to a standard that is owned by a single company.

CORBA

CORBA stands for Common Object Request Broker Architecture. Unlike COM, CORBA is an open standard, which means it is supported by a nonprofit organization (in this case the OMG, or Object Management Group) that any programmer or company may join.

This support carries two benefits to programmers. First, it gives them a voice in the development of the standard. And second, it keeps the development transparent so that programmers won't be given any surprises. Actually, the owner of a closed standard (like Microsoft with COM) would probably never deliberately make things difficult for programmers because that would be self-defeating. But everyone feels better when they have more direct control over the future.

SUMMARY

Three main kinds of software are system software, which includes all the programs necessary to run a computer; application software, which provides specific services to the user; and utility software, which enhances a user's computer experience. Malware, or malicious software, includes viruses and Trojan horses. The user must take care to avoid them.

The most important software on any computer is its operating system. Without it, the computer ceases to function and no other programs can be executed.

The operating system has a number of responsibilities.

First, it must keep all the programs and background tasks executing, which is known as process management. Second, it must provide file services such as reading, creating, and modifying files on storage devices. Third, it must allocate and deallocate blocks of main memory, which is memory management. A key part of memory management is virtual memory, in which a larger main memory is simulated through the use of the hard drive. Fourth, it must route events, such as user actions, to the appropriate program, and then route program actions to the proper output device. In general, this routing forms the connection between application programs and the devices in a computer system. Fifth, it must protect programs from interfering with each other or with files they should not access. Sixth, it must store key data about the system and applications that run on it.

A suite is a collection of applications sold together. Suites save the consumer money, and the applications they contain can benefit from each other's features.

A trend in software is component-based programming. Components are programs with standard interfaces that can communicate with each other even though they may have been developed by different programmers.

PROGRAMMING

PROGRAM LOGIC

The central task in computer science is the development of new programs. These programs are created through software engineering in a process similar to that of engineering for a building. The specifications of the program are laid out to determine *what* the program is going to do. Then the program is designed to decide *how* the program will achieve its goals. Only then is the program written.

At the design stage, the programmer determines the program logic using an *algorithm*, which is a series of instructions that define how to solve a problem. This definition may sound very similar to that of a computer program, but there's an important distinction. An algorithm is described "in English" rather than written in a computer programming language. Thus, an algorithm is written to be "human readable," whereas a program is written to be "machine readable." Put another way, an algorithm is the idea behind the solution, while the program is the actual implementation of that solution.

Computer scientists prefer to discuss algorithms when determining the best solution to a problem. Because programs are written by programmers—who have individual strengths and weaknesses—and are executed on computers, which may execute some kinds of instructions faster than others, a program can provide a misleading picture. Algorithms are a neutral proving ground for possible solutions.

While modern programming languages are widely varied, they all share the basic concept of *control flow*, which is the order in which the program instructions are executed. Control flow is determined by the *control structures*, which are the traffic cops on the program highway.

Although computers are capable of astoundingly complex tasks, even the most complicated computer programs are built using simple arithmetic operations and a few elementary control structures, coming together in nearly infinite combinations. These elementary control structures are discussed in this section using algorithms. While many algorithms involve the manipulation of numeric data, the algorithms below involve our computer science student, Todd, a young man with a very systematic approach to fun.

Sequential Execution

The sequence is the default control flow; it results from the lack of any control structure and is the easiest to understand. In a computer program, the instructions are executed as they are listed, from top to bottom, unless the computer is told otherwise. Executing instructions in the order listed is *sequential execution*.

For example, Todd uses a sequential execution algorithm when he grooms himself before going to a party.

"Pre-Party Grooming" Algorithm
Wash hair
Shave face
Brush teeth
Gargle with mouthwash
Apply "product" to hair, sculpt

When Todd executes this algorithm, he simply executes the instructions in order. The order is important to Todd. For example, he washes his hair first so it has time to naturally dry during the other steps before he applies his "product" (see Figure 5.1).

Todd always grooms himself the same way. Sequential execution is all that is needed when there are no choices to be made. In most cases, however, more is needed.

Figure 5.1—Todd's Grooming Ritual

Conditional Execution

In the previous example, all the instructions have to be executed every time the algorithm is used (every time Todd grooms himself for a party). In other cases an instruction or group of instructions may be optional. With *conditional execution*, an instruction is executed or skipped based on a condition tested when the instruction is reached. In most algorithms and programming languages, conditional execution can be spotted by looking for the word "if," as in, "*if* this condition is true, *then* do this step." For that reason, programmers often refer to conditionally executed instructions simply as "'if' statements."

Todd uses conditional execution when he executes his algorithm to dress himself for a party. Todd takes his clothing choices seriously, altering his outfit to match the party's attendees and locale.

"Getting Dressed for Party" Algorithm
Put on boxers
If party is downtown,
    Then put on dress shirt and khakis
Otherwise,
    Put on black sweater and jeans
Put on leather belt and dark shoes
If Marta will be at party,
    Then put on Movado watch she gave me
Put cell phone in pocket

Note first that sequential execution is still the rule. This algorithm is executed from the first instruction to the last, except for the "if" statements.

This example demonstrates two kinds of conditional execution. The first is a "two way" conditional. Todd dresses upscale for downtown parties, but relaxed when partying in the suburbs. Because he will always do one or the other—he's not going to attend a party in his underwear—he's choosing from two paths. The second conditional is a "one way." If his friend Marta will be at the party, he'll wear the watch she gave him. There's no alternative here. He either wears the watch or he doesn't.

Repetitive Execution

While conditionals are used to execute or skip an instruction, *repetitive execution* is used when the same instructions are executed more than once. In normal discourse, most programmers refer to repetitive execution as *looping*, from the idea of circling around to a previous position. Two ways to loop are counterbased and conditional.

Counting Loop

A counting loop is used when the number of times to repeat the code is known before the loop starts. Todd uses a counterbased loop when he attends parties where he will meet his neurotic, platonic girlfriend, Marta. If he doesn't talk to Marta at least three times, she will become moody and bitter for weeks. After fulfilling his duty with Marta, however, and being in no mood for further conversation, Todd turns up the music volume so that everyone can dance instead of talk.

"Mingle When Marta's Around" Algorithm

Repeat (three times):
    Locate Marta
    Ask her how she is doing
    Listen to response
    Spend ten minutes talking to other
      guests
End Repeat
Crank up stereo to drown out conversation

Note the use of the "End Repeat" to give an unambiguous ending point to the counting loop. All programming languages have something similar, so that even with all the extra spaces removed, there would be no doubt which instructions are "in" the loop and which are "out."

Conditional Loop

With conditional looping, a set of instructions is executed until a specified condition is met. Conditional loops do not require knowing how many times the loop will execute. Todd uses a conditional loop at parties when Marta is absent. Freed from any conversational obligations, Todd moves from group to group at the party, settling down with the first group that is not talking about politics.

"Mingle When Marta's Absent" Algorithm

Repeat these steps:
    Sidle up to new group
    Introduce self
    Listen to conversation for five minutes
Until conversation is not about politics
Spend hour chatting

Procedures

Using loops allows programmers to avoid having to repeat the same block of instructions several times in a row. In some cases, however, a program calls for the same process to be repeated, but now the repetitions are separated by other tasks. Or, two processes will be almost the same, but not exactly.

When Todd meets a young woman at a party (and the young woman, like Todd, is of legal drinking age), he likes to "break the ice" by making two martinis: a vodka martini for himself and a gin martini for the lady.

"Breaking the Ice" Algorithm (Original)

Fill shaker with $\frac{1}{2}$ cup ice
Add 2 ounces vodka
Add $\frac{1}{4}$ ounce dry vermouth
Shake
Strain contents into martini glass
Add olive

Dump ice from shaker and rinse shaker

Fill shaker with $\frac{1}{2}$ cup ice
Add 2 ounces gin
Add $\frac{1}{4}$ ounce dry vermouth
Shake
Strain contents into martini glass
Add olive

Figure 5.2—Todd Makes Two Martinis

This algorithm contains two sets of instructions that are very similar except that in the second step of making the first drink, Todd uses vodka, and in the second step of the second drink, he uses gin. Because the same exact series of instructions is not repeated, a loop cannot be used to simplify this algorithm. In a case such as this, the programmer (or Todd in this case) uses a *procedure*, which is a named block of instructions that, when referenced, results in execution of those instructions. Procedures allow the use of parameters. A *parameter* is a placeholder for an actual value in a procedure; the parameter's value is specified when the procedure is used. This allows the creation of generic sets of instructions for doing related specific tasks. Here is Todd's same martini algorithm using a procedure:

**"Breaking the Ice" Algorithm
(Using Procedure)**

Perform martini procedure *(alcohol is vodka)*
Dump ice from shaker and rinse shaker
Perform martini procedure *(alcohol is gin)*

Martini procedure (has alcohol as parameter):
Fill shaker with 1/2 cup ice
Add 2 ounces *alcohol*
Add 1/4 ounce dry vermouth
Shake
Strain contents into martini glass
Add olive

In this version, the instructions for making a martini are only given once. For the martini procedure, the type of alcohol is specified. The first use of the procedure adds two ounces of vodka in the second step; the second use of the procedure adds two ounces of gin (see Figure 5.2).

Besides avoiding duplication to instructions, using procedures allows programmers to break up complex tasks into smaller, named functional units, which makes the algorithms easier to follow. Look again at both versions of the algorithm. In the second version it's very easy to see that the overall purpose is to make two martinis. In the first version this is obscured.

SOFTWARE ENGINEERING

Software engineering consists of several phases for the development of the software, phases that can be combined into development paradigms.

Phases of Software Development

As discussed in Chapter 1, software engineering means using a specific method to create a program. The method includes five main tasks: specification, design, implementation, testing, and maintenance.

Specification

The first step in any software development project is *specification*, which determines exactly what abilities the finished software will have. In this phase, one asks the question, "What will the program do?"

This step is accomplished in different ways, depending on the destination of the software. Some software is created for use by a particular company or client. For example, a bank might have its own programmers develop new software for calculating mortgage amortization tables. In this case, the programming team can talk directly with the users to see what their needs and desires are.

Other software is called "shrink-wrapped," which literally means it's wrapped in plastic that shrinks to the size of the box, and in general means it's sold commercially. Here, the programming team can't simply ask the users what they need, because they won't know for sure who the users are until the software is available on the market. Instead they have to rely on market research and focus groups to see the program from the user's point of view.

Software specifications detail not only what features the program will have, but also what the program's interface might look like.

Design

In the specification phase, one asks, "What will the program do?" In the next phase, design, one asks, "How will the program do it?" The *design* phase creates the blueprint for the software's creation.

In the design phase, the programmers choose a programming language to work in, choose algorithms for different functions of the program, decide which members of the team will do what, make charts describing how the parts of the program will fit together, and so on.

Implementation

In the *implementation* phase, the program is actually written. The phase is so-named because the programmers are implementing the design that was made in the previous step. Most people—beginning programmers included—assume that the majority of software development is in implementation, but it's actually just a fraction.

Testing

In the *testing* phase, the programming team determines if the software meets the specifications and the design.

In fact, these are two different concerns. One concern is that the program works without error. The programmers do not want the program to halt prematurely (known as a *crash*) or to display erroneous results. Another concern is that the program is what the users want. A program could never crash and always produce correct output, but if it is missing a key feature, it's not a finished program.

Programmers talk of alpha testing and beta testing. *Alpha testing* is done by the members of the programming team. *Beta testing* is done by users or potential users.

Many different methods are available for alpha testing. It's not as simple as just running the program and seeing how it works. Consider a program that computes mortgage loan amortization tables. The inputs to this program are the type of interest accrued, the interest rate, the date the loan starts, and so on. With many different permutations of inputs, it would be impossible to test them all. Because most programs have more possible inputs than can ever be tested, systematic approaches to testing must be followed.

Two main categories of testing are white box and black box testing.

With *white box* testing, the programmer uses his or her knowledge of the program to pinpoint locations of possible failure. For example, suppose the programmer knows that one of two large blocks of the program will be executed based on some condition. In this case, the programmer contrives different sets of test inputs to force execution into both paths.

With *black box* testing, the testers do not have any knowledge of the inner workings of the program. This kind of testing relies purely on the specifications of the program. If the program's specification says it should do X when given Y, give it X and make sure it returns Y.

At first it might seem that white box testing is automatically better than black box testing, but this is not always the case. While having knowledge of the program's inner workings is useful, it can lead to unwise assumptions. The part of the program that originally appeared "easiest" might have been written less carefully, and, if it is tested less carefully as well, a problem could easily slip through.

Maintenance

Most programs need support and additional development after they have been released, which is known as the *maintenance* phase. Support can include training clients on the software, installing the software on a client's computers, or developing additional product documentation. Additional development is needed when errors are encountered. If an error is extensive, an entirely new version may need to be installed. Small errors can be fixed with a patch, which is a section of code that replaces a part of an already installed program and is usually downloaded from the software developer's Web site.

Even when no errors arise, the software may still need additional development. If a client purchases new computers with a new operating system, for example, the software developers may need to make modifications to the software. Or the business needs may change, meaning the original specifications are no longer exactly what the client needs. In some cases, changes are so extensive that development must start again back in the specification phase.

Development Paradigms

The phases of development listed in the previous section can be combined in different ways, or paradigms.

Waterfall

This first development paradigm is the most direct. In the *waterfall paradigm* the phases are performed in order. This does not mean that one phase must be finished before the next one begins, but that once a phase is finished it is not returned to.

This paradigm is called the waterfall model because it is like having a fountain with a series of basins at different levels. Water that falls out of one basin fills the one below. Similarly, when one has enough specifications together, even if they are not finished, one can begin design work; once enough of the design is complete, the implementation can begin.

The strength of this paradigm is its simplicity. Its weakness is its assumption that the development can proceed in such an orderly and linear manner. For example, specifications can often change in the middle of a project, because the user was misunderstood, or the implementation of the original specifications would be too expensive, or any number of other reasons. The waterfall paradigm doesn't easily accept such changes.

Rapid Prototyping

A prototype, in engineering, is a model of a device that can be used in tests before the production of the device begins. For instance, car makers often design a prototype of a new car that can be driven at test tracks and displayed at auto shows. The information gathered from these can be used to improve the design before the car is produced on the assembly line.

In computer science, a *prototype* is a rough version of a program, quickly created, that approximates the appearance of the final program but without all the final program's functions. The *rapid prototyping paradigm* has the programming team create a prototype as early in the process as possible.

This paradigm attempts to overcome some of the weaknesses of the waterfall model. One problem with the waterfall is that it is difficult to get the specifications correct when the user has nothing to look at. Most users are unable to visualize exactly what they want in a program interface, for example, but they will recognize a good interface when they see it. Often, the programming team spends considerable time creating detailed specification documents only to discover some fundamental misunderstanding has rendered much of the work useless.

With rapid prototyping, the team is not obsessive in capturing every detail in the initial specifications. Instead the specifications and design are painted with a broad brush to create a quick prototype. The users are shown the prototype, and their reactions to it help clear up any misunderstandings they may have had. Then more detailed specifications are created and development proceeds from there. Thus, this paradigm progresses through the first three phases twice, once quickly, and then again more slowly and carefully.

Prototyping also helps clarify the design. For example, if the program will use a technique the team hasn't used before, the prototype gives the team experience with the technique in a "throwaway" program. The team may then decide they need more information on the technique and additional training, or they may decide to return to another technique they know better.

One drawback to this paradigm is that creating the prototype adds to the development time. If the prototype uncovers problems in the specifications or design, the time spent on the prototype easily saves time elsewhere. But if the prototype uncovers no major issues, the team may believe the time was wasted. Also, if the prototype is too good—too close to the user's expectations—the users may press to have development continue using the prototype as a base, which horrifies the programming team because the prototype was not carefully built.

Spiral

In rapid prototyping, the first three phases are performed twice. In the *spiral paradigm*, the phases of development are repeated over and over. Initially the specifications and design are broad and the resulting implementation is mostly show, much like a prototype. As development progresses, the documentation becomes more specific and the program more detailed and functional. The term "spiral" is appropriate because it implies that the team circles around the program, coming closer to the desired result with each pass.

The spiral paradigm may seem very similar to rapid prototyping, but there are important differences. With rapid prototyping, the team creates a first program as a demonstration only, while in the spiral paradigm, there is no intention to throw away any of the work that is created.

The spiral paradigm, like rapid prototyping, may suffer from a perception of slow progress.

Extreme Programming

A more recent paradigm that is gaining popularity is *extreme programming*. This paradigm is built more upon specific tenets than a rigid process plan. Extreme programming requires the programmers to build testing into code modules. That is, when a programmer adds new features to a program, the programmer also adds another block of code to test the first. That way, the entire program can be tested at any time, which aids in regression testing.

Another interesting tenet is team programming. Extreme programmers work in two-person teams sharing one computer. At any given time, one person is programming and the other is checking the work of the first or checking a reference manual.

LANGUAGES

Computers understand machine language, but programmers use higher-level languages to create programs for the computer. A compiler translates from one language to another.

Compilation

In Chapter 3 we defined machine language as the set of instructions that a particular model of CPU understands. By definition, every program that a computer executes is in the form of its machine language, but that doesn't mean it was written that way. The instructions in a machine language are trivially simple, which means machine language programs require many instructions to accomplish even a simple processing task. Programming in machine language is therefore a tedious task that is avoided whenever possible.

You might wonder: If machine language is the language the CPU understands, how can one program any other way?

One can write in another programming language that is easier to use, then translate the program into the machine language of the CPU used to execute the program. These easier-to-use programming languages are called "high-level languages" because they are at a high level of abstraction from the actual machine hardware (see "Levels of Abstraction" in Chapter 1). The process of translating a high-level language into a machine language is called *compilation*.

For example, suppose that a programmer needs to write a loan application program for a bank. The bank will run this program on its loan officer's computer, which uses an Intel Pentium IV processor. The programmer doesn't want to write directly in the Pentium IV machine language, determines that the high-level language Visual Basic is the best choice for this project, and so writes the program in the Visual Basic language. When a program is in the form of a high-level language, it is called *source code*, because it is the source of the machine language program that is actually executed. The programmer compiles the source code using the Visual Basic compiler, which translates the program into the Pentium IV machine language. In the form of machine language, the program is known as *machine code*, or the *executable*.

The compiler is the central tool of the programmer. Having the compiler places the programmer on a higher level of abstraction.

The programmer can, to a great extent, ignore the hardware and concentrate on solving the problem at hand. Before solving the problem, though, the programmer must pick a programming language in which to solve the problem.

Programming Paradigms

The programmer usually works with procedural programming and object-oriented programming to create programs.

Procedural Programming

The original way of making programs, *procedural programming*, simply defines the control flow necessary to solve a task, using procedures to divide the source code into functional units.

Because procedural programs are similar to the algorithms they implement, this style of programming is considered easier for the beginning programmer to understand. However, pure procedural programming has weaknesses. Its straightforward "list the steps to solve the problem" model worked well when most programs simply consumed input and produced output. Today, most programs are interactive; they sit waiting for the user to tell them what happens next. The procedural paradigm does not match up well with this style of program. Also, procedural programs are often "loose" with data, sharing the data among all parts of the program. Allowing unfettered access to data has problems.

Object-Oriented Programming

In *object-oriented programming*, instructions are grouped together with the data they operate on. To understand what this means, consider the student records office at a typical university. The registrar is the official in charge of safeguarding students' official records and making any applicable changes to those records. Students come to the registrar and fill out forms for their various requests, such as having a transcript sent to another school, updating the student's address, or changing the student's enrollment in the coming semester. The students have no direct access to the records themselves; they may only hand their forms to the registrar, who then executes the request, which results in returned copies of records, changes in the files, or whatever the request might have been.

This situation illustrates the key principle of object-oriented programming, *information hiding*, which occurs when data is placed out of direct reach of the data's users. Here, the users are the students, the data are the records, and the registrar lies between them.

Information hiding has many benefits, the first of which is that it maintains the integrity and security of the data. Consider the problems that would occur if the students had direct access to the file room. They might file paperwork that was incorrectly completed because it would not have been reviewed by the registrar. Furthermore, each student would have access to all student files, not just his or her own, a serious security and privacy concern. By requiring all requests to go through the registrar, all paperwork can be checked for accuracy before filing, and all students can be required to show identification before they are provided copies of their records, assuring security and privacy.

Another benefit is the separation of the interface from implementation. The forms the students must fill out for their requests are the interface of the records system; the forms are all that the students see of the records office. The implementation is the method used to store the files. The files could be stored on paper in cabinets, on microfilm, in a computer database system, or even in different formats for different records. Because the interface and implementation are separate, the students do not need to know how the records are actually stored. Furthermore, the records office can change the filing system at any time without affecting the services to the student, as long as the forms the students use do not change.

A final benefit is reuse. Suppose that instead of only one records office for the entire university, each individual school at the university had its own. If the same forms are used at all records offices throughout the campus, a student who began in the School of Humanities but later transferred to the School of Mathematics will understand how to make requests of the new school's records office because the interface is the same at both.

The object-oriented programming paradigm gives all these benefits. Instructions and data that logically belong together are kept together, which allows sections of code to be reused in other programs without a lot of trouble. Certain procedures act as gatekeepers—like our registrar—which keeps the data secure. The interface is kept separate from the implementation so that, if a better algorithm for some problem is found, a new piece of program can be substituted without disturbing the rest.

Popular Programming Languages

Besides choosing a development paradigm, the programmer must choose the best language for a project. Popular programming languages include C, C++, Visual Basic, Java, and Perl.

C

C, a language with a minimal name, has been around since the early 1970s. By modern standards it is a very low-level language; it has a smaller set of simpler instructions compared to the other languages discussed here. C encourages "terse" programs that are short and often difficult to read for anyone who is not the original programmer. This language is strictly procedural and is most often used for systems programming, creating software that directly interacts with the hardware or any situation in which performance is paramount. By keeping everything simple, a C compiler can produce tight, efficient machine code, making C a high-performance language.

C++

The name C++ is pronounced as "C plus plus." In the C language, ++ is an operator that means "to increase by one"; thus, the name can be read as "one more than C." This reading is appropriate since C++ is an extension of the C language. Almost all of the instructions of C are retained (indeed, most C++ compilers can compile C source code), but new ones have been added to allow the use of the object-oriented paradigm. C++ is thus known as a *hybrid language*, one that does not enforce a single programming paradigm. The programmer using C++ can use both the procedural or object-oriented paradigms, even within the same program. C++ is a general-purpose language and is used for all types of programming.

Visual Basic

The Visual Basic language was developed by Microsoft, and its history is interwoven with that of the Microsoft Windows series of operating systems. Those systems provided a graphical user interface instead of plain text command entry, which made life easier for the computer user but more complicated for the programmer. Creating the user interface often required much more work than the underlying logic of the program.

Visual Basic changed that. More than just a programming language, it was a complete program design environment that itself extolled all the benefits of an intelligent user interface. It offered "drag-and-drop" interface design, which allowed programmers to design an interface by mixing and matching parts (like the Mr. Potato Head toy). This capability meant that programmers could spend their time on the core program logic. The language itself was based on an older language called BASIC, which stands for Beginner's All-purpose Symbolic Instruction Code. BASIC was designed as a teaching language and is easy to learn, with an instruction set resembling English more than other popular languages like C or C++. Putting all the features together, Visual Basic allowed the programmer with ordinary skills to create a good-looking program quickly.

For these reasons, Visual Basic became very popular for business program development. The language evolved as the Windows operating system went through its revisions, always allowing (or in some cases, forcing) the programer to make use of the latest Windows features. Eventually, the language attracted more "hard-core" programmers, who appreciated many Visual Basic features but complained that the language was too simplistic, hid too many important details from the programmer, and lacked important features like full support of object-oriented programming.

Microsoft listened to these complaints, and now Visual Basic is no longer a simple language. In its latest revision, it's truly a modern, object-oriented programming language. However, these changes have complicated the language, and development is not as easy as it once was. No language can please all programmers.

Java

Java is an object-oriented language with a set of instructions inspired by C++. It was originally developed for use in embedded systems. An *embedded system* is a computer and program in one self-contained package, for example, a "smart appliance" such as a DVD player. However, Java's popularity comes not from embedded systems but from its use on the World Wide Web.

Java is popular for the Web because of its distinguishing feature: platform independence. A *platform-independent* language produces programs that can be executed on different processors and operating systems. Java achieves this by not fully compiling the source code. Rather than produce machine code to run on a specific processor, a Java compiler produces "intermediate code," which is at a level between source code and machine code. On each system that runs Java programs, a special program called the Java Virtual Machine—called the VM for short—must reside, which *is* specific to that processor and operating system. The VM interprets the instructions in the intermediate code and performs the specific instructions needed for that system.

Platform independence is the key for programs on the World Wide Web because so many different systems use it. Even outside of the Web, the ability to write one program that can run on a Windows, Macintosh, or UNIX system is very powerful, saving time for the software developer. Java's motto is, "Write once; run anywhere."

The platform independence comes at a price, though, which is performance. Programs executing in a processor's machine code run faster than programs that must be interpreted on the fly. If a programmer only needs a program to work for a particular operating system, the performance loss may be enough to push development into another language.

Perl

One last language, Perl, is a *scripting language*, which refers to a language in which the source code is processed by a program called an interpreter, rather than compiled. Such languages are used for smaller tasks than compiled languages and are often used for "one-off" programs—special tasks that may only need to be done once. Perl is particularly suited for text manipulation, such as finding all the occurrences of a particular word in a document and exporting all the paragraphs in which that word appears to a second file. Perl is often used for programming tasks on a Web site.

Because Perl programs tend to be short but numerous, the language is very expressive. That is, the language incorporates the features of many other languages, so that programs can be written quickly. This means the language doesn't follow any particular paradigm, and Perl programs are not easy for others to read. As a general-purpose language, these problems would be serious deficiencies, but for the programs Perl is used for, they are not.

LANGUAGE NAMES

Computer scientists enjoy creating names for new technologies and ideas in the discipline, and programming language names are no exception. Some interesting choices include the following languages:

- *Ada* was named after Augusta Ada Byron, daughter of poet Lord Byron. She worked with Charles Babbage to develop plans for the Analytical Engine, the rudimentary analog computer described in Chapter 1.

- *APL* simply stands for "A Programming Language."

- *SNOBOL* is slang for an early language for business programming that was named COBOL (COmmon Business Oriented Language). The name SNOBOL is a play on the name, born from the developers' lack of faith in their language's popularity (as in, "it doesn't have a snowball's chance in . . .").

SUMMARY

The software development process is a journey from idea to implementation. Along the way, the programmer develops an algorithm or uses an existing algorithm.

Algorithms and programs use control structures to define the order for executing the instructions. The common control structures are sequential (execute instructions in order), the conditional (execute instructions only if some test is met), repetitive (execute instructions a specified number of times or repeat until some condition is met), and the procedure (a block of instructions referenced from elsewhere in the algorithm or program).

The programmer must use these control structures to define solutions to problems. Tasks that are intuitive when discussed generally are often difficult to describe in a formal algorithm. The best programmers are those who quickly can see a good solution to a problem in terms of the control structures and instructions of the specified programming language.

The programmer uses the algorithm to develop an actual program, which is called the source code. The source code must be translated into machine code by a compiler before it can be executed.

Software engineering involves different phases. The first step in any software development project is specification, in which it is determined exactly what abilities the finished software will have. The design phase creates the blueprint for the software's creation. In the implementation phase, the program is actually written. After it's written, the program must be thoroughly tested. Even once the program is released to a client, it may require modification or support.

Various methodologies for software engineering exist that approach these phases in different ways.

Different programming languages exist for different types of programming. Some programming languages are procedural and mimic the structure of the algorithm. Other languages are object-oriented and place instructions and data together in a way that protects the data and encourages code reuse.

Some languages are high-level and make quick work of developing the user interface. Other languages are low-level and offer higher performance but require more work from the programmer.

NETWORKS

NETWORK OVERVIEW

In Chapter 1 networks were defined as sets of computers connected together so they can share data. A company can make its current data, such as customer account information, available to all employees at any time. Networks allow resource sharing, file sharing, and enable different users to communicate with each other.

Concerning resource sharing, networks can allow one resource, such as a printer, to be used by multiple users. Without a network, a printer would have to be installed for every user who needs one.

Files can be shared without a network, but that means putting them on disk and walking them from one user to another (sometimes jokingly referred to as a *sneakernet*). But with a network, files can be shared without anyone leaving a chair. Users can then easily collaborate from their computers.

Networks allow communication. They allow users in different locations to communicate, either in real time (video conferencing) or not (e-mail).

In general, a network allows a group of computers to act in concert, to act as if they were one computer. From a user's point of view, if the network is fast and robust, the locations of data and other users are irrelevant; it's as if all the data on the network is on each user's computer.

Basic Parts of a Transmission

A network, then, is a mechanism for transmitting data from one computer to another. When data is transmitted across a network, it is referred to as a *message*. These messages may be fixed in size (a fixed number of bits of data) or of variable size, but there's always some upper limit. Because of this limitation, most blocks of data to be transferred are broken up into multiple messages.

In any single transmission, the computer that transmits the message is the *sender*, and the computer to which the message is transmitted is the *receiver*. This terminology refers to a single transmission only. In most cases, each computer is both sending and receiving.

Two computers both sending to each other at the same time is known as a *full-duplex* transmission. In some situations, both computers can send to each other, but not at the same time, which is a *half-duplex* transmission. A good example of this is a "push to talk" cell phone. When the operator of the phone pushes the "talk" button, the speaker on the phone cuts off as long as the button is pressed. When the phone is used this way, the operator can listen or talk but not do both at the same time.

If only one computer can send, it is known as a *simplex* transmission. If you have a dish on your roof for receiving television signals, you have a simplex communications link. The television data comes from your service provider, which beams it up to a satellite orbiting the Earth, which in turn beams it down to the ground to all the rooftop dishes. However, no mechanism sends data from the dish back up to the satellite; it's a one-way street.

Each computer connected to a network is known as a *node*. Some nodes are users' computers, some are devices (like a printer shared by users of a network), and some exist just to direct traffic to other nodes.

The network *medium* is the physical connection the message crosses to get from sender to receiver. Some networks use multiple media (the plural of the word "medium"). With satellite television, for example, the satellite beams signals through the air to the dish, which is one medium, but then the dish is connected to the television through wires, which is another medium.

Network Sizes

Networks come in different sizes. Some networks involve only a few machines that are all in the same building. Others involve thousands of computers or more, spread across the globe.

The smallest network, a *point-to-point connection*, connects just two computers (see Figure 6.1). A simple example of this would be someone who has two computers at home and wants to be able to easily share files between them.

A *local area network*, or LAN, connects computers in a single building or in adjacent buildings.

A *wide area network*, or WAN, connects computers that are widely separated, either in different parts of a city or in different countries.

The number of nodes does not determine whether a network is a LAN or WAN. While the average WAN has more nodes than the average LAN, either could have just a few nodes or many. What makes the difference is the physical separation between the computers. In both a LAN and WAN, the same organization owns or controls the use of all the computers on the network. In a LAN, the organization also controls the other network components, such as the medium. In a WAN, the organization cannot physically string cable to the other end of a city or continent. Instead it has to connect to some general carrier to provide the connection.

The situation is analogous to a company phone system. If an employee wants to call someone in the same office, the call can be placed only using equipment that resides in the office. If that employee wants to make a call to someone in the branch office in another state, then some long distance company like AT&T, Sprint, or MCI provides the connection.

Network Responsibilities

To be effective, a network has to fulfill expectations related to delivery, reliability, performance, and security.

Delivery

The first responsibility of a network is to deliver the message to the receiver. When the sender and receiver are directly connected to each other, this is not difficult. But in most

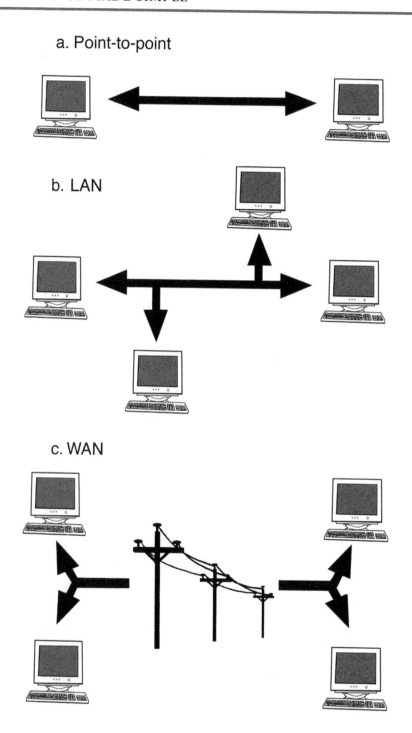

Figure 6.1—Types of Networks

cases there are many intermediate nodes between the sender and receiver, and then *routing* is important. This means what it does in general usage, following a "route." In this case, routing determines the path a message will take from the sender to the receiver, which involves determining the intermediate nodes the message passes through along the way.

Reliability

For a computer network, *reliability* means that the message that arrives to the receiver is the same message that left the sender. Unfortunately for computer networks, the world is full of things that can corrupt signals. If you have ever moved a telephone too close to a television or other electrical device and heard static on the line, you've experienced this problem firsthand. All electrical devices emit electromagnetic radiation, which can interfere with networks. In fact, two network connections can even interfere with each other, a phenomenon known as *crosstalk*. When you faintly hear someone else's phone conversation during your own, you're experiencing crosstalk.

In order to ensure reliability, networks must be designed both to reduce the influence of other devices and to safely handle the situation when a signal is corrupted.

Performance

For networks, *performance* means that the message arrives at the receiver on time. Note that performance is relative to the application. For example, it's acceptable for an e-mail to take several minutes to arrive at the receiver, but in teleconferencing, a delay of several minutes would make communication between the conference attendees so frustrating as to be unusable. Performance means getting the message there when it needs to be there, whenever that is.

Performance is a function of both the underlying physical media and the network rules for transmission. The amount of data a particular network can transfer in a given time frame is referred to as the network's *bandwidth*, which is usually measured in bits per second.

Security

Network security encompasses several points. First, a private network must prevent unauthorized access. If people could gain access to a bank's network, for example, they could potentially access the sensitive financial data of the bank's customers. Even on a public network like the Internet, security is a concern. If you do any shopping on the Internet, you know that at some point you are sending your credit card number in a message over the network. While you may trust the message's receiver—the merchant you are buying from—with that data, the message passes through many nodes along the way, nodes that you don't know or trust. Thus, a mechanism must exist for passing sensitive data through unknown hands.

NETWORK COMPONENTS

Now that you have some understanding of the transmission of data and the expectations for networks, look at the components that make networks work effectively.

Transmission Media

To transmit data, computers can be connected through twisted pair wires, coaxial cable, optical fibers, and electromagnetic waves.

Twisted Pair

The simplest way to connect computers is through copper wires. Two wires must be used to make a complete electrical circuit. When you see a pair of wires in a lamp cord, they run in parallel. Originally, network wires were made the same way, but not anymore. *Twisted pair* refers to two copper wires that are braided together instead of running in parallel.

The wires are braided to enhance reliability. As we noted before, electromagnetic interference is the bane of accurate transmission. However, it turns out that if the wires or a circuit are exposed to the same interference at the same level, the interference tends to cancel itself out. With parallel wires running past some source of interference, one wire is closer to the source than the other and gets a higher level of interference. But when the wires are braided, each wire tends to get the same overall level of interference, reducing the negative effects.

A twisted pair is sometimes covered with a metal mesh, at which point it is called *shielded twisted pair*, or STP. This shield tends to reduce interference even more. If it doesn't have this additional protection, it is known as *unshielded twisted pair*, or UTP.

The main advantage of twisted pair is its simplicity. It is easy for network technicians to work with because it is very flexible, can fit in tight spaces, and can easily be cut to different lengths. The technology is also very inexpensive.

Coaxial Cable

Coaxial cable refers to a construction in which one wire is placed inside the other. This is the same cable used in cable television. At the end of one of these cables, you'll see a thick wire in the center, and around that, a kind of nut that screws onto a connector on the television or cable box. If you cut the cable in the middle somewhere, you would see that the thick wire runs through the middle with some insulation, a ring of metal, and a plastic coating around it. The ring of metal connects to that nut on the end. A coaxial cable makes a complete circuit because the wire in the middle is one wire and the ring around the outside acts as the second wire.

Different grades of coaxial cable are available for different applications. They all have the same basic construction, but the width of the layers varies, or different materials might be used for one of the layers. Coaxial cable has a greater bandwidth than twisted pair. In general, the thicker the wire, the more data it can transmit at once, and cable uses thicker wire than twisted pair.

Coaxial cable has some disadvantages, though, that can offset the higher bandwidth. The cable is so thick that it cannot easily fit around tight corners, it is more expensive, and, compared to twisted pair, it is more difficult to cut and make connectors.

One problem that twisted pair and coaxial cable share is that signals in copper wires tend to fade over a distance. This explains why two televisions in a house on the same cable system can have varying reception: one television has a longer cable than the other. To combat this, network designers install *repeaters*, which are devices that read a signal on one wire and reproduce it on another. In this way, longer distances can be covered. The different wire types are shown in Figure 6.2.

a. Unshielded twisted pair

b. Shielded twisted pair

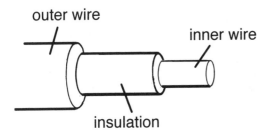

c. Coaxial cable

Figure 6.2—Types of Wires

Optical Fiber

Optical fiber transmits data as light along a thin glass or plastic filament. The nature of how light refracts in glass or plastic allows this. You may have seen tabletop novelty lights that use plastic filaments. These have ordinary lightbulbs in the base, but sticking out of the base are a number of plastic strands looking something like a porcupine. The ends of these strands glow the same color as the lightbulb. The strands guide the light from

one end to the other. Optical fiber works the same way. At one end of the fiber is a light source, and at the other end there's a light detector. To transmit binary data, the light can be turned on for each 1 and off for each 0.

The light source in less expensive systems is a light-emitting diode, something like the light on some keyboards that indicates whether the "Caps Lock" is on. More expensive optical fiber systems have a laser as a light source. The laser is better because it produces a tightly focused beam.

Optical fiber has a number of major advantages over copper wire technology. First, because it uses light and not electricity, optical fiber is immune to electromagnetic interference. Second, it has a much higher bandwidth than copper wire. Third, it can run much longer distances than copper wire. While repeaters may still be needed, they can be spaced much farther apart.

Optical fiber does have some disadvantages, though. The main issue is cost. The fiber itself is more expensive to make than a wire, and the equipment needed at both ends of a connection is more expensive too. Also, optical fiber is much harder to work with. It is fairly stiff and a lot easier to accidentally damage. A network technician cannot simply splice two fibers together the way two wires can be spliced.

Because of these disadvantages, optical fiber is often used for a *backbone*, which is a term for a major pathway in a network. For example, if a company has 100 nodes split evenly between two adjacent office buildings, the connection between two buildings might be optical fiber, while the connections within each building could be copper wire. The backbone would be optical fiber because it gets more traffic than any other connection. But connecting all the computers in each office building through optical fiber would be expensive and unnecessary.

Wireless

Wireless refers to transmitting data via electromagnetic waves through the air. These waves are categorized based on their frequency. Lower frequency waves are called radio waves; these include the frequencies used by AM and FM radio as well as those used by broadcast television. Higher frequency waves are called microwaves.

Wireless technology is not a general replacement for wires or fiber. Any time wire or fiber is practical, it is a better choice than wireless, which is used in special situations like long distance transmission. In fact, the long distance telephone network relies on microwave transmission towers.

Another situation is *broadcasting*, which refers to sending out a single message to multiple receivers at once. Unlike wires and fiber, which direct a signal to a particular destination, wireless transmissions are unguided. They may be aimed in a specific direction, but they are still broadcast to a wide area. The advantage is that any receivers in the broadcast area can get the message. This approach is more efficient than sending the same message to each receiver individually.

A final reason to use wireless is mobility. In a wired network, nodes can only be where the wires are. In a wireless network, the nodes can be anywhere in the transmission area.

Wireless has a couple of problems that the other media do not. One problem is that air is the conduit for the transmission, and the characteristics of the air are constantly changing. For example, weather, solar flares, and other natural phenomena more often affect wireless networks. The other problem relates to security. Because the messages are broadcast, they are easily intercepted. This makes the security built into the protocol especially important.

Protocols

Every network needs a set of rules, or *protocols*. These function for the network the way traffic rules and knowledge function for the highways. To drive from one place to another, you have to know where the roads are (using a map on paper or in your head), the rules of the road (drive on the right, red light means stop, and so on), and be able to make decisions while on the road (if an accident stops traffic on the freeway, what is the next best way to get to your destination?). The network protocol does the same things for the network.

Protocol functions include data linking, error detection, routing, and bridging.

Data Linking

A *data link* is the direct connection between two nodes in a network. In a network with thousands of nodes, a message may go through many intermediates to get to its destination, but that trip is still managed one data link at a time.

The data link part of a protocol is concerned with reliability, with ensuring that the message made it to the other side. A common way to achieve this is through an *acknowledgment*, or ACK, which is a short message sent in the opposite direction of the original message.

If node A sends a message to node B, when B receives it, it sends an ACK back to A. If a specified period of time passes without an ACK, node A assumes something went wrong with the original message and sends the original message again.

Such a scheme gets more complicated when the network is busy. Node A may need to send many messages to node B faster than B can reply to the first message. B must then indicate which message is acknowledged when it sends an ACK, and A must "check off" successful messages and resend the unsuccessful ones. This checking is similar to balancing a checkbook at the end of a month, checking off the cashed checks.

Error Detection

When node B sends acknowledgments, it should only acknowledge a packet if it arrives in the same form that it left node A. The trick is how node B knows that a message was damaged. If a person receives a wet or smeared paper memo, the damage is easily seen. But a message in a network is just a pattern of bits, 1's and 0's. Any damage to the message, from the receiver's point of view, simply changes some 1's to 0's or vice versa. The damage is not self-evident.

Error detection refers to rules in the protocol that help identify whether some bits have been changed during transmission. A simple scheme is redundant transmission. Send the data in the message multiple times. The receiver checks the copies to see if they match. If they do, the ACK is sent, but if the copies differ, then some of the bits must have changed. Some protocols would send a NACK, or *negative acknowledgment*, to indicate that the message was garbled, but it's not necessary.

Another scheme is called *parity*, in which the sender counts the 1's in the message, and then attaches a 1 to the end of the message if this count is odd and 0 if it is even. This means that in the final message sent, the number of 1 bits is always even. For example, if the message originally has six 1 bits, a 0 is added, which means there are still six 1 bits, an even number; but if there are seven 1 bits, a 1 is added, making the total eight, an even number. Then the receiver just has to count the number of 1 bits and see if the count is even.

More advanced schemes can even do *error correction*, which allows the original message to be recovered even with some corruption of bits. Redundancy is one way to do this. If the message is sent five times and four messages arrive alike and the fifth is different, it's safe to assume the fifth message is corrupted and the other four represent the correct message.

Because error correction requires sending so much extra data, it is usually not implemented. The overall performance of the network is better when the occasional corrupted message is sent again. The exceptions to this occur when the transmission time is so long that retransmission becomes a problem. The NASA Mars Rovers are examples of this. Because it takes so long for a message to get from Earth to Mars, or the reverse, it is better to correct the message than to resend it.

Routing

Once the network can successfully transmit between nodes that are directly connected, the network needs the ability to transmit from any node in a network to any other node. One of the important details at this level is routing: determining the path a message will take across the network. A *router* is a special node that forwards packets toward their destination. Networks are built by connecting users' computers to routers—a single router can support multiple users' computers—and then connecting routers to each other.

When a router receives a message, it must determine which connection to send it along. This is easy if the destination is a computer it is directly connected to, but if it's not directly connected, it has to make educated guesses. Most routers configure themselves as they go along and do not have a picture of the entire network. The problem is similar to deciding which plane to get on at the airport when none of the flights go directly to your destination city and you don't know the flight schedule for any other airport.

The solution is for the routers to share information with each other. Usually the information shared is what's known as a *hop-count*, which is the number of nodes a message must pass through to reach a particular computer. For example, suppose router W is directly connected to computer A (Figure 6.3). Then W's hop-count to A is only one. Suppose W is also connected to routers X and Y. Periodically W sends all the hop-counts it knows to X and Y. When X and Y find out that W's hop-count to A is one, they decide that the hop-count to that computer is two; that is, it will take one hop to get to W and then another hop to get to A.

When X sends out its own hop-counts to another router, Z, the other router updates its hop count for A to three, and so on.

This system also allows the network to eventually rout around routers that have malfunctioned or have been taken down, albeit slowly. Normally the router sends the messages to the

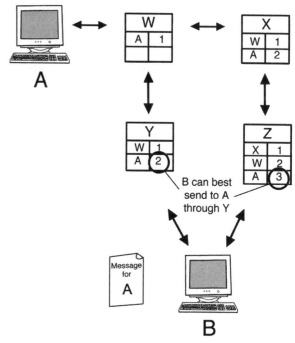

Figure 6.3—Routing

directly connected node with the lowest hop count to that destination. But if an adjacent router is down, the router picks the next best. The problem is that other routers may still be sending traffic intended to pass through the down node.

For example, if some distant router thinks the fastest way to send a message to A is to go to Z, it does so even if X is down because it is not directly connected to X and therefore has no way to know this has happened. Z routes this message as best it can, but in the worst case, it may send the message back the way it came. Eventually Z's routing table reflects that it is not the best intermediary for a message going to A, but this takes time.

Because bad news travels slowly around the network, messages that come in a time when tables are inaccurate could be sent on wayward trips or even be caught in an endless loop where routers keep passing the same message among themselves. To keep a message from floating around the network indefinitely, messages generally contain their own hop-count, that is, the count of nodes they have passed through already. Once that count exceeds a specified value, it's assumed the message is doomed and it's discarded.

Bridging

A *bridge* is a node that logically divides a network into smaller subnetworks. In an office LAN with ten computers, for instance, a bridge could be used to divide the LAN into two LANs of five computers each. Although the two networks are logically separate, nodes in one LAN can send messages across the bridge to nodes in the other LAN. In some types of small networks, because smaller networks are more efficient than larger ones, the use of bridges can improve network performance.

A *gateway* is a kind of bridge that connects two different kinds of networks. For example, an office may use a LAN technology for the inter-office network, yet want to allow office users to access the Internet, which uses a different protocol. In this case, the gateway translates LAN messages to the Internet protocol and vice versa.

Because gateways are often a LAN's point of connection with "the outside world," they are special security risks. Much care must be taken that messages that are not responses to requests from LAN users are not let "into" the LAN.

Flow Control

Networks must also provide *flow control*, which is a method for allowing the receiver to control how often messages are sent by the sender. A good example of why flow

control is needed is a printer attached to a network. The printer receives messages across the network and stores the data to be printed in RAM. As each page is printed, the space in RAM is reclaimed.

However, even a fast printer takes a few seconds to print a page. During those seconds, the data for several pages arrives. The printer cannot remove data from RAM as fast as it is coming in. Without flow control, the printer's RAM would overflow. Flow control allows the printer to tell the computer sending the print job to "hold on," and later to tell it to send more data.

Sometimes the mechanism for flow control is part of the mechanism for error control. One such mechanism is called *stop-and-wait*, which is when the sender sends a single message and does not send another until the first message's ACK is returned. This method is slow because the sender spends most of its time waiting, not sending.

A more advanced implementation is called *sliding window*, in which the sender and receiver agree to a set number of unacknowledged messages that can be in transit at any time. For example, if that number is five, the sender sends out the first five messages it wants to send without waiting for an ACK. When the ACK for the first message is returned, the sender sends the sixth message; when the ACK for the second message is returned, the sender sends the seventh message; and so on.

Encryption and Authentication

Messages sent across a network often contain sensitive information, such as credit card numbers. Unscrupulous people might try to intercept these messages. Preventing the interception is not always possible because the message might pass through nodes that are not under the control of the sender or the receiver. For security, some mechanism must be in place so that intercepted messages are useless to the interceptor.

Encryption refers to encoding a message so it can only be read by the intended receiver. Encryption works by processing the data with a special value called the "key," which results in a new message. The new message cannot be returned to the original (cannot be decrypted) without the use of a key. The entire process is referred to as *cryptography*.

There are two categories of cryptography.

In *private-key cryptography*, the encryption key is the same as the decryption key. This approach means that for the sender to transmit an encrypted message, the receiver must already have the sender's secret key. The sender cannot transmit the key to the receiver because then any possible interceptor of the encrypted message could intercept the key also. That would defeat the purpose of encryption.

In the second category, *public-key cryptography*, the encryption key and decryption key are different. Each receiver maintains a private key, which it does not share. Each private key generates a public key, which is then "published," which means it's shared with any node that asks for it—by posting it on a public Web site, for example. Messages that are encrypted with a public key can only be decrypted using the matching private key. For instance, if node A wants to transmit to node B, node A uses B's freely available public key to encrypt the message. The resulting message can only be decrypted by B's private key. Thus, no matter

who intercepts the message, only B can decrypt it.

What makes public-key cryptography work is the mathematical relationship between a private key and public key. The public key can easily be computed from the private key. However, the reverse computation, though possible, is so time-consuming that it is believed to be intractable even for a computer. (In the 1992, Robert Redford movie *Sneakers*, a scientist supposedly finds a computationally "easy" way to do the reverse calculation, which would make a lot of secure data suddenly insecure.)

Public-key cryptography solves the problem of safely getting the keys to the right nodes, but it introduces another problem, *authentication*, which means confirming the sender's identity. Even if messages can only be read by the receiver, it doesn't mean they were all sent by the expected sender. An imposter could hijack a conversation by sending messages using the receiver's public key, confusing the receiver. For example, if someone could send messages to your bank that your bank thought came from an ATM you were using, the messages could tell the bank to transfer money from your account to the imposter's.

Thankfully, authentication can be achieved in several ways (Figure 6.4). One solution is to give the sender a private key also and have it publish a public key (just as the receiver must publish its public key). The sender then encrypts messages, first with its own private key and then with the public key of the receiver. Remember that a message locked with one key of a public/private pair must be unlocked with the other member of the pair. Thus, when the receiver runs the message through its private key, the resulting message must be processed

a. Secure Transmission

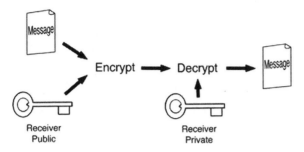

Message and Public Key: must be decrypted using private key.
Only the owner of the private key can read the message.

b. Authenticated Transmission

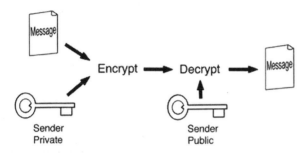

Message and Private Key: must be decrypted using public key,
so only one one owner of the private key could send the message.

c. Secure and Authenticated Transmission

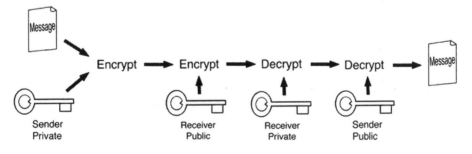

Secure and Authenticated Transmission uses both techniques on one message.

Figure 6.4—Secure and Authenticated Transmissions

again with the sender's public key. Because the message decrypts in the end with the sender's public key, it proves it was originally encrypted with the sender's private key, which only the sender has; hence, it proves the sender sent the message.

Authentication works well when the senders and receivers all know each other and where to find each other's public keys. If you want to make a purchase over the Internet, though, the merchant can't find your public key even if you had one. In those cases, a combination of public-key and private-key cryptography is used. A form of public-key cryptography is used initially, and through this the sender and receiver create a temporary shared secret key. The secret key is used until the sender is done sending messages and then it is discarded.

Compression

One way to improve network performance is to send less data over it. Like a highway, a network runs more smoothly when it isn't congested. Of course, asking users to put less traffic on the network to improve performance is self-defeating, but there is another way.

Compression means reducing the size of stored data. *Decompression* means returning compressed data to its original state. Compression is of two types.

Lossy compression loses some part of the original data, so that when the data is decompressed, it is a little different than it was originally. Compressed audio and image file formats often use this kind of compression, because the loss isn't noticeable to the human ear or eye.

Lossless compression returns the data to its exact original form. Many network protocols do this automatically to reduce the traffic on the network. At first, lossless compression seems like a trick. How can data be reduced and yet still keep track of the parts that are gone?

Suppose our college student, Todd, has to call his cable company with a dispute over his bill. Before the company can help him, it wants to know his account number. Unfortunately, Todd's account number is long:

94019294965700598729101022076572020
39075

Slowly reading this number over the phone takes Todd a long time. The next day, Todd's friend Marta notes a problem with *her* cable bill and has to make the same call. Marta's account number is just as long, but it has a definite pattern.

5555555559999999999999990000000000
00000

Instead of actually reading this number out digit by digit, Marta says, "it's nine fives, then fifteen nines, then fifteen zeroes," which is a lot faster.

What Marta is using is a technique called *run-length encoding*, in which repetitions of the same number are replaced with a special notation. She could write her account number in a shorthand notation like 9:5, 15:9, 15:0, which takes up a lot less space and can be easily converted to the original form whenever she needed it.

In a computer network, the only numbers involved are 0's and 1's, but the concept is the same. Although other compression schemes may use a technique other than run-length encoding, they all work on the principle of finding some pattern in the data and replacing that data with a shorthand notation for the pattern.

CURRENT NETWORKING TECHNOLOGIES

Current networking technologies include Ethernet, Frame Relay, and Bluetooth.

Ethernet

Ethernet, one of the most popular LAN technologies, refers to a number of related LAN protocols that use different media and have different capacities.

On the low end are 10BASE-T Ethernet, which uses unshielded twisted pair media, and 10BASE-2 Ethernet, which uses coaxial cable. Both support data rates of 10 megabits per second (that's what the *10* in the names refers to), which is a little more than 1 megabyte per second. To put that in perspective, this level of network could transmit the contents of a full CD-ROM in about ten minutes.

On the upper end is Gigabit Ethernet, which, as the name implies, can transmit a gigabit, or 1,000 megabits, per second. That means it could transmit an entire CD-ROM in about six seconds. There is even a 10 Gigabit Ethernet that would reduce that to half a second! Gigabit Ethernet can use multiple copper wires but most often uses optical fiber.

In Ethernet, nodes compete for the use of the network. As you've seen in other types of networks, each node shares a data link with adjacent nodes, and some nodes act as a message forwarding service. In Ethernet, all the nodes on the network share a common link. All the nodes share the medium, are always listening, and can send messages at any time.

You might wonder how the nodes schedule the use of the network. The answer is that they don't. Any node can use the network as long as it does not detect another message on the network. A *collision* could occur when two nodes try to send at the same time, the result being garbled data. Because it takes time for a message to propagate down the line, if node A

starts to send a message, there is a short delay before node B senses this message on the line. If node B sends its own message during this delay, the collision occurs.

Fortunately, nodes can sense when a collision has occurred. The nodes that tried to send will wait a random amount of time and then re-send the message if the network is clear. Because the wait is random, usually one node starts retransmitting first and then the other detects it and waits. In this way, Ethernet allows the nodes to share the network without directly communicating with each other about the details.

If a node were to send out its entire message before a collision occurred, even though it could sense the collision, it would not realize that its own message was affected and would instead assume a message from other nodes caused the collision. Because of this erroneous assumption, it would not resend the message. If the wires connecting the nodes are short, this situation cannot happen because the first part of the message reaches every node before the sender sends the last part of the message. Any collision must occur within that time because nodes only send when they haven't sensed another message on the wire.

The *collision domain* is the maximum distance of wire between two nodes so that the beginning of a message from one node reaches the other before the end of the message is sent. When Ethernets are designed, they must ensure that the wiring used doesn't exceed this length from one of the nodes to the other.

Unfortunately, if faster Ethernet versions are used, messages travel faster, and the collision domain is smaller. A smaller domain means a shorter network, probably with fewer nodes, which sounds like a bad deal because with more nodes, one wants more speed. The solution is bridges, which we discussed previously. By placing bridges strategically throughout the Ethernet, the overall network becomes a set of mini-Ethernets, each one well within the confines of its collision domain.

Frame Relay

Frame Relay is a high-speed network protocol used for connecting LANs to make a WAN.

WANs were originally created by leasing dedicated backbone lines from long distance service providers. If a company has an office in New York and another in Albany, it would lease the exclusive use of either a bundle of wires or an optical fiber that ran between the two points. This sort of lease was wasteful, though, because the company would have to lease based on its maximum usage of the line. In other words, if it occasionally needed to send a gigabyte of information in a few seconds, the company would have to buy a line that could support that even if most of the time it didn't use the line much at all. When a sender transmits a lot more data than its average rate, on the other hand, it is known as *bursty data*.

Another problem is that if the company had multiple offices, it would have to lease lines to connect each office to every other office. While a company with two offices needs one line, a company with five offices needs ten.

What was needed was a WAN that could handle bursty data without requiring excess bandwidth and that could simplify connections between multiple offices. Frame Relay does both. A long distance service provider that offers Frame Relay is essentially allowing all the WANs it supports to share the use of all of its cables or optical fibers. There's plenty of bandwidth for bursty data as long as all the WANs are not bursty at the same time.

A disadvantage of Frame Relay is that individual messages experience variable delays in reaching their destinations. This delay makes it problematic for applications like real-time video because the image data must be chopped up into small messages to be sent, and a delay in any of the messages can prevent the video from being displayed properly.

Bluetooth

Bluetooth is a network protocol for short-range wireless communication. It is an open standard, which means any company can make Bluetooth-enabled products. It is named in honor of Harald Bluetooth, king of Denmark in the tenth century who united Denmark and Norway a millennium ago.

Other wireless networking technologies existed before Bluetooth, but they had a different design goal, such as putting a permanent network in place in a building where it was not feasible to run a lot of cabling. Bluetooth networks are not intended to last very long, but instead are created spontaneously and disappear quietly.

Previously, wireless networks connected the same sorts of devices as wired networks, such as desktop computers and printers. Bluetooth, though, appears in hand-held devices like cell phones, television remotes, and personal digital assistants. There is even a Bluetooth-enabled pen; when the user writes, nothing shows up on the paper, but the writing can later be transmitted to a computer for storage.

Most networks are installed by skilled technicians, but Bluetooth can't work that way, because the whole point is for the devices to be carried around everywhere. As a consequence, Bluetooth networks have to "install" themselves.

As long as a Bluetooth device is turned on, it is constantly seeking other Bluetooth devices. Each device sends out radio waves in the same frequency range used by cell phones, garage door openers, and others. The signal uses very little power, which limits the range to about thirty feet. When two Bluetooth devices sense each other's presence, they form an ad hoc network called a *piconet*. One device is designated a master, and the other device a slave. The master drives all the communication in the piconet.

If other Bluetooth devices come into range, they can be added to the piconet as additional slaves; up to seven slaves can be attached to a single master. If even more devices come into range, multiple piconets can link together, with the master of one piconet playing the role of slave in another, an arrangement known as a *scatternet*. When the devices fall out of range with each other, the piconets and scatternets dissolve.

To get an idea of how useful Bluetooth could be if it were widely adopted, consider the following scenario. Marta attends a seminar on robotics given by one of her university's professors. The professor uses a Bluetooth-enabled computer in the presentation, and Marta has brought along her Bluetooth-enabled PDA. She takes no notes because her professor's computer automatically transmits them to her PDA during the lecture. To get back to her apartment, Marta takes the subway. As she passes the station gate, her PDA is sent an update schedule by the local transit authority. When she gets home and turns on her desktop computer, the professor's lecture is copied to the "Robotics" folder on her computer.

This is a scenario that imagines the future, but it's a future that may arrive soon.

SUMMARY

Networks allow users to share resources, files, and data, and to communicate—all without leaving their computer.

Networks come in all sizes. A point-to-point connection connects just two computers. A local area network (LAN) connects computers in a single building or in adjacent buildings. A wide area network (WAN) connects computers that are widely separated.

A transmission of data involves a sender, a message, and a receiver.

Networks are commonly connected with twisted pair, coaxial cable, or optical fiber, which are called the network media. In general, the less expensive the media, the less bandwidth the network has, and the more susceptible it is to interference. Twisted pair is cheap but fairly slow, and optical fiber is faster but much more expensive. Wires are also easier to work with than optical fiber. Fiber is often used for high-speed backbones connecting sets of computers connected by wires.

Other networks transmit data through the air and are called "wireless." Such networks are useful when the devices on the network will not remain in the same location for long.

The set of rules for transmission for a particular network is the network's protocol. Mechanisms in the protocol are responsible for making sure that the message actually arrives at the destination and that it hasn't been corrupted from its original content. Protocols also determine how much of the network's bandwidth is in good use and help prevent unauthorized access to network data.

Special devices on networks help direct traffic. A bridge splits a network into two logical networks. A router connects computers and decides what path a message should take to get to its destination. A gateway connects networks with different protocols.

To keep messages from being read except by the intended recipient, they are encrypted by the network. In private-key cryptography, the encryption key is the same as the decryption key, so the sender and receiver must somehow be given the key without anyone else knowing what it is. In public-key cryptography, the encryption key and decryption key are different. Any receiver can safely publish its key, allowing any sender to transmit a message that only the receiver can decrypt and read. Public-key cryptography can also be used to authenticate the sender.

Currently popular networking technologies include Ethernet, which is used for local area networks, Frame Relay, which is used to connect local area networks to form a wide-area network, and Bluetooth, which creates short-range wireless networks automatically as devices come close to each other.

THE INTERNET

HISTORY OF THE INTERNET

The *Internet* is a worldwide network that
connects many networks in many disciplines.
Before you learn about connecting to the Internet and examine its uses, look briefly at
the Internet's fascinating history.

ARPANET

The network that became known as the Internet began as a project of the U.S. Department
of Defense. In 1969 the department's Advanced
Research Project Agency (ARPA) established a
wide-area network with two nodes using leased
lines called ARPANET, which was called an
internetwork, or a network of networks, which
was shortened to the term *internet*. The nodes
on this network were universities and private
research facilities working under ARPA con-
tracts. The thought was that researchers could
better share data if the communication was
easier.

At first, the network was a raw data transfer
device with none of the applications users
now take for granted. The applications came
later, out of need. By 1972, for example,
enough nodes existed that users needed the
ability to send text messages about the state
and future expansion of the network. Because
of this need, someone wrote a program that
allowed text messages to be sent from one
node to another. Electronic mail was born.

While ARPANET quickly gained popularity
in research and academic circles, many years
passed before the public at large became aware
of it. This delay may have been a good thing
because the network was created, in part, to test
the ideas of internetworking as well as to use
them. The design and protocols of the network
went through many iterations, some of which
were so fundamental as to cause a *flag day*,
which in computer science jargon is a change
that is not backwards compatible, thus requiring all users to implement the change on the
same day. Such changes were trouble enough
when there were only a few nodes on the network, but would be almost impossible now.

Commercial Internets

ARPANET spawned imitators, creating inter-
networks for those not working for ARPA.
Soon it seemed every group of researchers had
its own internet. One internet, for instance,
was devoted to magnetic fusion researchers
working for the U.S. Department of Energy.
Another new internet was NSFNET, founded
in 1986 by the National Science Foundation
(NSF). The original purpose of this network
was to connect five supercomputers that the
foundation had commissioned at schools
across the country, but this goal was quickly

amended to support all forms of scholastic use. The NSFNET used the protocols of the ARPANET but had a much larger scope. It eventually reached every major college and university and became publicly known in a way ARPANET never was.

These developments soon attracted commercial interest. Even at this early stage, it was easy to see possibilities in the technology well apart from campus use. The NSFNET charter, though, limited its use strictly to academic pursuits. In response, private companies developed their own networks to allow commercial traffic. When they arrived, the Internet, with a capital *I*, was born. The current *Internet* refers to the worldwide network that developed out of the NSFNET project. The term internet, with a small *i*, is a generic term for a network that connects other networks.

Because these private networks captured all of the burgeoning commercial traffic, they quickly grew in capacity, to the point where the original internets that inspired them were superfluous. Eventually both the ARPANET and NSFNET were dissolved, leaving all traffic in the hands of commercial networks.

Early Applications for the Internet

What drove the popularity of the Internet wasn't the raw ability to transfer data across the globe, but the new applications that used that ability. In technology, it's always the software that drives the hardware. Customers wouldn't buy a DVD player if some of their favorite movies weren't available on DVD. What is always needed with a new technology is a *killer app*, an application that convinces people to buy the technology.

When the Internet was still a cottage industry, it lacked a killer app. E-mail was useful, but not enough people had e-mail accounts to make it exciting. What the Internet needed was an application that would allow users to publish documents and other files so that anyone who needed them could find them and access them. Then the Internet could become a giant repository of information.

One of the first steps in this direction was *FTP*, or *File Transfer Protocol*, which, as the name implies, is a mechanism for transferring files across the Internet. FTP allowed users to publish files on a particular computer and allowed others to copy these files to their own computers. Files could be made available to all or could be protected by a password.

However, to access an FTP file, users would have to know the address of the computer where it resided. Just as with RAM, where every byte of memory has an address, each computer on the Internet has an address. If users aren't given the address where a particular file is located, they can't find the file. The situation would be akin to a library whose books are ordered on the shelves by ISBN instead of by subject and author. No one would be able find anything that way without using the library's catalog.

The next step, then, was creating a catalog for the FTP files. In 1989, McGill University in Montreal developed a tool called "Archie," the name a play on the words "archive" and "archivist." This tool would regularly contact all the FTP file locations it knew about, request their file directories, and compose the file list into a searchable index. Thus, Archie can be considered the first Internet search engine. (A *search engine* is an application that allows users to find particular records or files from a large collection.)

The tool did not solve all the problems. It could only search FTP addresses it had been given; it could not find new FTP locations on its own. Also, Archie wasn't easy for nontechnical people to use. In addition, the program was developed for UNIX systems, and like most UNIX programs of that era, depended upon a certain level of user savvy.

Another problem is that although Archie allowed searching for files, it did not allow browsing. To continue the library analogy, searching with Archie is like using the card catalog to find titles on a specific subject, and browsing is like wandering the stacks to see if any of the titles on the spines sound interesting. Also, libraries often make displays—like "Fun Books about the Olympics!"—but there's no equivalent way to group titles using FTP and Archie. In short, no real system of organization existed among the FTP files.

Then, in 1991, the *Gopher* system was introduced, so named because it was developed at the University of Minnesota, whose mascot is a golden gopher. Instead of allowing users to simply publish files, Gopher was a mechanism for publishing both files and menus on the Internet. Rather than being presented with a list of files, the user accessing a Gopher site was given a menu with options like: "1. Files on Prussian Military History." Menus could have submenus, and submenus could have further menus below them, and so on (Figure 7.1).

Thus, Gopher was easily used by nontechnical people and allowed easy browsing. This system also allowed one Gopher site to reference another. Users who published a list of Prussian

a. FTP: unconnected files

b. Gopher : Files organized into menus. Each menu can link to other file locations.

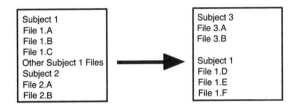

c. World Wide Web: links embedded in documents themselves.

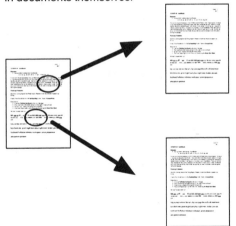

Figure 7.1—FTP, Gopher, World Wide Web

military history files could include menu items that would take them to other Gopher sites that had files on the same subject.

As with FTP, search engines were developed for Gopher, the first being called "Veronica." Officially, this was an acronym for "Very Easy

Rodent Oriented Netwide Index of Computerized Archives," but the name, clearly inspired by the FTP search engine Archie, was a play on the character Veronica from the Archie comic book. (Another search engine introduced later was called "Jughead.")

Because Gopher sites referenced each other, it allowed search engines to find new Gopher locations on their own. A *spider* is a program that "crawls" through references on Internet sites (like those in Gophers) to find new sites and material. Through the use of spiders, search engines could eventually index all the Gophers in existence.

All the pieces were falling into place, but the Internet still lacked its killer app. Though Gopher was easier to use than FTP, it was still far from the mouse-based graphical interfaces that users enjoyed on the Macintosh and in Windows.

While Gopher was being developed, a physics researcher, Tim Berners-Lee, led a team that suggested organizing documents using hypertext. A *hypertext* document contains embedded links to other documents. This is similar to the Gopher concept except that the documents and references to other documents are integrated, not separated into menus and files. Note that at this stage, the documents were all plain text, and the links between documents were chosen using the keyboard, not the mouse.

The final piece came into place with Mosaic in 1993, which was a hypertext program that displayed documents graphically and in which users selected links to other documents with the mouse.

Soon everyone was creating hypertext documents and linking them to each other. The links among these documents formed a kind of spiderweb, and the entire collection of interrelated hypertext documents is now called the *World Wide Web*, or *WWW*, often just called "the Web."

The Web was the Internet's killer app. While the Internet had long been the playground of researchers, college students, and hard-core computer enthusiasts, it now had a purpose that was so powerful and easy to use that the public couldn't help but notice. The popularity of the Web caused an explosive growth in the Internet. The number of connected computers seemed to double overnight. Even today, to many people, "the Internet" and "the Web" are the same thing, because to them there's no point to the Internet without the Web.

The Future of the Internet

Where does the Internet go from here? While some researchers are looking for more killer apps for the existing Internet, others believe it's time for a new, faster Internet. To this end, a consortium of universities and government agencies is working to develop *Internet2*, the next version of the Internet.

In a way, this is history repeating itself, with universities banding together to test technologies that may one day be used by all. The current network created by Internet2 is called "Abilene," named after a railhead in Abilene, Texas, that when built in the 1860s was the gateway to the frontier. Abilene provides higher-speed transmissions with lower delays than the current Internet. In a speed trial, the network was able to send the equivalent of a dozen CD-ROMs worth of data in under a minute. While that's in the same class as a Gigabit Ethernet, consider that this wasn't over a LAN, but over cables that stretched for thousands of miles. The Internet2 group believes important applications exist that can work only on such a network.

One bane of the current Internet is real-time video; for example, having a camera in New York transmit video to a user in Los Angeles. The current Internet is capable of transmitting video, but because of various possible delays and problems in transmission, most video data must accumulate before it can be passed on to the user. This *buffering* means that the video player waits until it has several seconds (or more) of received images before it begins playback. The delay allows it to recover small glitches in transmission without interrupting the user's video playback.

While buffering is fine in some cases, it hampers participation. If you're trying to participate in a conversation that is taking place on the other end of the network, you need the ability to respond to what's happening now, not what happened thirty seconds ago. Furthermore, to reduce problems further, most video sent across the Internet is small and uses few images per second, which results in a choppy playback.

Such problems have limited the development of video applications for the current Internet. If technologies from the Abilene project are adopted by the wider community, though, the way people use the Internet could change dramatically again. No one knows what killer apps could exist for the next Internet.

CONNECTING TO THE INTERNET

Common ways to connect computers to the Internet are through T-lines, dial-up technology, and cable lines.

T-lines

To use the Internet, businesses, schools, and other organizations first must connect their own computers together using a LAN technology, such as Ethernet. One of the nodes on the LAN is the gateway. As described in the previous chapter, a gateway translates from one kind of network to another. In this case, the gateway translates from Internet protocols to those of the LAN.

Then the gateway must be connected to the Internet. Because all the computers on the LAN must communicate with the Internet through this one connection, the connection needs a lot of bandwidth. A common solution is a *T-line*, a line leased from a service provider that comes in different levels for different bandwidth needs. (Originally, the provider would have been AT&T, which created these designations.)

A *T1 line* is usually a twisted pair and provides about 1.5 megabits per second, or about 190 kilobytes per second. That means it could transmit the contents of a CD-ROM in about an hour. At one time a T1 line was considered fast, but that is no longer the case.

A *T3 line* is a bundle of T1 lines and provides about 44 megabits per second, or about 5 megabytes per second. That means it could transmit the contents of a CD-ROM in about two and a half minutes.

Dial-up Connections

Home users originally connected to the Internet through ordinary phone lines, known as voice lines in the industry, and often still do. The phone system works on analog principles: As a person talks on one end, the voice vibrates a speaker coil, which produces an electrical level that varies as the vibrations vary. On the other end, the electricity is applied to another speaker coil, which produces the same vibrations in the air at that location, reproducing the sound of the original voice. Except for using electricity, the process is the same as the childhood game where two tin cans are connected by a string. Because computers communicate digitally and phone lines are analog, a conversion is required.

A *modem* is a device that can convert a digital signal to an analog signal and vice versa. The name comes from MOdulator/DEModulator; modulation is digital-to-analog conversion, and demodulation is analog-to-digital conversion.

When someone uses a dial-up connection, a modem must exist in the computer system and at the other end of the connection. An *Internet Service Provider*, or ISP, actually provides the connection to the Internet. Each message sent over a dial-up connection is digital until it gets to the sender's modem, where it is converted to analog, transmitted over the phone line to another modem, which converts it back to a digital message, reformats it to the Internet's protocol, and starts it on its way to its ultimate destination.

Phone lines do not support a high range of frequencies, which is why people heard over a phone once sounded like they were in a box. This low-frequency range results in low bandwidth. Dial-up connections can only support a speed of 56 kilobits per second, which means it would take more than a day to transmit the contents of a CD-ROM. Even this speed is only available in one direction—from the Internet to the user's computer. In the other direction, the speed is only 33 kilobits per second. The term

downstream refers to the direction from the Internet to the user's computer, and *upstream* refers to the direction from the user's computer to the Internet. In many methods of communicating with the Internet, the downstream bandwidth is much higher than the upstream bandwidth. In many applications this is no problem, but some applications, such as video conferencing, require the same bandwidth in both directions.

DSL

The weakness of a dial-up connection comes from its use of analog phone equipment, not the wires used for phone lines. A *DSL*, or *Digital Subscriber Line*, transmits data digitally over normal phone lines and thus allows much higher data transfer speeds.

Unlike a dial-up connection, which is available to anyone with a phone line, DSL requires that your phone company install special equipment. A phone line is a pair of wires leading from a home or office to a building known as a central office, or CO, and each pair from the CO to a phone is known as a *local loop*. You have probably seen these windowless one- or two-story CO buildings, either with a phone company's name on the outside or no markings whatsoever. The DSL equipment must be installed at a CO to provide DSL service to all the lines that connect to that CO so the line never passes through analog switches.

The performance of DSL is heavily dependent on the length of the local loop. The longer the wire, the more the signal degrades, and if the speed isn't lowered, too many errors occur for the connection to be useful. Therefore, the closer the home or business is to a CO, the better the DSL will perform.

Unlike a dial-up connection, because DSL uses a higher range of frequencies than is used for voice communication, it doesn't tie up the phone line. Someone can talk on the phone while the DSL is in use without any interference between the two.

DSL comes in different bandwidth arrangements. DSL for home use is usually ADSL, where *A* stands for "asynchronous," which has a much higher downstream bandwidth than upstream bandwidth. (If the bandwidth is the same in both directions, the two directions are synchronized; if they are different, they are asynchronous.) This arrangement makes sense for home users because the most common home use of the Internet is the Web, where lots of data in documents is sent down to the user's computer but little data is sent back up (often, just the name and location of the next document the user has selected). A Typical ADSL service offers a 1.5-megabits-per second downstream (equivalent in that direction to a T1 line), and a 256-kilobits-per-second upstream, which, although slower, is still about eight times faster than a dial-up connection's upstream.

DSL services intended for business use offer even higher downstream rates, such as 3 megabits per second or more. At these speeds, they are a good alternative to a T1 line.

Cable

Another popular way to get a high-speed connection to the Internet is through the "cable company," the same company that provides a home with cable television. Access is through a box known as a *cable modem*, which, despite the name, is not a modem at all, because there is no digital-to-analog conversion. Instead, a cable modem is a gateway, converting between two different LAN protocols so a computer can communicate over the cable line.

The cable modem has two connection ports, one for the cable itself and one for the connection to the user's computer. The computer and the cable modem usually communicate through Ethernet—it's a miniature LAN. Some cable modems connect through a USB port (see Chapter 3) on the computer. The cable modem communicates with the cable company with a different protocol; like Ethernet, though, the connection is shared with other users. A device called a CMTS, or Cable Modem Termination System, is installed by the cable company for a set of subscribers in an area. The CMTS is another gateway, pulling data from the cable line and translating it into the Internet's protocols, or vice versa.

If you've ever used a cable modem, you may have noticed an "activity" light that comes on even when you are not sending to, or receiving from, the Internet. This light indicates some activity between your CMTS and all the cable modems it serves, not just activity involving your cable modem.

It is this sharing of the local cable that limits transmission speed. The cable company actually builds transfer limits into the system. If one user could use 100 percent of the cable, the speed would greatly outclass that of DSL, but because it must be shared, the speeds are "throttled" to something similar to DSL, in a range of about 700 kilobits to 2 megabits per second or more. Because the "throttle" is built into the system, the cable company can offer tiers of service. Thus, users can pay for just the bandwidth they need.

Both DSL and cable modem connections to the Internet are often referred to as "broadband," but this term is more advertisers' talk than anything that has technical meaning. In networking, "broadband" refers to a signal that uses a wide range (a broad band) of frequencies. In the vernacular, though, broadband simply means a connection that's a lot faster than a dial-up connection.

INTERNET PROTOCOLS

The protocols used by the Internet are called IP and TCP and operate at different levels. IP, which simply means Internet Protocol, is the lower level protocol and allows raw communication between two nodes on the Internet.

Internet nodes are identified by a numerical address known as an *IP address*. This address is written as four numbers in the range of 0 to 255, which makes 256 possibilities (remember "powers of 2" from Chapter 2) separated by periods; for example, 170.171.1.150. Each node on the Internet at a given time must have an IP address for other nodes to have access to it.

Because remembering the IP address of another computer would be difficult for users, each node is also given a unique *domain name*. A node cannot directly use a domain name to send data, but it can use it to acquire the IP address it needs. A special computer called a *domain name server*, or DNS, can return the IP address for a given domain name. For instance, when you type a name like www.broadwaybooks.com into a Web browser, before the browser can retrieve the web page, it must first check with a DNS. If you type a nonexistent name into a browser, the error message displayed tells you that the DNS search failed.

Because so many computers use the Internet now, most home users are not given a permanent IP address in the way that a Web site is. Instead, each time the computer is connected to the Internet, a computer at the user's ISP provides a temporary IP from a range of addresses assigned to that ISP.

IP is a low-level protocol that only provides what is known as a *best effort delivery* service, which means it performs no error checking, does not track the message, and doesn't ensure that it is delivered. Because this service is not good enough for most applications, a higher-level protocol, called *TCP*, or *Transmission Control Protocol*, is used alongside IP to provide reliable transmission from sender to receiver. TCP provides for message tracking, retransmitting, and error checking.

WORLD WIDE WEB

As stated earlier in the chapter, the World Wide Web is the Internet's killer app, what makes the Internet as popular as it is. The Web is successful for several reasons.

First, compared to other ways to share information electronically, the Web allows the publisher of new material to decide how the material is organized and displayed. Just as a phone book is organized differently and has a different style than a treatise on the mating habits of penguins, different subjects on the Web can be organized and displayed in a way most conducive to the material.

Second, Web publishing is cheap. Most ISP accounts provide some amount of Web space at no additional charge. This means that most Web users are potential Web publishers. Even a professional Web hosting contract can be had for well under $100 a month. Because Web publishing is so inexpensive compared to other ways of disseminating information, the total content of the Web grows quickly.

Third, the Web is easy to use. No special technical knowledge is needed to find information or browse someone's material. Even young children have no problem with the Web.

HTML

The atom of the Web is a single document called a *web page*, which is a text document written in a special format called HTML. Groups of web pages stored under the same Internet domain are referred to as a *Web site*.

HTML (Hypertext Markup Language) is a combination of plain text and specially formatted instructions that indicate how the text should appear. The term "markup" refers to those special instructions. Just as a typesetter or layout editor may indicate with a red

A NOTE ON CAPITALIZATION

The term World Wide Web, or Web for short, refers to a unique global entity and should properly be capitalized. Not every web page is on the Web, though. You could store a copy on your own hard drive for safekeeping, for example, and some companies create groups of web pages for their LAN (company policies, for example), not for publishing on the Internet.

In short, when referring to an HTML document that may or may not be available on the Internet, "web" is fine, but when referring to the World Wide Web itself or anything on it, "Web" is better.

pen how a plain block of text is to be formatted on a page, HTML indicates how a web page is formatted on the screen when viewed through a program called a *Web browser*, or just *browser*.

An HTML document is "marked up" using special instructions called *tags*, which are distinguished in the document using the keyboard symbols and which, in this context, are called "angle brackets." Here's a simple example marked up in HTML:

I <b>must </b>have doughnuts, <i>right now!</i>

When displayed, this text would appear as:

I **must** have doughnuts, *right now!*

In the HTML, the <b> tag indicates "start displaying the text in boldface," and the </b> indicates "stop displaying the text in boldface." Similarly, the <i> and </i> indicate where to start and stop the display of text in italics.

HTML tags can be divided into four categories.

Character Formatting Tags

Character formatting tags change the appearance of the text itself. The <b> and <i> tags shown in the above example are character formatting tags. This category includes most of the same options that would appear on the "Font" menu of a typical word processor, including font face, font size, bold and italics, and so on.

Choosing a font, though, is a more complicated decision than with a word processor. When you use a word processor, it only allows you to pick a font that is actually installed on your computer. When designing a web page, a designer cannot know for sure what fonts are installed on all the computers that will view it. If a page designates the use of a font that is not on the computer, the browser picks the font it thinks is the closest match or falls back to a default font. The text is always seen, but it may appear very differently than what the designer intended. Because of these unknowns, designers tend to stick to a few common fonts.

Layout Tags

Layout tags determine how the text flows across the page. These tags say where one paragraph ends and the next begins, and are used to divide the page into different sections; for example, to make multicolumn layouts.

Web designers have some of the same issues with layout as they do with fonts. Users may freely resize their browser window, and, if the window is dramatically narrower or wider than the designer expects, the layout could turn out badly.

Link Tags

Links are what make hypertext. HTML can make two kinds of references to material outside the document.

One kind is a link to another web page or a different place on the same page, which is called an *anchor tag*. Anchors can be used to make a link to another page or to make a place where other pages can link or do both. For example, a page summarizing the history of the Olympic Games might have a paragraph for each Olympics with an anchor tag for each, so that another page could have a link directly to, say, the 1980 Olympics. Furthermore, that same page might have a series of links at the top so users could jump directly to the part of the history they're interested in. Without any

anchors, other pages can only link to the page itself, which means the top of the page.

Another type of link is to other media, like images. Beyond using photographs and other graphics to better convey the material, web page designers use images to enhance layout and make up for other shortcomings. If a designer wants to use an unusual font for a title at the top of a page, knowing it's unlikely that the font will be available on most users' computers, the designer can create an image of that text in the chosen font. Because images require more bytes to store than an equivalent amount of text, though, such techniques must be used sparingly.

Designers can also embed other media, such as sounds or video. Finally, the page may link to other documents for which HTML is not an appropriate format. The IRS, for example, makes all the U.S. tax forms and instructions available on its site, but doesn't store them in HTML. Instead, it uses the *portable document format* (PDF), which was developed by the Adobe Corporation to provide document designers with the kind of control unavailable in HTML. It avoids the font problem by allowing the document designer to include the font data in the document. This makes the file much larger, but means it's not important what fonts are installed on the user's computer. It avoids the layout problems as well, allowing the document to be scaled to fit the user's window or zoomed into at the user's request. PDF is an excellent choice for standardized forms, which may be printed by the user, such as the ones the IRS provides.

Special Tags

Other tags exist for items that don't affect the page itself. For example, the web page can specify what is displayed in the browser's title bar. Other tags, called *meta tags*, don't have anything to do with the display, but provide information about the page's content. This information can be useful for indexing the pages and may also aid browsers in displaying the page properly.

HTML Tools

Creating web pages is complicated work. It combines the skills of a graphics designer with those of a programmer. Early HTML documents were created using a text editor; the designer had to actually type in all those tags. This approach is troublesome for large pages because in text form an HTML document looks very different than when it is viewed in a browser. If you want to see how different, most browsers have an option—in Internet Explorer it's under the "View" menu—to view the "source" of the page, which is the HTML document in text form. Do this for any large page on the Web and you'll quickly see the difficulty.

Thankfully, tools now allow direct editing of HTML. These programs work like a page layout program or advanced word processor. The designer just drags the text to where it needs to be, sets the font sizes and faces, drops in the images, and so on, and the editor creates the HTML without the designer even having to see it.

Also helpful to designers is the addition of stylesheets to HTML. A *stylesheet* is a document that an HTML document can reference to determine how its text is displayed. For example, a web page for a news organization could have a stylesheet that defines a "headline" as a 20-point, bold, Times New Roman font; a "byline" as a 12-point Arial font, italicized; and a "story body" as a regular 12-point Arial

font. Then a web page with a news story indicates that it is using that stylesheet, declares that "Costumed Crusader Saves City" is the headline, "Jimmy Dugan, Cub Reporter" is the byline, and the rest of the page is the story body. The browser then formats the text according to the stylesheet.

If a Web site has only one page, a stylesheet doesn't save any time. But when a site has dozens or hundreds of pages with similar elements, a stylesheet allows the text formatting to be designated in one place instead of over and over in each page. If the designer later decides that 20-point headlines are too big, or not big enough, the only document that needs to be changed is the stylesheet. Without it, every page on the site would have to be changed.

Browsers

As mentioned earlier, web pages are displayed in an application called a browser. Internet Explorer, Netscape, Mozilla, and Opera are some of the many browsers available. Besides displaying the page, the browser is responsible for retrieving it, usually across the Internet. The browser must also sometimes send user information back across the Internet, as happens when a user has filled out a form.

Browsers also contain utility functions to improve the user's experience, such as maintaining a history of recently viewed pages. To improve performance, most browsers also have a cache. As we noted in Chapter 3, CPUs have caches to keep recently used data nearby so that a request doesn't have to be made to main memory if the data is needed again soon. A Web cache employs the same principle, keeping a copy of recently viewed web pages on the user's hard drive and displaying the copy of a page when the user requests to view it, rather than waiting for it to cross the Internet again.

Still, the most important thing the browser does is display the page. In a perfect world, all browsers would display the same page in exactly the same way. Unfortunately, this is not the case. Early in the history of the Web and HTML, the companies developing browsers were in a hurry to introduce new features, moving faster than the organization responsible for developing HTML itself. They created their own flavors of HTML (adding their own tags), and this tactic encouraged designers to create pages that wouldn't display properly except in that company's browser.

The situation isn't quite as bad now. It's rare to find a web page that displays properly in one browser but is unreadable in another. Still, some differences remain, and they're enough to make a good layout turn ugly. Sometimes these differences can exist even between older and newer versions of the same browser. These differences leave the designer two choices. One choice is to declare that the web page has been designed for a particular browser and that any problems with other browsers are the user's problem. The other choice is to check each page in a cross section of popular browsers and avoid tags and designs that are known to cause problems.

Web Programming

Some Web sites have pages that change so frequently, it's not feasible to run each one through an HTML editor when the changes are necessary. A *dynamic web page* is a web page that is generated when the user requests it, rather than created once and subsequently merely copied to the user. Dynamic web pages allow form to be separated from content even more than style sheets do. For example, in a news organization, a template for a page can be created that essentially says, "Main story goes here," "Top sports story goes here," "Advertisement goes here," and so on. When the user requests to view the page, the Web site's server fills in the template with the current stories, a randomly selected advertisement, and everything else.

EXACT LAYOUT VS. GUIDELINES

When the Web and HTML were first gaining momentum, a debate raged over how specific the markup tags should be. Essentially, the debate was between those who thought the tags should specify as much as possible and those who thought they should be more like guidelines.

For example, rather than using a <i> tag for italics, those in the latter camp preferred to use an <em> tag, which is short for "emphasis." In most browsers, text marked with <em> would still display in italics, but the browser could render it in boldface, or in a bright red color, or any other way that would clearly emphasize the text. A tag like <em> is a *logical tag*, which describes how text relates to the document, rather than how it actually appears.

It appears that the "exact layout" camp won out over the "logical guidelines" camp. For graphic designers, exact layout is a good thing, because they have more precise control over the appearance of each page, but for some users this choice is a bad thing. Exact specifications cause problems with *accessibility*, which refers to ease of use for people with disabilities. For example, a designer who uses tags to highlight important blocks of text in a different color isn't helping a viewer with color blindness.

Dynamic web pages are an example of *server side scripting*, which is programming performed on a Web server using a scripting language (such as Perl, discussed in Chapter 5). *Client side scripting*, in contrast, embeds small pieces of programming code in a web page, which is run on a user's machine in response to user interaction. When you fill out a form on a Web site and click the "Submit" button, you are executing a piece of client side scripting.

Server side scripting is also used for handling user data once it reaches the server. For example, a Web site for paying an electric bill may request that the user enter an account number. The server side scripting can check with the utility company's database to determine if the account number is valid and, if so, retrieve the account data, at which point it generates a dynamic web page to return to the user.

Client side scripting can perform only basic tasks. To execute a server side script requires a "round trip"; that is, data must travel from the user's computer to the Web server and back again, which takes time. For faster and richer user interaction, some designers include embedded programs that run on the user's computer inside the web page. Two common mechanisms for providing embedded programs are the Java programming language (described in Chapter 5), which allows the creation of "applets,"—small programs with full graphical interfaces—and Macromedia's Flash software, which allows nonprogrammers to create animations and interactive programs in a style that is well suited to tutorials.

E-MAIL

E-mail refers to messages, most often text, sent across a network from one user to one or more users. On the Internet, e-mail is usually accomplished through the use of two protocols, SMTP and POP3.

SMTP, which stands for Simple Mail Transfer Protocol, is used by the program that sends the message. *POP3* is the third version of a protocol called POP, or Post Office Protocol, and is used by the program that receives the message. In addition to receiving the message, the POP3 program is responsible for storing it until the user actually retrieves it on his or her computer.

The SMTP and POP3 programs don't reside on the computers of the users who compose and receive the mail. Instead, each user is given an account on an SMTP or POP3 server provided by the user's ISP. If you look under the setup options of any e-mail client, such as Outlook, you will see where the domains of the SMTP and POP3 servers are specified. Often, the domains have names like smtp.myISP.com, or mail.myISP.com, where "myISP" is the user's ISP.

When a user sends an e-mail, a chain of events takes place. The user's e-mail client communicates with the user's designated SMTP server. The SMTP program locates the IP address of the e-mail's recipient using a DNS server and then sends the e-mail to the POP3 server at that address. The POP3 server receives the message and then stores it on the server. Eventually, the recipient checks his or her e-mail using an e-mail client, and the POP3 server sends the message to that user, erasing its copy.

This mechanism may seem to have more steps and computers involved than is necessary, but e-mail would not work as well as it does without it. Because the POP3 program is on a server that is always running, a user's account can receive an e-mail at any time. If the POP3 program were on the recipient's computer, that user could only receive e-mail when the computer was on. At any other time, attempts to send e-mail to that user would fail.

When an e-mail fails to reach its destination, it's known as a *bounce*, because one of the mail servers usually returns the e-mail to the original sender with an explanation. Bounced e-mails are why the SMTP program must be on its own always-running server too. Because of transient problems in the Internet, a valid e-mail address may be temporarily unavailable. The SMTP server can retry a troublesome e-mail several times before calling it quits. Even after a sender has shut down his or her computer, the SMTP server may still be trying to send out the user's last batch of e-mails.

E-mail is a very inexpensive way to communicate, but like all good things, it can be abused. The most common abuse is *spam*, unsolicited e-mail messages that are usually commercial in nature and sent in bulk to multiple addresses. Spammers harvest valid e-mail addresses from various sources, or even pay legitimate companies for their customer mailing lists. Spammers also "guess" e-mail addresses, appending randomly generated names to known domain names. The spam itself is usually an offer to buy some dubious (or even illegal) product or service.

Spam is an increasing problem. Once enough spammers begin sending to a particular address, the spam will crowd out the real e-mail, making the account almost useless. To protect themselves, users must be very careful about whom they release their addresses to, and they need to use filters designed to delete spam before it hits the user's in-box. Still, no method is completely effective. The only way spam will go away is if no user ever responds to it, which would make it unprofitable for the spammers to send it.

CHAT AND INSTANT MESSAGING

Chat refers to applications that allow a group of people to type text messages that are seen by everyone in the group. Chat allows clubs and other organizations to exist with members that span the globe.

Some chats are Web-based and run using an embedded program written in a language like Java. A user who has something to say types a message, hits the "Enter" key, and the Java applet sends the text to the Web server, which then relays it to all the members of the group.

IRC, or *Internet Relay Chat*, is an Internet-based protocol for chatting. IRC doesn't require the user to go a particular Web site, but instead to run the IRC client, which works for IRC like an e-mail client works for e-mail. Just as with e-mail clients, users have a number of IRC clients to choose from.

Chatting is an example of how technology has social side effects. People can connect in ways they never could before. Suppose you enjoyed collecting ceramic figures shaped like a mariachi band. There are probably not enough like-minded people in your city, or any city, to form a sustainable Mariachi Ceramics Club. But there are probably enough people in the world to support such a club. Through applications like chat, the club could meet online.

A similar application is called *instant messaging,* in which two users can exchange text messages and have the messages arrive immediately. A single user can be receiving messages from several other users, but that isn't considered chat because each message only goes to one user at a time. For this reason it doesn't require a central location to distribute messages; it only requires two users with compatible messaging clients. Instant messaging also allows users to be notified when users on their "friends list" are connected to the Internet.

SUMMARY

The Internet began with the ARPANET, a project of the U.S. Department of Defense. ARPANET spawned the NSFNET, which, because it did not allow commercial traffic, was soon overtaken by private networks operating under the same protocol. These private networks form the backbone of what is now called the Internet.

Early file-sharing applications, such as the file transfer protocol and Gopher, were popular on college campuses and in research centers but unknown to the general public. The World Wide Web, which connected users to a vast array of information through a graphical, mouse-based interface, changed that, and as it grew, so did the Internet.

Users connect to the Internet through an Internet Service Provider. Businesses often connect through a T1 line, which is a twisted pair, or a bundle of T1 lines called a T3 line. Business and home users both use DSL lines, which send digital signals across the existing phone lines. Dial-up connections also use the phone line but must convert the computer's digital signals to analog and back, which limits their effectiveness. Finally, cable television providers also offer Internet connection through their coaxial cables.

The Internet uses two protocols, IP and TCP, to provide data transmission services. IP provides a raw and unreliable service, while TCP offers a higher-level service with error correction and retransmission.

The World Wide Web consists of interlinked documents called web pages, which are text messages in a special format called HTML. The HTML format specifies tags—commands in the text, enclosed in angle brackets—that indicate how the text should appear and how it should be laid out across the page.

E-mail is sent across the Internet using the SMTP protocol for transmitting messages and the POP3 protocol for receiving them. This arrangement allows the sender and receiver of the message to be off-line while the message actually transmits.

Chat and instant messaging allow for real-time business collaboration and socializing.

COMPUTER GRAPHICS

KEY TERMS

phosphors, pixel, resolution, bitmap, bit blit, lossy, lossless, anti-aliasing, double-buffering, frame rate, rendering

2-D GRAPHICS

Computer-generated graphics are one of the most obvious expressions of modern computing power. When someone says they are amazed by what a computer can do now, it's more often because of seeing a computer game or a computer-generated film like *Toy Story* rather than the latest version of Microsoft Word.

First, look at some basic concepts of 2-D graphics, and then methods for drawing and animation in 2-D. You need to understand how 2-D graphics are created before you can understand how they can be extended into 3-D graphics.

Basic Concepts

Graphics are all about dots organized into grids of color. It's all about phosphors, pixels, bitmaps, and image files.

Phosphors and Pixels

As described in Chapter 2, a computer monitor, either a CRT or LCD, creates its images out of countless red, green, and blue dots. On a CRT, these dots are called *phosphors*. LCD screens don't have phosphors, but the concepts work the same. At any given time, each phosphor is either visibly glowing its given color to some degree or not. A computer monitor is only capable of creating these three colors at varying intensities. It's up to the human mind to do the rest.

In the nineteenth century the French painter Georges Seurat developed a technique called pointillism, in which he painted his canvases with different colored dots. If you look at these paintings closely, you can easily see these individual brush strokes, but from a distance you cannot, since the colored dots blend together, forming colors in your mind that are not the same color as any individual dot.

Computer monitors work the same way. Although any one phosphor can display only green, red, or blue, when packed tightly together they can display a huge range of colors. For example, if one area of the monitor has all the green phosphors fully lit, none of the red phosphors lit, and the blue phosphors fifty percent lit, the result is a color that's about two-thirds bright green and one-third blue—"teal," perhaps.

The number of phosphors on a monitor screen is an important factor in determining how sharp the images appear on it. When a monitor is advertised, one of the specifications is the *dot pitch*, which indicates the distance between phosphors of the same color. A common dot pitch is 0.28 mm, which means each red phosphor is about a quarter millimeter away from the nearest neighboring red phosphors, and the same is true for the green and blue phosphors.

As with other measurements in computer science, dot pitch should not be used as an absolute indicator of quality. While most monitors arrange phosphors in red-green-blue triangles, which means the nearest phosphors of the same color are positioned diagonally, others arrange the phosphors in neat columns. For those monitors, the dot pitch is the distance from one red column to the next, which in comparison makes the dot pitch higher even if the overall phosphor density is the same.

As described in Chapter 3, the phosphors are lit by an electron beam that scans the interior surface of the screen. The monitor's *refresh rate* is the number of times per second this happens; the number is given in *Hertz*, abbreviated Hz, which just means cycles per second. For example, a monitor with a 60 Hz refresh rate is scanning the screen sixty times every second. Common refresh rates are in the 60 to

EXPLORATION: COLOR

Not every person perceives color in the same way. Here's an experiment you can try if you have access to a Windows-based computer.

Open your Display properties window by finding an empty spot on the desktop, right-clicking the mouse, and then selecting "Properties." Then click the "Desktop" tab and find the button labeled "Color." Click that and then click "Other" to display the standard Windows "color chooser."

On one side you will see a selection of basic colors, but on the other side you'll see a block showing all the colors the computer can display. You will see two sets of numbers. One set has Red, Green, and Blue, and the other has Hue, Saturation, and Luminance. Values for all of these range from 0 to 255.

These are two different ways to describe a color numerically. The red, green, blue directly matches how the computer handles color. Try putting in 250 for red, 100 for green, and 20 for blue. Do you think this results in the color "deep orange"?

Try to find colors around you by guessing different red, green, and blue values, and not by picking them from the chart. How close is your first guess?

The other set of numbers (hue, saturation, and luminance) is a way to describe colors that most people find a little more intuitive. The hue value can be thought of as how far along the color is on a rainbow. A rainbow is red, orange, yellow, green, blue, indigo, and violet. A hue of 0 is red, by 15 it is into orange, and by 40 it is well into yellow, and so on. Saturation is the strength of the color. With a saturation of 0, any color is gray, or no color at all; and at 255, it is as colorful as a cartoon. Finally, luminance describes how bright the color is. Think of it as describing how bright the light is in the room when you look at the color. With a mid level, you see the color as it is; with a high level, everything gets white; and at a low level, everything becomes black.

Try finding some of the same colors you tried before using hue, saturation, and luminance. Are your first guesses closer?

85 Hz range. The lower the rate, the more the screen appears to visibly "flicker," because the phosphors have been too dark for too long before the electron beam comes around again.

Computer programs don't directly deal with an individual phosphor. The smallest logical element of the display from a program's perspective is the *pixel*, which is short for "picture element." A pixel, like a phosphor, is essentially a dot, but a pixel encompasses many phosphors. Therefore, a program can set a pixel to an intermediate color (like teal), and the graphics card and monitor will set the phosphors in that area of the monitor to make it the specified color. Whereas a phosphor is a physical entity, a pixel is a logical entity.

Each pixel has its color stored by the computer in a block of memory called the *display buffer*. The graphics card accesses this buffer to produce the signals to send to the monitor. Depending on the capabilities and current settings of the graphics card, the range of colors could be small or large, but most computers today display in what's called "true color," which in theory offers all the variations in colors that a human eye can distinguish. To do so, each pixel has 256 levels each of green, red, and blue. For example, the color defined as Red: 250, Green: 100, Blue: 20 is a deep orange. With 256 levels of each of the three mixing colors, over 16 million combinations are possible.

Bitmaps

A monitor's *resolution* is the number of pixel rows and columns it is displaying. For example, a 1024 × 800 resolution means the monitor has 1024 rows of 800 pixels, or 819,200 pixels total. The maximum resolution of the monitor is determined by the number of phosphors, or the equivalent of phosphors for LCD and plasma screens, and by the capabilities of the graphics card.

Users do not usually set the resolution to the maximum possible, however. Higher resolutions negatively impact computer performance. One issue is main memory. The current color of each pixel must be stored in RAM. A pixel in true color is 32 bits, or 4 bytes. If the display has 819,200 pixels as in the example above, more than 3 megabytes are needed to store the display data.

Another issue is that when the display changes, more pixels mean more time to update the display. Suppose a program running in a window covers the entire left half of the screen, and you move the window to cover the right half of the screen. This means that every pixel in the display must be updated and that the CPU has to execute several instructions per pixel. The more pixels there are, the more instructions the CPU must execute, and the longer it takes.

Programs reference a particular pixel using a Cartesian coordinate system, which is a complicated way of saying it is identified using its column and row numbers. For example, on a display with 1024 × 800 resolution, (0, 400) means column 0, row 400, which would be along the left edge of the screen, halfway between the top and bottom, and (512, 400) would be right in the middle of the screen.

This is called *2-D graphics* because it involves a coordinate pair to reference a pixel.

A rectangular block of pixels that can be referenced using coordinates is called a *bitmap*. The main display itself is one large bitmap, but smaller bitmaps are used to build the main display. Very small bitmaps are called *icons*. One of the most common graphical tasks performed is copying one bitmap into another. A word processing program, for example, might have a button the user can click to print the current document that is identified by a drawing of a printer. That drawing is an icon, and the word processing program and operating system work together to place that icon in the right spot on the screen.

Image File Formats

In addition to drawings like icons, photographs and other illustrations are also stored as bitmaps. Because images are so common in computing, different file formats have been developed for different kinds of images. The most straightforward way to store an image is to store all the pixels' color data directly, which is known as a bitmap file. In the Windows operating systems, these are BMP files.

Other file formats employ some form of data compression. As stated in Chapter 6, compression can either be lossless, in which the compressed file reproduces the original file, or lossy, in which the compressed file, when decompressed, creates a file very similar to the original file but not an exact copy.

Lossless File Formats. A *GIF file* uses lossless compression to store an image with a maximum of 256 different colors. The word GIF stands for Graphic Interchange Format and is pronounced with a hard G, as in "gift." The GIF format was predominant in the early days of the World Wide Web but has fallen out of favor. One major problem was that the file format was protected intellectual property of CompuServe, an early dial-up network something like today's America Online. Developers of every program that displayed files of that format owed CompuServe royalties. The other problem was that as graphics grew more sophisticated, 256 colors weren't enough.

A *PNG file* uses lossless compression to store images, and unlike GIF files, PNG supports true color. The PNG format, which is an open standard, has none of the legal issues attached to GIF. It was developed to supersede the GIF format on the Web, and to some extent this has happened.

Lossy File Formats. A *JPEG file* uses lossy compression to store images of any color range. Lossy compression means that the restored image has some artifacts of the compression. JPEG offers variable amounts of compression so the user can decide between smaller file sizes and image quality. At low levels of compression, most people could not tell the difference between an original bitmap photographic image and the bitmap produced from a compression JPEG of the original.

JPEG stands for Joint Photography Experts Group, which tells you what this format is made for: photographs. Digital photography takes a lot of space on hard drives, but the JPEG format allows photographers to reduce the size of these files and, in effect, decide for each picture how much quality to trade off for the size reduction.

JPEG does excellent work with photographic source material, but for illustrations and images that include text, it is not a good choice. For photographs with lots of subtle variations of color, its compression method is difficult for the eye to see, but this method produces poor results when used on images with only a few colors and clear lines, like logos and illustrations. GIF and PNG, because they are lossless, have no issues with image quality. However, while they can compress illustrations well, photographs do not compress very much under the algorithms they use. Therefore, most photographs are stored as JPEGs and most illustrations are stored as GIFs or PNGs.

TIFF Files. A *TIFF file*, or Tagged Image Format File, supports both lossy and lossless compression. It's intended as a kind of universal format that can use the types of compression in GIF, PNG, or JPEG files. The format is thus very flexible. The problem is, because it supports so many different data formats, it's difficult for programs to work with. Compatibility can also be a problem because TIFF is so complex that some programs only support some of its included compression methods. A user can save a TIFF file and send the file to another user who has a program that is supposedly TIFF-compatible who nonetheless cannot open the file.

Drawing in 2-D

To draw 2-D graphics, you need an understanding of bit blits, alpha blending, descriptive graphics, and anti-aliasing.

Bit Blits

The copying of one bitmap into another is called a *bit blit*, which is short for "bit-block transfer." When you use a program with a graphical interface, bit blits are occurring almost constantly. A good example of this is the mouse pointer, which is an icon, a small bitmap that can be an arrow or a vertical bar or something else. As you move the mouse around the screen, the mouse icon must be bit-blitted to every location you pass.

This operation is complicated by having to restore the screen to its original state when the mouse has passed. That is, whatever the

mouse is currently "covering" on the screen must be "uncovered" once the mouse has moved on. To handle this restoration, the operating system may keep a copy of the entire screen in memory, minus the mouse pointer. When the mouse moves, the operating system first bit-blits from the clean copy in the area where the mouse was to the bitmap actually seen on the screen, effectively "erasing" the mouse. Then it bit-blits the mouse in its new location.

As computer displays have grown more sophisticated, so have the bit blits. An operating system might give the user the option of making certain icons larger or smaller. Unless the computer has different-size icons stored, the operating system is required to scale the bitmaps as they are copied.

Alpha Blending

Another new trick for operating systems is the use of menus and boxes of text that seem to "fade" into and out of existence. This trick is an example of *alpha blending*, in which a value called alpha is used to indicate a bitmap's transparency.

For example, suppose an icon is said to be thirty percent transparent. In a normal bit blit, each pixel in the icon replaces each pixel on that part of the main display. With alpha blending, when the icon is bit-blitted onto the main display, each pixel's color is determined by adding seventy percent of the icon pixel color to thirty percent of the main display's color. This blending allows the icon to be seen clearly, but a little of the original background will seem to "bleed through" the icon.

To make something appear to fade in the screen, it is repeatedly bit-blitted to the same location on the screen, each time with a lower transparency value. This technique is computationally intense, because it replaces what would have been a single bit blit with a series of them. That explains why these kinds of "gee-whiz" features weren't used before on personal computers; it's not that no one knew how to do them, but that they weren't thought to be worth spending the processing time on.

The same technique is used to create the appearance of nonrectangular bit blits. Although every bitmap is a rectangle, that's not always the appearance that's desired. Returning to the mouse pointer, that icon is stored in a rectangular bitmap, but the shape is that of an arrow. If the bit-blit operation just copied each pixel onto the screen, then instead of an arrow that seems to float above the background, you would see an arrow inside a black rectangle. The solution is per-pixel transparency. Each pixel in the mouse's bitmap tells not only how red, green, and blue that pixel is, but also how transparent it is. All the pixels that make up the arrow are given a zero percent transparency, and the areas outside of the arrow are given a 100 percent transparency.

Remember that the common "true color" displays use 32 bits per pixel. Actually only 24 bits are needed for the color information because 8 bits for each color gives the 256 possible levels of each color. The other 8 bits per pixel are called the *alpha channel* and are used for extra information like transparency.

Descriptive Graphics

Copying bitmaps around the screen is one way to create 2-D graphics, but not the only way. Graphics can also be described and generated through programming. Operating systems offer programs the capability of drawing points, lines, curves, rectangles, circles, and other shapes, which are collectively known as *graphic primitives*.

Consider a money management program. One of its features might be a bar chart that shows the user's net worth month by month using a series of rectangles, the height of each proportional to one month's net worth. There's no way for the programming to produce this chart using bitmaps alone because the details of the chart change based on the underlying financial data. Instead, the programmer creates this graph one element at a time, using commands that tell the operating system things like "draw a rectangle, outlined in black and filled with yellow, with one corner at (100, 200) and the other corner at (120, 400)."

Besides the ability to base drawings on changing data, graphic primitives offer advantages over bitmaps.

First, graphic primitives are easier to scale and rotate. To display a bitmap over a larger area than was intended, the computer has to duplicate some of the pixels in the image, which makes the result look blocky. With drawing primitives, if a program wants an illustration to be twice as large, the program just moves all the coordinates twice as far from each other, and the result looks just as good. Primitives are also easier to rotate. With the use of a little trigonometry, the coordinates can all be moved to new locations.

Second, graphic primitives can take up less space than the same size bitmap. If the bar chart in the previous example filled an entire 1024 × 800 true color display, it would take over 3 megabytes to store as a bitmap. To be able to re-create the chart again, though, the program only needs to store the coordinates and colors of each line and rectangle involved, perhaps only a few hundred numbers.

Descriptive graphics are used heavily with fonts. A *font* is a set of styles for each possible character, including letters, numbers, and punctuation. Computers originally used bitmaps for each character in a font, but this meant you either had to have a new font for every size of character you needed or you had to accept that characters larger and smaller than the bitmaps were likely to be ugly or unreadable.

Fonts are now stored using descriptive graphics. It's as if the font is a record of the pen strokes necessary to write each character. If a user wants very large text for the title of a report, that's no problem. The computer just draws the strokes farther apart and with a wider pen.

The two most common font formats are True Type and Type 1. The True Type format was developed jointly by Apple and Microsoft, and the Type 1 format was developed by Adobe. Both define font characters in terms of lines and curves. They also provide additional information, such as *kerning*, which indicates how characters should be spaced relative to each other.

You might think that all characters in a word would have the same amount of space between them, but that actually looks "wrong" to the eye. Pairs of letters that can visually "snuggle" against each other, like AW, are given less space between them than pairs like RD, which cannot.

Although both font formats are highly refined, Type 1 is often regarded as the choice for the professional graphic artist, while True Type is the choice for routine display tasks.

Anti-Aliasing

When a computer "draws a line" or any other shape, what it is really doing is changing the colors of some of the pixels in the display. Suppose the computer draws a thin black line over a white background from column 1, row 1, over to column 9, row 3. This means the area the line crosses is three times as wide (in terms of pixels) as it is high.

One way to draw this line would be to change three of the pixels in each row from white to black. This does make a visible line, and indeed it's how lines were once drawn on computers. But the line has a jagged, artificial quality. It doesn't look like a line drawn on paper.

The solution to this problem is called *anti-aliasing*, which uses subtle shadings of pixels to smooth out the appearance of curves and lines. The technique is demonstrated in Figure 8.1. In each of the three parts of this figure, each square represents a pixel. If you imagine that the pixels' boundaries aren't there and you could draw a "perfect" line of this width, you'd have the situation in part (a). Now, look at how the line interacts with the squares representing the pixels. Notice how the pixels on the ends are completely covered by the line, but most of the pixels are only partially covered to some degree. Rather than color each pixel completely black or white, the anti-aliasing technique colors each pixel in a range from white to black, including all the grays in between, based on how much of each pixel would be covered by the "perfect" line. Part (b) of Figure 8.1 shows the percentage of each pixel covered by the "perfect" line. In part (c), each pixel is given a lighter or darker shading (here approximated with cross-hatching) based on these percentages. Thus, the pixel in the lower-left is 90% darkened, while the pixel above it is only 10% darkened.

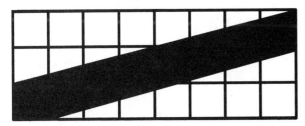

a. "Perfect" diagonal line

0%	0%	0%	5%	10%	25%	75%	90%
10%	25%	75%	85%	85%	75%	25%	10%
90%	75%	25%	10%	5%	0%	0%	0%

b. Percentage each pixel is covered by "perfect" line.

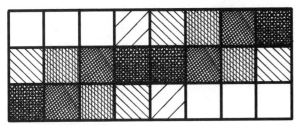

c. Anti-aliased line

Figure 8.1—Anti-Aliasing

Just as your eye mixes the red, green, and blue dots on the monitor to form new colors, it will mix the different shades of gray that the pixels show and will recognize a smooth black line on a white background. If the line is colored and the background a complex image instead of a plain white background, the process is more complex but follows the same concept.

Anti-aliasing is also used with fonts, since they are, after all, just a collection of lines and curves. The technique works well on larger text, but for small letters it just makes the text look blurry and hard to read.

EXPLORATION: CAN YOU ANTI-ALIAS?

Get a piece of graph paper, or make a grid yourself on a paper using a ruler. What you want is a 6 × 6 set of boxes. If the boxes on your graph paper are small, you may want to consider each 2 × 2 block a single box.

Your first goal is to make a circle that just fits in this 6 × 6 grid, by completely coloring in some of the boxes. Your circle probably doesn't look very round. Your first attempt might look more like a stop sign. Now try using the anti-aliasing technique. First, draw a circle freehand, as well as you can, over another 6 × 6 area. Note which boxes are completely in or out of your circle, and with those that are partially in, see how much is in or out.

If you can find different shades of the same color in a set of pens or pencils, use them. If you just have a single color, you can make multiple shades of darkness by using diagonal strokes in one direction for the first level of color, then making diagonal strokes in both directions for a second level of color, and so on.

Use the technique to make the boxes in the circle's interior completely dark but those on the edges of the circle less so. Look at your freehand circle. If twenty percent of a box is in the circle, try to color the matching box in your anti-aliased drawing about twenty percent dark. When you're done, take a step back from your paper and see how much more rounded the shape looks now than it did after the first attempt.

Some techniques in graphics are specific to the display technology used. One of these techniques is *subpixel font rendering*, which is an anti-aliasing technique developed for improving text display on LCD monitors. Microsoft's ClearType display option, built into Windows XP, is an example of this.

On an LCD monitor, each pixel is made of three LCD elements, one each of red, green, and blue, arranged in rows like this:

```
RGBRGBRGB
RGBRGBRGB
RGBRGBRGB
RGBRGBRGB
RGBRGBRGB
RGBRGBRGB
RGBRGBRGB
```

Each repetition of RGB represents one pixel, which means three pixels in each of seven rows shown above. Suppose the computer displays the letter Z, white on a black background, in this grid. Setting each pixel to black or white means turning on red, green, and blue in some pixels and leaving all three off in others. The letter Z appears like this:

```
RGBRGBRGB
        RGB
     RGB
     RGB
  RGB
  RGB
RGBRGBRGB
```

Here, where the letters remain, the LCD elements are one, making white pixels. As you can see, this Z lacks definition because there aren't enough pixels to give it a clearer shape. If the computer knows how the colored elements of the pixel are arranged, however, it can use this knowledge to smooth the display by only turning on part of a color. The result here is:

```
RGBRGBRGB
        BRG
     GBR
     RGB
  BRG
  GBR
RGBRGBRGB
```

In the second row above (highlighted), the middle pixel of the three is set to 100 percent blue, which turns on just the blue element in that pixel, and the rightmost pixel is set to a bright yellow, which turns on the red and green elements but not the blue one. The resulting mixture of bright blue, red, and green elements appears white, but instead of mixing these colors in one pixel, part of one pixel and part of another are mixed. Hence, the term "subpixel" is used for this technique.

Animation

In animation, icons and other graphics appear to be moving across the screen. The basic idea is the same as an animated film. By presenting slightly different images to the eye in rapid succession, the brain fills in the missing motion and sees the objects whose positions have changed as smoothly progressing across the screen. Animation is used in noninteractive presentations (like PowerPoint) and in interactive programs like computer games.

Animation requires the combination of a number of techniques, the most important of which is bit-blitting the moving part of the image to new places on the screen, as described earlier with the mouse pointer. When lots of items are moving around the display, though, a more comprehensive technique, *double-buffering*, is used.

In double-buffering, all the graphics are drawn to an off-screen bitmap, which then becomes the display buffer. For example, consider a program that is animating a dozen colored balls bouncing across the screen. If the screen is set to a 1024 × 800 resolution, the program performing the animation creates a second bitmap, also at 1024 × 800. Now there are two display buffers, one actually being displayed (call it A), and one off-screen (call it B). The program draws all twelve balls in B and then alerts the operating system that it has finished. The operating system then switches the roles of the two buffers so that now B is visible, and the program draws twelve balls, in updated positions, in the A buffer, which is now off-screen. Then the operating system switches the buffers again.

It's as if there are two chalkboards, one on an easel in front of an audience, one on the lap of the artist who sits behind the easel. When the artist finishes each drawing in the story that's being told, the chalk boards are switched. In this way, no one sees a drawing in progress.

Each complete drawing cycle is called a *frame*. The number of buffer switches the program performs in a second is known as its *frame rate*. The frame rate determines how smooth the animation appears to the user's eye. A film in a movie theater is only 24 frames per second, but for an interactive program like a computer game, that's too low for most people because there's a small delay between when the user performs some input (like pressing a button on the mouse) and sees the effect on screen. Such a delay can cause a form of motion

sickness. A frame rate of 40 per second, or even 60 per second or more, is desirable.

Why is double-buffering necessary?

The first reason is that it can save processing time. When there's only a mouse pointer to move around the screen, it's easy to replace part of an image to "erase" the mouse before redrawing it elsewhere. But if there's movement across the whole screen, this technique becomes wasteful, and it's easier to redraw the entire image from scratch, from the background elements to the foreground.

Redrawing the whole image leads to a second reason, which is that double-buffering allows the animation program to have multiple moving parts that overlap. By deciding the elements to be drawn first determines which items appear to be "in front of" others. This becomes especially important in 3-D graphics, as described in the next section.

A third reason is that the animation looks better with double-buffering. When the operating system switches between the two buffers, it doesn't do so at arbitrary times. Instead, it does so during the monitor's vertical refresh, which is a short delay between when the monitor has finished the last update of the screen's phosphors, or LCDs, but before it has begun the next one. By making the switch at this moment, the animation is as seamless as possible. If the animation program drew directly to the main display buffer, it might draw a new location for the bouncing ball right at the spot where the electron gun was passing. The top half of the ball would then be where the gun had just drawn it in the previous position, and the bottom half would be after the update in the new position. Thus, the two halves of the ball would have slid away from each other. This kind of visual artifact occurring when part of an old frame is shown with part of the new is known as *tearing*.

An important point is that because the electron beam scan is what changes the image, the refresh rate determines the maximum frame rate. If the monitor is refreshing the screen seventy-five times per second, there's no point in the program animating any faster than that.

3-D GRAPHICS

The term 3-D graphics does not refer to images that seem to reach out from the screen like Vincent Price in *House of Wax*. Instead *3-D graphics* refers to descriptive graphics like those described in the previous section, except the descriptions use three coordinates instead of two. Equally important for 3-D graphics is how 3-D graphics are rendered into 2-D graphics and how color, texture, and animation are used.

Basic Concepts

To understand differences between 2-D graphics and 3-D graphics, begin with coordinates and rendering programs.

Coordinates

A coordinate in a 2-D graphics system uses two values, indicating the row and column of a particular location on the screen. A coordinate in a 3-D graphics system specifies a location in an imaginary three-dimensional space.

To get a basic idea of how this works, imagine holding a stiff, blank piece of paper out in front of you. Because all parts of the paper are about the same distance from your eye, the paper appears to be a perfect rectangle. Now, suppose you tilted the front of the paper away from you. Because the top of the paper is farther away than the bottom, the top appears shorter from your point of view and the sides of the paper lean inward as they go up (see Figure 8.2).

In a 3-D graphics system, each coordinate has a "depth" value in addition to values similar to a row and column. In the first view of the piece of paper, each of the four corners has the same depth, but in the second view, the top two corners have greater depth than the bottom two. The graphics system would use this depth data to draw the appropriate shape on the screen.

Rendering

The process of generating a 3-D image begins with a description of the scene. Most scenes are described using flat triangles. Rectangular shapes, like the piece of paper, would be created out of two right triangles connected along their long sides, as shown in the illustration in Figure 8.2.

Imagine if you were a set designer for a school play and you had to make the entire set out of flat triangular pieces of plywood that you could glue together in any way. Simple shapes on the stage, like a couch, could be fairly easily built, but consider trying to create something round like a beach ball. You'd have to cut up huge numbers of tiny triangles to get the appearance of a ball from perfectly flat shapes. The graphics system has the same strengths and weaknesses.

It's important to note that a 3-D graphics system needs a 2-D graphics system to work.

a. Paper held out flat

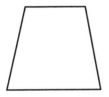

b. Paper tilted away from viewer

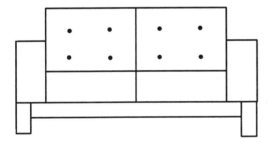

c. Sofa viewed head-on

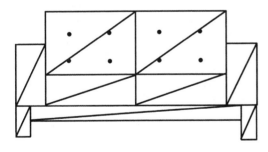

d. Sofa broken down into triangles

Figure 8.2—Perspective and Triangles

The 2-D graphics system is still responsible for setting the color of individual pixels. The 3-D system takes the scene description and the desired perspective on the scene and determines how each triangle should appear on the screen. This process of transforming the 3-D description of a scene into a 2-D bitmap for display is called *rendering*, and programs that perform this task are called *renderers*.

As you might expect, this process is complicated. Unlike a lot of areas of computer science, where programmers can get by with no more mathematics than that covered in first-year college algebra, 3-D graphics involves liberal doses of trigonometry and calculus.

The first complication is that some triangles may lie in front of others. If you describe every item in a room using triangles, from any given perspective some triangles would block others. For example, in the stage set, from some points of view the sofa blocks the view of the beach ball, and in others the beach ball blocks the view of part of the sofa. If all these triangles were fed into a computer and every one was rendered, it would look like everything was crystal clear (like Wonder Woman's plane). The first step toward making realistic, opaque objects is to remove parts of triangles that are obscured by others, a process known as *hidden line removal*.

Color

Stopping at this point, you'd have nothing more than the outline of the triangles. To make a scene look more real, you need color. You could color the edges and the inside of every triangle a particular color, like coloring the triangles in the sofa a bright pink, but this wouldn't look very real. Instead, every object needs to be given an apparent color, and then light sources must be placed in the scene, representing lamps or the sun. The graphics system must calculate, for each point, how much light is reaching that point, and determine the final color accordingly.

Each surface also needs a level of reflection. The difference between chrome and cardboard, for example, isn't just that chrome has a silver color and cardboard is brown, but that chrome is shiny and "glints" in bright light, whereas cardboard is dull.

This model is computationally expensive and still not all that realistic. One of the things the example ignores is the effect objects have on each other. If you place your hand near a green wall, your skin will appear a little green itself. Every surface that's not completely black reflects some light onto neighboring surfaces. More advanced renderers must track light not just to each triangle, but from each triangle to nearby triangles as well.

Some renderers use a technique called *ray tracing*, which calculates individual rays of light emanating from each light source, plotting their progress as they bump off each surface like billiard balls. Ray tracing can handle tricky situations like mirrors, which have no color of their own and merely reflect another part of the scene, and thick glass, which distorts images seen through it.

Texture

At this point the scene would be colored but every object would be made of solid colors. In fact, not many surfaces in the real world have solid colors. Wood objects have grain, for example, and a one-color carpet nevertheless appears to have dots of lots of different colors. The next step is a technique called

texture mapping, in which a picture is applied to an object.

To see how this works, imagine that the college student, Todd, has moved into a new apartment with a long, blank white wall in the living room. To make the room more interesting, Todd takes a picture of a brick wall and has the picture made into a slide. He then sets up a slide projector to project the brick wall onto his blank white wall. Now, the white wall appears to be a brick wall (see Figure 8.3).

Texture mapping works similarly in a graphics system. The computer is given a picture in the form of a bitmap and a solid surface and told to project where each pixel in the bitmap would appear on the surface. As with Todd and his projector, if the surface is flat, this is a lot easier to get looking right than if the surface is curved.

One problem with this technique is that a picture has no "depth." Todd's wall might look good from a distance, but if you got close to it and looked across the wall, it wouldn't look right. In an actual brick wall, the bricks stick out a little more than the mortar lines, and if you stand near a brick

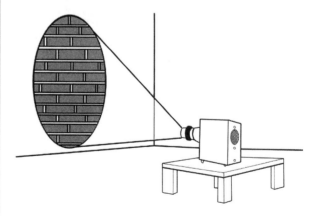

Figure 8.3—Todd's Texture Mapping

wall and look across it, the bricks hide the vertical mortar lines. This won't happen with the picture of bricks on Todd's wall.

Animation

The most important question in 3-D animation is how fast each frame in the animation needs to be generated. In *real-time animation*, the frames are generated as the user watches them. If you want an animation that runs at 40 frames a second or faster, then there's only 1/40th of a second or less to create each frame.

During this time, the computer must first place all the triangles in the appropriate place in the scene for this frame. For every object that has moved since the last frame, the appropriate triangles must be repositioned in the 3-D coordinate space. The computer determines which triangles can be seen from the specified perspective. The scene must be lit, probably from multiple light sources, and the triangles must be texture-mapped or colored. All of this needs to happen in 1/40th of a second or less.

It's not surprising, then, that real-time rendering must often sacrifice realism for speed. Animation created for noninteractive applications has the luxury of greater time. In making a computer animation for a film, for instance, the filmmaker can generate a single image over any period of time, transfer the image to one film frame, then start over with the next frame. In the film *Monsters, Inc.*, for example, the filmmakers had not one computer, but a network of computers, and rendered frames not in a fraction of a second, but over a period of six hours. This allowed them to do about a million times more calculations per frame than would be possible for real-time animation on a home PC.

GRAPHICS HARDWARE AND SOFTWARE

As you've seen, computer graphics requires computers to do a lot of work. Good results in this area are the result of specialized hardware and tightly written software.

Graphics Cards

In many personal computers, the most complicated piece of hardware in the system is not the CPU, but the processor on the *graphics card*. Originally, graphics cards were just called "display adapters," because all they really did was adapt (convert) the data in the display buffer to a signal format that the monitor could display. Now, they are responsible for much of the rendering process.

Some manufacturers of graphics cards use the term *GPU*, or Graphics Processing Unit, to refer to processors specialized for rendering 3-D scenes. Where a CPU is a general processor capable of many different tasks, the GPU on a graphics card is optimized for the rendering task. The GPU has circuits for moving triangles in a scene around, for applying textures to triangles, for anti-aliasing, and for all the other operations noted in this chapter.

To achieve the necessary speed for complicated real-time renders, GPUs have to work on multiple pixels at the same time. This is possible because of the limited operations of the GPU versus a CPU. In other words, a CPU is like a single, highly skilled, multitalented employee, but a GPU is like a group of diligent employees with talent in only one area. In the circuit space required to make all the CPU's talents available, several less talented GPU circuits can be placed. When you read a review of a graphics card, the reviewer often refers to the number of "rendering pipelines" on the card. This is the number of parallel circuits in the GPU.

Specialized graphics hardware is most important for real-time graphics, where performance trumps realism. Even in situations where the card will not be used for the final rendering (as for film animation), however, a graphics card is often used for fast "test" renders to allow the animators to preview a lower quality version of the frame before investing hours of rendering time in a finished frame.

Commercial Graphics Software

Computer graphics is both art and science. The characters and scenes displayed come from the mind of an artist but must be turned into a form the computer can use. To do so requires specialized software.

The most basic tool is an illustration program, such as Adobe's Illustrator. An *illustration program* imitates an artist's traditional tools, paper, and something to color the paper, be it paint, chalk, ink, or something else.

Another important tool is an image manipulator. The most popular program for *image manipulation* is Adobe's Photoshop. Originally, these programs were used in place of traditional photography techniques like cropping (cutting off part of a photograph), blowing up, airbrushing, and so on. Now, there are general image manipulators for creating all kinds of effects, whether or not the original image was a photograph. An image manipulator could color a black-and-white image, drain the color from a colored one, make a picture look like it was drawn in chalk even though it was painted, blur a picture, sharpen it, or use

a host of other visual tricks. In the hands of a skilled user, the manipulation becomes its own art form. Just as a musician can reinvent a song by "remixing" it in a studio, a photo manipulator remixes the original image into something new.

For 3-D graphics work, a modeling program is a must. Modeling is the computer graphics equivalent of sculpture. The user draws shapes in three-dimensional space and applies colors, textures, and other features. The program then stores all this data in a file format that renderers can later use. Discreet's 3D Studio Max is probably the most popular modeling program.

Renderers

As you might imagine, 3-D graphics requires some complicated programming. While the operating system handles some of the work, the applications are still responsible for most of the effort to get a 3-D scene rendered. Many companies would rather purchase rendering software than create their own. For some applications, this software saves considerable time and expense.

The RenderMan software is the best known high-end renderer. It was originally developed by Lucasfilm, the company founded by George Lucas of *Star Wars* fame. Lucas's ILM (Industrial Lights and Magic) was the leading company for producing "special effects" for film, using traditional methods like models and lab processing. The RenderMan software was seen as the vanguard of a new kind of special effect, where computer-generated imagery would be matched to traditional photography. Lucas spun off the RenderMan division, selling it to Apple cofounder Steve Jobs, who calls the new company Pixar.

RenderMan is now used by Pixar, ILM, and other special effects houses around the world to produce many of the fantastic effects seen in today's films. The dinosaurs in *Jurassic Park*, the wraiths in *The Lord of the Rings*, and the world inside *The Matrix* were all created using RenderMan. Pixar also used the software to produce a series of popular films that were entirely computer-generated, starting with *Toy Story*.

In addition to films, 3-D graphics are popular in computer games. Given the challenge of producing these games and getting them into the marketplace faster, game developers recognize the crucial work of renderers. Usually, the company developing the rendering engine develops one game to use it, and that game gives the renderer its name. The games "Quake" and "Unreal," while popular in their own right, were also demonstrations for the Quake and Unreal renderers, which other companies license for use in their own games.

SUMMARY

Computer graphics are created using dots of three different colors. When the intensity of each primary color is varied in a given area, a wide variety of colors can be perceived by the user. A pixel is the smallest logical group of colored dots that a program uses.

The graphics display of a computer is a rectangular grid of pixels, each comprising many colored dots. These grids are called "bitmaps," and their size is the resolution of the display.

Images can be stored as complete bitmap data or be compressed in some way. Compression that doesn't distort the original picture when decompressed is called "lossless," while lossy compression loses some of the original data in the compression/decompression cycle.

Copying all or part of one bitmap onto another is called a "bit blit," which is the basis for all computer animation. An example of a bit blit is the mouse arrow in Windows. Bit blits can replace one rectangular block of pixels with another, or the two areas can be blended together.

Although all graphics are displayed as blocks of pixels, sometimes graphics are described and stored using lines, curves, and other shapes. Fonts are good examples of this approach, being stored as a series of pen strokes. A black line drawn on a white background often looks artificial, though, because each pixel is either entirely black or entirely white. Anti-aliasing techniques help soften these visual artifacts by using different shades of color to blend harsh edges.

Animation usually involves double-buffering, in which graphics are drawn to an off-screen bitmap, which is then switched with the on-screen bitmap. The quality of animation is determined in large part by the frame rate, which is how often the bitmaps are switched.

Three-dimensional graphics involve describing a scene using countless flat triangles, which are then filled with color or covered with a small bitmap called a "texture." The process of transforming a 3-D scene description to a single 2-D bitmap is performed by a renderer. This type of graphics is very computation intensive and benefits from specialized hardware.

ADVANCED COMPUTER CONCEPTS

DATABASES

The most common type of business application that a company manages is a *database*, which is any machine-readable collection of facts that is organized for easy retrieval and modification.

Most database applications are client/server applications. A server, or set of servers, actually stores the database. On the user's computer, a client program accesses the server's data across a network. This is analogous to how the Internet works. Web servers store the web pages, and the client program (Web browser) displays the pages to the user. Database development involves standard programming techniques on the client side, in addition to some special skills unique to database development.

Database Design

As with programming languages, various paradigms have evolved for database design. The *relational database* is the dominant paradigm in use today. This consists of a set of one or more tables of data with specifically defined relationships between the columns in one table and the columns in another.

The tables must be constructed carefully to avoid redundancies in the data, which prevent efficient storage and can result in data that logically conflicts with itself. The process of refining data tables into the form best suited for the database is called *normalization*.

Consider a music store, the Tower of Rock, that wants to normalize its inventory records. Initially all data is contained in a single table.

For each album, this table stores the name of the musical artist, the album title, the quantity currently in stock at the store, and the name and address of the distributor of this particular title—who must be contacted when it is time to reorder. Each row in a database table is known as a *record*.

The problem with this design is that it contains redundant data. A few sample items of data show this easily. Each distributor is responsible for more than one title. This kind of storage leads to what are known as repeating groups in the rightmost two columns. Each time a particular distributor name appears, the same distributor address is associated with that name in the column to the right.

This redundant data wastes space in the record store's database. More important, if the address of a distributor changes, it must be changed in every music title that is ordered from the distributor. If this is not done, or is done incorrectly, the database will be logically inconsistent, and some of the titles will not be

Artist	Title	Quantity in Stock	Distributor Name	Distributor Address
Presage	Winter's Tales	10	Marksman	123 Glub Street
Porkrind Briefcase	Last of the Apache	5	Marksman	123 Glub Street
Samson	Don't Cut My Hair	8	New York Music Gear	485 W. 95th
M.C. Chalupa	Mild, Hot, and Fire	2	New York Music Gear	485 W. 95th

Tower of Rock, Initial Table Design with Sample Data

properly reordered because their rows in the table still reflect the old address.

To normalize this database, the original table must be split into two smaller tables. The first table will contain every column from the original table except the distributor address. The second table will contain only the distributor name and address.

Now, each distributor address is only stored one time, so if it changes, it only needs to be updated in a single place. Also, if thirty new music titles are added, all from existing distributors, the addresses won't have to be repeated in the database another thirty times.

Another consideration is the uniqueness of data. If two titles have the same name—consider how many artists have a record called *Greatest Hits*—then confusion is possible. When a copy of Abba's *Greatest Hits* is sold, it must be deducted from its quantity in stock and not from that of the Red Hot Chili Peppers' *Greatest Hits*.

Title Table

Artist	Title	Quantity in Stock	Distributor Name
Presage	Winter's Tales	10	Marksman
Porkrind Briefcase	Last of the Apache	5	Marksman
Samson	Don't Cut My Hair	8	New York Music Gear
M.C. Chalupa	Mild, Hot, and Fire	2	New York Music Gear

Distributor Table

Distributor Name	Distributor Address
Marksman	123 Glub Street
New York Music Gear	485 W. 95th

Tower of Rock, Normalized Table Design with Sample Data

Database developers talk about a *unique key*, a value that identifies a single record in a table. In the case of the Tower of Rock, each title in its store could be assigned a number not assigned to any other title. Abba's *Greatest Hits* could be #39853, and the Red Hot Chili Peppers' *Greatest Hits* could be #96037.

The requirement for a unique key in each record has driven one of the negative aspects of the computer revolution: identifying everything in the real world with a number. When you have to write your account number on your check when mailing a payment to some company, it's because the company needs that unique key so if the check and statement are separated, the company can be sure that the payment is applied to your account and not to someone else's account with the same name.

Most unique keys are just arbitrary numbers. In the Tower of Rock, the first title it stocks could be assigned #00001 and the numbers could increase from there. Other keys are partially derived from other data in the record. The first two digits of an insurance policy number, for example, could indicate the state in which the policyholder resides. If different policy rules are in effect in different states, it allows the company agents to know what rules are in effect even before the record is retrieved from the database. It's a good bet that when a unique key is much longer than necessary (as when a company with 10,000 customers assigns each a sixteen-digit customer number), the key isn't there just to identify a record, but to store data as well.

Database Manipulation

Having a database is useful only if the data can be easily retrieved or updated as data changes.

SQL Queries

To *query* a relational database is to request a subset of its data. The simplest types of queries produce a single record when given its unique key. A little more difficult is finding a record when the key isn't known. To find the record for the M.C. Chalupa title *Mild, Hot, and Fire* without a key means examining every record in that table.

The standard way to query a relational database is *SQL*, which stands for Structured Query Language. The acronym is usually pronounced like the word "sequel." SQL queries are text commands sent to a compliant database server, which then returns the results in the form of a *recordset*, which is just what it sounds like—a set of records. The recordset can be thought of as a temporary table.

To give an example of the flavor of SQL, if you wanted to pull the entire record for the *Mild, Hot, and Fire* title, the query would look something like this:

```
SELECT * FROM TitleTable WHERE Title =
"Mild, Hot, and Fire"
```

The asterisk (*) in this case means "all columns," because a query can specify one or more specific columns for the database to return. If you only needed the quantity in stock, for example, you could use the following query:

```
SELECT QuantityInStock FROM TitleTable
WHERE Title = "Mild, Hot, and Fire"
```

Because it always starts with the same word, SQL queries are also commonly called *select statements*. Users do not usually enter select statements themselves. Instead they operate the client program, which issues the proper SQL command to the database server based on user input and then formats the recordset the database returns. The database and the program that the user sees are two separate programs, and SQL is the language they use to communicate.

More complex queries are needed when the data needed is scattered across multiple tables. A database in an orthopedics office, for example, might need a report that shows all the patients who have seen Dr. Carlisle and who carry Blue Cross insurance. The basic patient information, including the patient's insurance carrier, would be in one table, while information about patient visits would be in another table. To make this report, patients with Blue Cross insurance are identified from the first table and then are matched with records for patient visits with Dr. Carlisle in the visitation table.

A *join* operation matches rows in two different database tables based on a specified column they both share, like "patient" in our example, which appears in the "patient information" table and the "patient visit" table. Joins are used in cases like this report, where data from two tables must be merged. Because each row in the first table must be compared against each row in the second table, joins are expensive operations, and so database designers are careful to optimize queries that involve joins.

Most queries involve several steps, and the order in which the steps are carried out can have a dramatic effect on how fast the query executes. In the doctor example, it may be that Dr. Carlisle is one of eight doctors at this office. If a new recordset with just the patient visits that involve Dr. Carlisle is made and joined with the "patient information" table,

the overall time would be much lower than if the tables were joined first and then all the Dr. Carlisle records were selected. In the latter case, the join would spend most of its time combining records that have nothing to do with Dr. Carlisle.

Indexes

Since queries are time consuming, database designers often create an *index* on certain items. An index is a table that relates a single item (like the title) back to the records in which the item is found, and it is designed to be quickly searched. For example, rather than search the entire title table for *Mild, Hot, and Fire*, the index is searched for a reference to the sought-after record in the full table.

Indexes can be designed in different ways, and in our record example, one way to design an index is to keep the records in it sorted; album titles would be in alphabetical order. The database designer has to work closely with the intended users of the database to make sure that the proper indexes are created. By analogy, a phone book allows you to quickly find someone's phone number using the person's name, but it's of no help in finding the name of a person if you just have the phone number.

Updates

In addition to retrieving data, the database needs a mechanism to allow programs to alter, add to, or delete the data. SQL also has commands for these operations. If the Tower of Rock needs to change the quantity of *Mild, Hot, and Fire* to ten copies, the following SQL command could be used:

UPDATE TitleTable SET QuantityInStock = 10 WHERE Title = "Mild, Hot, and Fire"

As shown, the update command alters data in the database. Although in this case the intention is to update a single record, note that if other "Mild, Hot, and Fire" titles were in the table, they would *all* have their quantity set to ten, which is why this kind of update would almost always be done using a unique key, as described above. In addition to the update command, SQL has commands to add a new record to a table, or to delete one or more records.

Updating data adds new levels of complication to database design. If two users try to retrieve and update data at the same time, which is not an unusual occurrence for databases, logical errors can result if the database doesn't handle the situation carefully. For example, suppose two different clerks at the Tower of Rock sell copies of the same record at the same time. The programs in both cash registers would look at the current inventory, see that it is currently ten records, and then decide it must now be nine after the sale. Both would set the inventory to nine, but after both sales it should be eight.

If the sales happened several minutes apart, the process look like this:

1. Cash register 1 asks the database for the current quantity of the record, is told 10

2. Cash register 1 tells the database to update the quantity to 9

3. Cash register 2 asks the database for the current quantity of the record, is told 9

4. Cash register 2 tells the database to update the quantity to 8

But if both cash registers do their "asking" before either does any "telling," the result would be:

1. Cash register 1 asks the database for the current quantity of the record, is told 10

2. Cash register 2 asks the database for the current quantity of the record, is also told 10

3. Cash register 1 tells the database to update the quantity to 9

4. Cash register 2 tells the database to update the quantity to 9

This problem can be prevented in many ways. One solution is to make a *transaction*, which is a set of commands that must be executed in a block. Each of the cash registers could execute a transaction of the form:

Begin Transaction
    Ask database for current quantity
        of record
    Tell database to set quantity of record
        to 1 less than current quantity
End Transaction

By having each cash register package the "ask" and "tell" parts together in a block that is executed as a unit, each one will in essence be saying, "Set the current quantity to one less than it is now." There's no way for one cash register's process to get between the "ask" and "tell" of the other; thus, one cash register's transaction will be performed in full, setting the quantity to nine, and then the other will be performed in full, setting the quantity to eight.

Data Mining

Some of the more interesting projects in computer science involve huge databases and discoveries of knowledge hidden within them. More and more companies are becoming involved in *data warehousing*, which aggregates low-level data from multiple sources for further analysis. For example, if the Tower of Rock later expanded into a chain of 200 stores across the country, a database at company headquarters could be built from the data collected and stored at each store. Not all of each store's data would need to be duplicated in the data warehouse, just whatever data the company's management could use to make decisions.

A related area is *data mining*, which involves extracting hidden knowledge from the relationships among data. Suppose the Tower of Rock lets customers enter their addresses into the store database so they can receive a monthly "What's New in Music" newsletter along with some coupons. Having gathered the addresses, though, the company might discover that a good percentage of its customers come from a certain neighborhood across town. If it wanted to open another store, that could be the place to do it. If the company cross-referenced the customer list with purchases, it might further determine that the new store should stock more "acid house" dance records because that's what's likely to be popular.

OLAP, which stands for On-Line Analytical Processing, is a methodology that allows efficient data mining. OLAP essentially creates a second, higher-level database that combines tables from the main database in many different ways so that, when a particular kind of comparison is requested (as between customer zip codes and items purchased), much of the work has already been done. This technique allows for much faster analysis than if the reports were generated from the raw data for every request.

Popular Database Technologies

An exhaustive list of database technologies would take up most of this chapter, but a few can be singled out. As stated before, most database applications are made of a server, which actually houses the database and provides the data manipulation services, and a client, which is a program on the user's machine that gets the user's request and formats the data in an easy-to-understand way.

On the server side, two market leaders are IBM and Oracle. IBM's database is DB2, while Oracle's database is simply called Oracle Database. Other major players in this arena include Microsoft, whose database has the moniker SQL Server (remember that SQL is pronounced like "sequel"), and Sybase, whose database is currently titled Sybase IQ.

Because all of these databases provide querying and updating through SQL (although each has a slightly different version), the products don't distinguish themselves through base functionality, but rather, through performance (especially with large numbers of users and huge databases), ease of installation, ease of maintenance, reliability (how long the program tends to run without crashing or needing to be restarted), documentation, quality of support services, and ease of integration with other applications.

Another popular database server is MySQL, an *open-source* application available under the General Public License (the same as Linux, discussed in Chapter 1). "Open-source" means its use is free as long as certain rules are followed. MySQL goes hand in hand with Linux, but it is available for all the major operating systems. Combined with Linux, and Apache, which is an open-source Web server application, MySQL allows a company or organization to produce a professional, database-driven Web site with little upfront software cost.

Multitiered Database Design

Consider a firm with a large file room for its customer files, and several vice-presidents who make reports based on the data in those files. Suppose the vice-presidents themselves go into the file room, pull the files of the customers relevant to their reports, copy the needed data, and then create the reports from this data. Besides the oddity of having employees at the vice-president level pulling files, this work model has serious flaws.

First, it requires that all the vice-presidents be given direct access to the file room, which makes it easy for files to be mislaid. And second, if the company devises a different method of storing files (for example, microfilm), then all the vice-presidents have to be trained on the new method.

If you remember the discussion of programming paradigms in Chapter 5, you'll recall that this sort of problem led to the development of object-oriented programming. A similar solution is used for database design.

In a *multitier database*, the application is broken into three layers: data storage, business logic, and interface. To see what these layers mean, consider again the firm we were just discussing, only with more employees. In addition to the vice-presidents, there's a file clerk, who is the only person with access to the file room, and a runner, who runs from the executive offices down to the file room and back again. When a vice-president needs to make a report, he or she outlines the needed data to the runner. The runner delivers the request to the file clerk, who provides the raw data on a piece of paper. The runner formats the data the way the vice-president likes it. Finally, the vice-president creates the report from the runner's formatted data.

Note that if the company switches from paper files to microfilm, the only job that changes is the file clerk's. As long as the file clerk can provide a copy of raw data in the form of a piece of paper, it doesn't matter in what form the files are actually stored. The file clerk is the data storage layer in the multitier database.

The runner is the business logic layer. Business logic is simply the rules specific to that business's data. For example, if a vice-president were to create a new customer file but forgets to check the "new/returning customer" box, the runner would be expected to catch this and not file it until the data is complete.

Each vice-president is part of the interface layer, and through the reports creates easy-to-understand snapshots of the underlying data. Note that each of the vice-presidents may be looking at the data in a different way, but they all interact with the data through the runner. By separating the interface task from the data retrieval and formatting tasks, a new vice-president only needs to know how to create reports, and nothing else.

An actual multitier database works the same way. Because the data storage layer is separate from the rest of the application, the data is safer and the company can switch to a different database product without having to rewrite all its software. Because the business logic is a separate layer, it's easy to alter the software when business rules change (as when a company changes the number of days that an account can be overdue before it charges interest). Because the interface is a separate layer, it too can be changed easily as technology improves, and different employees can have different views of the data.

ARTIFICIAL INTELLIGENCE

Artificial intelligence is an unusual field in computer science, in part because it's not always clear whether something involves artificial intelligence or not. A general explanation could be that a program involves artificial intelligence if it performs a task that was previously thought of as a task only a human could do well. Thus, a program that plays chess as well as most humans is artificially intelligent. This definition has problems, though, because as computers advance, expectations change. Before the census was taken over by computers (see Chapter 1), many people probably couldn't imagine that a machine could perform the tabulations. But no one today would consider such "number crunching" worthy of the name artificial intelligence.

Within the field, there are different schools of research. Some researchers focus on designs that are biologically inspired, which means their function, however crudely, is an analogy of a human brain or thought process. Other researchers have no concern over the method

employed to produce a result, and only care what the result is (winning the chess game, for example).

The term "artificial intelligence" itself doesn't suit everybody. Some people don't like the idea of declaring a machine "intelligent" and would rather reserve its use for human intelligence only. The notion that an intelligent being can be created seems impossible to some people and blasphemous to others. Reactions like these led some researchers to try to define "intelligence" itself, which isn't easy to do without using other hard-to-define terms like "the ability to reason."

An early researcher in this field, Alan Turing, developed a famous test, which is named after him, to determine if a machine is intelligent. Turing wasn't interested in the philosophical issues as much as with coming up with a practical way to test machine intelligence. In the Turing test, three computers are set up in three different rooms (Figure 9.1). In the first room, a human being is running a text-based message program like an Internet "chat." In the second room, a possibly intelligent computer has been programmed to hold a text-based conversation. In the third room, another human communicates with the other two rooms through the chat software. The human in the third room, by having conversations with the other two, tries to determine which one is the human and which one is the computer. This trial is repeated many times, and if the humans guess right only about half the time, the computer is deemed intelligent.

Turing thought it was likely that some machine would pass his test by now, but that hasn't happened. Programs that attempt to

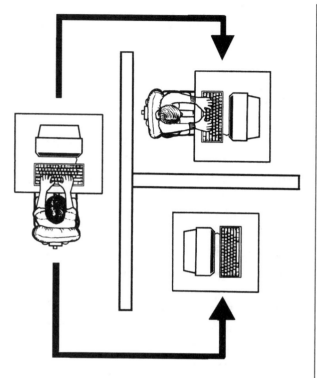

Figure 9.1—Turing Test

mimic human conversations rarely fool anyone for long. However, most researchers today are looking for more practical problems to work on, rather than trying to develop a fully thinking machine.

Reasoning with Facts

One type of artificial intelligence involves facts and logical rules. Computers can be very good at this kind of intelligence, much better than the typical human, but there are limitations on the effectiveness of "hard" facts and rules.

Knowledge Bases

Imagine a company that is developing software for use by genealogists. Genealogy is the study of family connections and history, and its facts involve events like marriage and birth, such as:

Fact: Fred Barnes wed Tabitha Wilkins on March 14, 1934.

Fact: Ralph Barnes, son of Fred Barnes and Tabitha Wilkins, was born on January 20, 1937.

Fact: Ingrid Barnes, daughter of Fred Barnes and Tabitha Wilkins, was born on April 19, 1940.

In addition to simple declarative facts such as these, logical rules can also be created. Everything that can be said about the facts must be encoded into rules, even those facts that humans would take for granted. For example, because Ralph is Fred's son, you could say that Ralph is Fred's child. This seems obvious, but it must be stated. Once the notion of a child is defined, further rules can be based upon it:

• "Child" Rule: If person A is the daughter or son of person B, then A is B's child.

• "Sibling" Rule: If person A and person B are both children of person C, then A and B are siblings.

• "Grandchild" Rule: If person A is person B's child and B is person C's child, then A is C's grandchild.

• "Cousin" Rule: If person A and person B are grandchildren of person C, and A and B are not siblings, then they are cousins.

Broader rules than these could define terms like "ancestor" or expressions like "in the same family."

Facts and rules are organized into a repository called a *knowledge base*. As the name implies, it's a database where the data consists of facts and logical statements. Having a complete knowledge base is the first step in this kind of artificial intelligence.

Inference

Once the knowledge base is in place, it can be queried, the same way a database is queried. The difference is that a database is just returning a subset of its data, while the knowledge base has logical rules to apply. The kinds of queries used in artificial intelligence are ones like: "Are Ralph and Ingrid siblings?" The process of reaching a conclusion through logical rules is called *inference*, and a program that follows this process is called an *inference engine*.

To see what's involved, here are the logical steps in answering the query, "Are Ralph and Ingrid siblings?"

1. By the "child" rule, Ralph is Tabitha's child, because Ralph is Tabitha's son.

2. By the "child" rule, Ingrid is Tabitha's child, because Ingrid is Tabitha's daughter.

3. By the "sibling" rule, Ingrid and Ralph are siblings because they are both children of Tabitha.

In most cases, the inference process is not so direct. The logical steps shown are how you would probably answer this question if it were asked of you, but you have advantages a program doesn't have. For example, you already know that Ralph and Ingrid are siblings and why this is true. You know that the "grandchild" and "cousin" rules are not needed to

answer this question. When a program begins an inference, it must consider all the rules in the knowledge base, which means it may try using some rules that have no consequence to the outcome. To minimize this effect, the program employs strategies to help decide which rules are tried first. Two common strategies are forward chaining and backward chaining.

Forward chaining starts from the base facts and tries to progress toward the goal. In the example, the forward chaining strategy says, "We are trying to determine something about Ralph and Ingrid. The only facts we have about them are who their parents are, so let's try to do something with those facts."

Backward chaining works in the opposite direction. It starts with the goal and works back toward the facts. In the example, the backward chaining strategy says, "We are trying to determine whether two people are siblings. To use the sibling rule, we need to know who is a child of whom. Let's go from there."

In simple yes/no queries like the example, either strategy works, but some queries seem more suited for one or the other. If the chief of police asks a detective to tell him everything known about the Smith murder case, the detective will probably employ a forward chain, listing all the facts the police department has gathered and all the conclusions those facts can support. If the chief instead asks the detective how good the evidence is on Williams, the detective could employ a backward chain, starting first with the conclusions that would have to be true for Williams to have committed the crime—he would have had to be at the scene and had a motive, for example—and then working backward to show how the facts supported those conclusions.

Reasoning with Probability

Not all intelligence can be done on the basis of absolute facts. One problem is that some terms do not have absolute definitions. Consider the word "rich." Some people, such as Microsoft chairman Bill Gates, are undeniably rich. Other people are undeniably poor, which means they are certainly not rich. But how much money must someone have before he or she is considered rich? Is someone with a net worth of $500,000 rich?

Fuzzy Sets

Many subjective terms, such "tall," "hot," and "fast," might be used in creating a knowledge base. For example, in creating a knowledge base for plant species, a certain plant could be described as medium-tall, growing in hot climates, with bright green leaves, flowering in late spring, and so on. Each plant in the knowledge base would be described using subjective terms. Someone using this knowledge base might enter the characteristics of a found plant to determine which species it could belong to. These characteristics could be things like, "found in Tennessee," "leaves are green," and so on. The problem is to determine whether Tennessee is hot, and whether green is the same as bright green. Because no absolute answer is possible, the best solution is to determine the likelihood that the plant matches a species in the knowledge base.

One solution is to create fuzzy sets for each category. A *set* is a group of items that share some quality. The set of numbers from 1 to 5 is {1, 2, 3, 4, 5}, for example, and the set of animals includes "dog," "bear," and "rattlesnake." An item must be entirely in a set or not in a set; the number 5 is in the set of numbers from 1 to 5, and the number 6 is not. A *fuzzy set*, in contrast, offers partial membership. In a "rich" fuzzy set, Bill Gates could be a 100 percent member, while someone with $100,000 in the bank could be a twenty percent member.

If Florida is defined as ninety percent in the "hot" category and Tennessee as sixty percent hot, then it means a plant found in Florida is more likely to match a species described as "hot" in the knowledge base. The result of queries to this kind of system is not a direct answer, but an answer with a confidence level, as in, "there's a seventy-five percent chance this plant is quercus rubra, or red oak."

Probability Systems

Uncertainty can arise even without subjective terminology. Suppose a technical support employee is told that a computer seems to have completely failed. When the power switch is turned on, nothing seems to happen. Several possible causes could explain this situation. It's possible a fuse has blown and no power is running through that outlet. Or, the outlet could be fine and the computer's power supply has failed. The computer's power switch itself could be the culprit or any number of circuits on the motherboard could have failed.

The tech support employee, based on previous experience with the company's computer and office infrastructure, may decide that there's only a fifteen percent chance for the first choice, a blown fuse, and a greater chance, say thirty percent, for a problematic power supply inside the computer, and so on. This kind of uncertainty is different than what was discussed in the previous section. Absolute facts, and not fuzzy sets, underlie this uncertainty. If there's no power at the outlet, a computer cannot work, for example. The problem is that when only the effect is known—the computer doesn't come on—not enough is known to determine the cause.

In general, the problem is incomplete information. You may lack information because of your inability to gather it. For instance, if you buy a used car and don't know its history and a mechanic asks you if the oil was regularly changed, you won't be able to answer. You may lack information because there's randomness involved, such as playing backgammon in which possible moves are determined by the roll of a die. Information may not be available because its acquisition is too expensive, as when a doctor thinks the symptoms described don't warrant the use of an expensive MRI scan. With incomplete information, only educated guesses can be made based on past experience.

Artificial intelligence often must do the same, assigning probabilities to events and making conclusions from this imperfect knowledge. As with absolute reasoning, both facts and rules can be created, only with percentages, like:

Fact: There's a 1% chance some computer in the office will fail to come on for any given day.

Rule: There's a 15% chance that a computer not coming on indicates a blown fuse.

The first statement just gives a probability that could be used at any time. The second statement gives a conditional probability: if you know one thing, there's the chance something else is also true. Some rules tend to reinforce or counteract each other. If the tech support person goes into an office with a failing computer and sees that a clock plugged into another outlet has stopped, that greatly increases the possibility of a blown fuse, but if the clock is running, it decreases that chance.

Expert Systems

The techniques described come together in an *expert system*, which is a program with a knowledge base derived from a human expert and is used to make decisions in that expert's area. Expert systems are a good example of a practical application of artificial intelligence.

Knowledge bases in expert systems are determined by asking experts questions, having them fill out questionnaires, or simply observing them do their work. The most common form of expert system uses this knowledge base to guide the user to a decision with a series of branching questions. If you have ever used a "troubleshooter" program, you've seen something similar. The program begins by asking about the general issue involved and then asks multiple-choice questions, like, "Is the power light on?" The questions get more specific, and eventually the program suggests a course of action.

Expert systems can allow users to get by without the human expert for questions an expert would find routine. An interesting by-product of the process of making an expert system is that the expert may find out more about his or her own expertise. Many people who perform tasks well don't have to think about what they are doing. When they do, they are surprised by their own thought processes, perhaps even discovering a better way to work.

Computer Vision

An exciting area of artificial intelligence is *computer vision*, which is having a computer recognize real-world objects in still and moving images. Computer vision can be thought of as the opposite of computer graphics. If computer graphics means turning a description of a scene into a picture of that scene, then computer vision means turning a picture of a scene into a description.

Computer vision is not an end in itself, but rather, a way to give input to another process. For example, a biologist might want to determine what percentage of a certain area is forested. The biologist could feed an aerial photograph of the area to a computer program. The program would find the forests and determine their boundaries. That's the computer vision part of the problem. From there the computer would have to calculate the area of the irregularly shaped forests and add these areas together.

Computer vision has many applications. For example, Toyota has introduced a car that can parallel-park itself. The driver pulls alongside the car in front of the parking space (as you would if you were parallel parking yourself) and checks a small monitor in the dashboard, which shows the view from a camera pointed out the back of the car. Superimposed over this image is a rectangle where the computer thinks the parking space is. The driver checks this rectangle, altering it if it's misaligned, and then clicks a button. Then the car drives itself into the space using the moving camera image as a guide.

Computer vision is also used in analyzing camera satellite photographs to determine if the image contains anything of interest. Depending on the use of the satellite, an interesting item in a picture could be a hurricane, a clump of trees, or a tank division. Computer vision is also used in automation and robotics to guide computer-controlled armatures.

"Seeing" is something most humans take for granted without having to think about how

it is done. Like many aspects of human cognition, it's a process that's poorly understood. How an image registers itself on the retina seems clear enough, but how the mind understands what's in that image is not.

To understand the difficulties researchers face in this area, consider this simple task: recognizing an apple. If someone shows you a photo of an apple, you would instantly recognize it as such. If you were asked how you know it's an apple, you might reply, "Because it's red, and it has this distinctive shape." But if the apple is green, as some apples are, and even if the photograph is black and white, you would still recognize it. If the apple is shown from a completely different angle (from below, for example), you would still recognize it, as you would if the apple in the photograph were partially obscured by a box in front of it.

On some level you have internalized the "idea" of an apple and can recognize its image in endless permutations. How this is accomplished is a mystery that has yet to be solved. Computer vision currently works best in a restricted environment, such as one in which all the objects in front of the camera are of known shapes, for example, in a system that examines parts coming along an assembly line and rejects those that are misshapen or oriented in the wrong direction for the automatic packing system down the line.

Some vision problems involve turning the data back into graphics again. Good examples of this are various medical scanning procedures that allow doctors to have a three-dimensional view inside a person's body. A *CAT scan* produces a three-dimensional view using X rays. CAT stands for Computerized Axial Tomography. In an X-ray photograph, areas are lighter or darker depending on the density of the material they pass through. Because bones are about the densest thing in a body, they block more X rays, which is why bones show up as the whitest parts of the photograph. A single X-ray photograph gives only a "flat" view of the body. If two things in the body overlap from the chosen perspective, nothing in the X ray indicates which item is "on top" of the other.

The "axial" in Computerized Axial Tomography refers to a camera that rotates around a center line in the body (an axis) taking digital X-ray photographs at regular intervals. By combining the density data from all these X rays, the CAT scan software can pinpoint where the dense

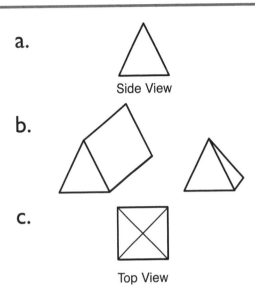

Figure 9.2—Combining Views

EXPLORATION: FINDING A SHAPE

A classic puzzle is similar to the process a computer must use in a CAT scan. A number beside each row and column in a grid shows how many dots in that row or column are filled in—how "dense" the dots are in that direction. From that information, you have to determine the shape. For example:

```
    0   1   3   1   0
0
1           #
3       #   #   #
1           #
0
```

Here the five numbers across the top indicate the first column has zero dots, the second has one, the third has three, and so on. The numbers along the side tell the same story for the rows. The shape indicated with the # symbols is the only one that fits these numbers. In some cases, more than one pattern may fit. You can use certain logical rules to figure this out with-

out trying a lot of combinations. The third column has three dots, but you don't know which rows those appear in. But because the first row has no dots and the last row has no dots, there are only three rows in which those dots in the third column could appear. That tells you exactly where they are. The same thing happens with the third row, which also has three dots that can only appear in one place. See if you can find patterns to fit the following:

A	B	C
03230	22522	12345
0	5	1
3	1	2
2	1	3
3	1	4
0	5	5

Hints: Pattern A can be solved using the idea from the example, above. In patterns B and C, start with the "5" rows and columns.

objects occur in three-dimensional space instead of just in two dimensions. Consider the objects in Figure 9.2.

In the first view of this object, you can see that, viewed from the side, it looks like a triangle. Below this, you see two different shapes that could produce this side view. Without further information, any one of them is possible. The second view of the object, from the top, eliminates one of these possibilities. Other shapes still could reconcile with this side view and top view, but the more views that are shown, the fewer possible shapes there are. The CAT scan works similarly, determining which three-dimensional representation is consistent with all the two-dimensional pictures.

ROBOTICS

A *robot* is a machine with moving parts controlled by a computer. The term was first used in this way by Czechoslovakian playwright Karel Capek in his 1921 play, *R.U.R.*, which stands for "Rossum's Universal Robots." The word "robot" was derived from the Czech word *robota*, which means tedious labor or drudgery. The "robots" in this play were not machines, though; rather, they were genetically engineered variants of humans, making the story more in the line of *Frankenstein*. Still, it presaged a future in which humankind would create beings to do its rote work.

Most people associated the term "robot" with sentient, humanoid creatures from science fiction stories, like C3PO from the film *Star Wars*, but most robots make no attempts at artificial intelligence. Industrial robots are used to perform repetitive tasks that humans would find tedious or dangerous. Robots that

paint automobiles are a good example of both. The robot can apply the paint to the car evenly, putting the same amount of paint on each car. In addition, the robots can suffer no health problems from long-term exposure to paint fumes.

At the most general level, many of the devices in a personal computer are robots. The mechanisms used to move a read/write head in a hard disk drive, for example, are conceptually no different than those used in large-scale robots.

Robots are also used in entertainment. There's no more obvious example than the robots at Disneyland and Walt Disney World. Although highly advanced, they operate on principles similar to a player piano. On a player piano, a roll of paper has holes in it to indicate when certain notes are struck—compare this concept to that of Jacquard's mechanical loom from back in Chapter 1. Similarly, these Disney robots were originally controlled through a continuous loop of audiotape. The tape was logically divided into multiple "tracks." Some tracks were ordinary audio, such as the "speech" that would emanate from a speaker in the robotic character's mouth. Other tracks had signals that controlled the hydraulics to move the robots' limbs and facial features. Because of their reliance on audiotape, Disney dubbed their robots "Audio-Animatronics." Though the robotic movements are now stored digitally on a hard drive, the name remains.

Most robots are rooted to a spot, but some can move about freely. Because walking on two legs is a very difficult task to design a robot for, most mobile robots run on wheels or treads, or have a lot more than two legs. An eight-legged robot, for example, can move by keeping four legs on the ground while the other four legs move. Thus, it's always as secure on the ground as a kitchen table. A robot with two legs has to balance on a single leg while the other is in motion, which is much more difficult. Still, some robots have achieved this.

ASIMO, which stands for Advanced Step in Innovative MObility, was developed by the car maker Honda as part of a long-term robotics project. ASIMO can walk on two legs with a natural-looking stride and even climb stairs. An interesting note: Honda made ASIMO smaller than its prototypes so that its "eyes" would be at the level of a seated person, and thus, if it is used in an office setting, it wouldn't appear threatening when it came in the room.

SUMMARY

The most common kind of database is a relational database, which organizes data into tables. The tables are designed to avoid including the same piece of information twice, which reduces the chance of inconsistent data.

Data is retrieved from a database with queries. SQL is the standard language for writing queries to the database. Because queries are often slow, some tables have secondary tables called "indexes" that allow fast access to records with a given key.

As databases grow large, they often contain evidence of relationships between data that the database designers never imagined. Data mining is the process of sifting through the data looking for these hidden relationships, like discovering that customers purchasing product X are more likely to purchase product Y, which suggests that the two products should be located together.

A multitier database divides the application into the data access layer, the business logic layer, and the interface layer. Separating these functions makes changes possible at different layers without having to rewrite the entire application.

Artificial intelligence is a difficult field to pin down. What seems like artificial intelligence now may not seem so intelligent later. Two major areas of artificial intelligence are fact-based reasoning and probability-based reasoning. Fact-based reasoning uses logical rules of the form, "If we know these things are true, then this other thing must be true also." These rules can be used to derive new conclusions from known facts. With probability-based reasoning, rules that are true only some of the time, like, "If it rains three days in a row, there's a fifty percent chance the creek will flood," can be used. The results are not absolute facts, but possibilities. Expert systems use facts and probability to model the opinions offered by a subject expert. Computer vision systems either turn images into descriptions or combine multiple images into one detailed image, as with CAT scans.

Robots are used throughout computer science, if you consider that the mechanism of a hard drive functions like a robot. Some robots are used where humans couldn't or shouldn't work, and others are used to entertain us.

COMPUTERS IN SOCIETY

GOVERNMENTAL ISSUES

As computers become ubiquitous, inevitably
the government must get involved, and just as
inevitably, no decision the government makes
can please everyone.

Privacy

From the discussion on databases in the
previous chapter, remember the concept
of data mining, where vast stores of data
are sifted for information about customer
spending habits. A retailer could notice that
a certain credit card is often used to purchase
product X, cross-reference the name on the
card with the address in the retailer's catalog
mailing list, and send the customer a cus-
tomized flyer when product X goes on sale.

For some people, this sales tactic would be
a case of excellent customer service. Many
customers, however, do not want their spending habits analyzed in this way. Some feel
that this smacks of being watched by "Big
Brother," from George Orwell's novel *1984*.
They don't like records of their purchases
being stored forever in some digital vault,
and consider this kind of tracking an invasion
of their privacy.

People do not necessarily object to a company
making secondary use of data they have
provided, usually to improve the marketing
of products and services. But they do object
when data is shared among companies or
linked to other data. For example, a bank
stores data on all its depositors. From the
amount of deposits, the bank can make
some assumptions about the overall financial
status of the depositor and may target offers
based on these assumptions. To most people,
this practice crosses no boundary. If, however,
someone receives a mailing from Big Lots
because the bank has identified him or her
as a small depositor and passed this information on, the person may feel that a trust has
been violated.

Laws exist to protect direct transfers of sensitive
data like financial information, but with computers, data can also be acquired indirectly.
EPIC, the Electronic Privacy Information
Center, uses the term *reidentification*, described
as "the process of linking anonymous data to
the actual identity of an individual."

Suppose a political pollster conducts a phone
interview with a voter. The voter does not give
his name, but in response to the demographic
questions, indicates he is a Hispanic man,
born in 1968, owns three cars, and lives in
the zip code 35243. He then answers a series
of questions regarding his political beliefs in
which he expresses left-of-center attitudes
regarding gun control and taxation. The poll
provides its data in both aggregate and raw

form. It does not identify any voter by name, address, or phone number, only by the demographic data listed above. However, the voter turns out to be the only Hispanic man born in 1968 in that zip code with three cars. He can be reidentified by any data miner who has already connected him with his demographics. The previously anonymous data becomes "Mr. Hernandez is a liberal," and two weeks later Mr. Hernandez wonders why he is receiving a complimentary subscription to *Mother Jones*.

Some believe the government should step in and prevent any exchange of personal data between companies, even in aggregate form, without the explicit consent of the consumer whose data is being exchanged. Many companies have adopted their own policies in this direction, but these policies may only require that the consumer be notified when the data is exchanged, or the policy itself may become void if the company is merged with another.

Protection of Children

The Web is a fantastic resource, but it is also awash in pornographic and violent images that many parents don't want their children exposed to. These parents have often banded together to call upon the government to help protect children from inadvertent viewing of objectionable Web sites.

Lawmakers are willing to help, but it has proven difficult to craft laws that will actually help protect children without running afoul of the U.S. Constitution. The situation at first seems the same as with pornographic magazines, but the reality is quite different. Laws exist in municipalities that prevent the sale of "adult" material to minors. This is fair to shopkeepers because they can require a driver's license or other form of identification as proof of age before selling the adult material, the same way they check for proof of age before selling alcoholic beverages. The Web has no equivalent to "carding" someone at the corner store, however.

One law the U.S. government enacted in this area is called CIPA, or the Children's Internet Protection Act, which specifically targets "adult-only" material on Web-enabled computers in libraries. This law requires libraries to install filtering software on publicly accessible computers to receive federal library grant money.

The filtering software is intended to prevent access only to objectionable Web sites, but no filtering is perfect. Some filters that work through automated examination of a Web site's contents can be overzealous and block access to a site that frequently uses the word "breast," even though the site may be offering information on breast cancer prevention instead of erotica. Others use manually chosen lists of objectionable sites, but these lists can fall out of date.

It is important to note that CIPA does not require a library to do a specific level or type of filtering, and that it allows for the filtering to be bypassed for a library patron who asks a librarian to do so. Even so, the law is controversial. Some have argued that any intentional abridgement of information is counter to the spirit and purpose of a public library, and that filtering software is so unreliable that patrons with legitimate research needs will have the sites they needed to access blocked. The law was challenged in court, with the case eventually reaching the U.S. Supreme Court, which upheld the constitutionality of the law in a 6–3 decision.

INTELLECTUAL PROPERTY ISSUES

Copyrights and patents are collectively referred to as "intellectual property." Some interesting problems have arisen from applying existing laws and standards in these areas to software.

Copyright

Software is protected by *copyright*, just as books, plays, music, and films are. A copyright is a legal right to produce and sell a "work," such as a book or program. Any copies of that work that are not authorized by the copyright holder are illegal. While it's difficult and costly to make illegal copies of a book or to make any money by putting on an illegal performance of a play, copying software is often very easy.

Software piracy refers to installing software without remuneration to the copyright holder, and it's a large and growing problem for computer science. Thirty-six percent of all installed software on computers in 2003 was pirated, according to a worldwide study conducted by the Business Software Alliance, an industry antipiracy group. This represented a loss of $29 billion to the software industry. In some parts of the world, such as China, considerably more software is illegally copied than legally purchased.

Software piracy has existed as long as commercial software has existed. Software publishers have tried different tactics over the years to thwart software pirates. *Copy protection* refers to techniques that prevent unauthorized duplication of software or renders unauthorized duplicates useless. During the 1980s, when software was distributed on floppy disks, publishers inserted incorrectly formatted data into certain disk sectors—a set of data that would normally only be produced if the physical medium was failing. When the program executed, it would check that sector on the disk and make sure the error occurred before continuing. If a pirate copied the disk using normal methods, the operating system would skip the "bad" sector, and the resulting copy would have all the program data but wouldn't run.

This approach worked in an era where you ran a program directly off a floppy disk. When hard drives became common, users wanted to install the programs onto their hard drives, then put the floppy disks (later, the CD-ROM discs) in a box and forget about them. For a while error encoding went away and most software was unprotected. Some expensive programs used a *dongle*, which is a device that plugs into a computer port (like a printer or USB port) and must be present for a particular program to execute. Software can also be copied by computers with dongles.

Currently, the industry has developed variants of the error encoding idea. Many programs, especially games, require the user to keep the CD-ROM in the drive while using the program. A popular copy protection scheme for CD-ROMs is Macrovision's SafeDisc. While Macrovision doesn't release a lot of details to the public, its technology seems related to what was used with floppies: introduce nonstandard data into certain areas of the disc that CD-ROM burners will have trouble duplicating, modifying the application so it won't work unless those sectors are present on the disc.

An application encoded with SafeDisc can be installed on a hard drive, but the disc must be present in the CD-ROM drive or the application will not start. Furthermore, the application may make regular checks on the drive to make sure the disc is still present. While this arrangement benefits the software publisher, it penalizes the user who legally purchases software. The user must find the disc for the application for each use. Furthermore, the authentication process makes the application slower to start. (Macrovision's documentation estimates ten to twenty seconds to initially authenticate the disc.)

Software publishers must therefore walk a fine line between protecting their copyrights and annoying users too much. One problem is that copyright law in the United States allows a user to make one copy of a program for archival purposes, to protect the user from loss if the original CD-ROM is damaged beyond readability. With copy protection in place, users have no way to make an archival copy.

In the past, some users might have resorted to *cracking*, which means modifying a program to remove its copy protection features. The legality of this practice was in question until the *Digital Millennium Copyright Act*, or DMCA, was signed into law in 1998, which added a number of provisions—some of them controversial—to copyright law as it applies to technology. One provision makes it illegal to remove copy protection or to tamper with technology used to prevent unauthorized access to copyrighted material.

Soon after the law was passed, it was clear that a literal interpretation of its wording would cause problems. In 2003, for instance, the Library of Congress released a set of exemptions that included the situation in which someone has software locked by a dongle (as described above) but the dongle is broken and the company that made the dongle no longer

exists. The exemption allows the user to crack the protection, because the user has a right to use the software and there is no other remedy.

As Internet access became the norm for home computers, yet another copy protection scheme was developed, one in which a company maintains a central repository that lists the computers on which its software is installed. The software won't execute unless it's first registered with this repository.

Microsoft uses this technique with their flagship software, the Windows operating system. Each CD-ROM package has a long string of letters and numbers on it, called the "CD key." When the user installs Windows, he or she must enter the CD key. The installer takes this number and sends it to a server at Microsoft, which then returns a matching value. This process is similar to the authentication process used for public-key cryptography as described in Chapter 6. In short, it would be difficult for anyone other than Microsoft to generate the matching value for a particular CD key, but it is easy for the Windows installer to verify that the key and the value returned by Microsoft match. If they don't, then Windows will cease functioning until it has that value.

This approach allows Microsoft to store all the CD keys that have been used to activate a product and thus know when the same CD key has been used more than once, which indicates that one of the copies is illegally installed.

Software Patents

An even thornier issue than copyright is the idea of a software patent. A *patent* grants an inventor the right to limit who produces or sells an invention. A key provision of patent law is that patents are granted for inventions, not ideas. For example, if you come up with the idea of a car that runs on kitchen waste, you cannot patent the idea unless you can actually demonstrate to the patent office the method under which the car works. It's this mechanism, and not the general idea behind it, that would be patented.

Furthermore, some things that are "pure ideas" cannot be patented at all. An example of this would be a business practice. If McDonald's determines that employees work best when scheduled in five-hour shifts that alternate from morning to afternoon every other day, there's nothing they can do to prevent Burger King from adopting this practice.

A final consideration of patent law is that only nonobvious inventions can be patented. If everyone thinks of a simple idea when faced with a certain problem, no one can get a patent just by being the first one to file that invention with the patent office.

Thus, legally, software programs are protected by copyright, and patents extend this protection to software techniques such as specific methods of cryptography or data compression. This means that a programmer cannot copy instructions from an existing program that implements these algorithms, nor create a new program that uses one of these algorithms.

Many computer scientists have argued that software patents should not exist at all, that such patents come too close to patenting an idea and not a specific invention. For example, some programs that work with text color-code the text to help the user understand what's being shown. This color-coding is not difficult for a programmer to do—it involves no new algorithm—but until fairly recently most programmers didn't think to do it. Is a program that color-codes text in a new way simply a new idea or a new invention?

Another problem is the definition of "obvious." A famous software patent involves spreadsheet recalculation. In a spreadsheet, the screen is divided into cells with numbers of labels in each cell. A good example is a grade book, with a row for each student and a column for each homework assignment and test. At the end of each row is a cell with a formula that computes that student's average, which determines the student's final grade in the course. Another cell at the bottom of that column computes the average score for the whole class, which the teacher could use to determine if the coursework for this term was too easy or too hard (see Figure 10.1).

Suppose the teacher needed to update a student's score for a homework assignment. This new score would affect both the average for that particular student and the overall class average. If the teacher is working this out by hand, he or she has to recalculate the average for that student before recalculating the average for the whole class, since the

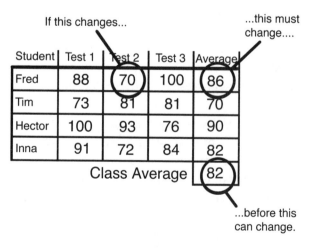

Figure 10.1—Natural Order Recalculation

latter value depends on the former. Early spreadsheets always recalculated from top to bottom, regardless of which cells depended on which other cells. Processing the cells in this fixed order meant that the spreadsheet would often have to cycle through the recalculation procedure several times before all the cells got the right values. With natural order recalculation, only one cycle is necessary, and soon all spreadsheet programs worked that way.

A patent was granted for this "natural order recalculation" idea. The patent was eventually overturned, but until it was, there was the possibility that every spreadsheet program would accrue some royalties for the patent holder. To most programmers, and even non-programmers, the natural order recalculation seems like an obvious idea, and that's all this patent is—an idea—because it does not describe a specific algorithm for actually doing the recalculation. Yet the patent was granted.

Patents in other fields encourage innovation. A pharmaceutical company must invest millions of dollars to develop and test new drugs. Drug patents allow the company to recoup its investment by being the sole provider of the drug for twenty years after it is introduced. Without this protection, any other company could immediately copy the formula, which means the company would have no incentive to develop the drug in the first place.

This situation does not seem to be paralleled in the software industry. Software developers distinguish their products not by the algorithms they employ, but by their implementation. Hundreds of word processing programs exist, for example. Every user has a favorite, which is typically based not on some innovative (and possibly patentable) feature, but on how well it provides the common features the user works with every day.

The patent office has issued so many broadly worded software patents that large software publishers are forced to stockpile patents (buying them from smaller developers if necessary) so that if they are threatened by another patent holder, they can agree to share patents rather than pay exorbitant licensing fees. This tactic means that the smaller publisher, the "little guy" you might hope that patents are supposed to protect, is in the worst position, with no patents to trade.

ETHICAL ISSUES

Although the Hippocratic oath does not use the exact words, "First, do no harm," that's the sentiment leading computer scientists want to instill into all areas of computer science.

Critical Software

At first, perhaps it's not clear why ethical issues in computer science are so important. Because a doctor, for instance, has the lives of patients in his or her hands, it is easy to see why ethics are so important in medicine. It's easy to forget, though, that bad software can be as dangerous as a bad doctor. Computer software runs the air traffic control system, calculates stress loads in construction projects, and stores the data that tells a doctor that a patient is allergic to penicillin. If an antimissile battery fails to fire at an incoming target because of a software glitch, lives will be lost.

Many other programs have dire (if not deadly) consequences for failure, from the software at the bank to the software that runs the roller coasters on Space Mountain. Even software as pedestrian as that which generates the bills for a telephone company could cause havoc with thousands of people's lives if a serious failure sent customers' bills to the wrong addresses.

As stated in previous chapters, computer scientists are starting to take software development as seriously as architectural engineers take construction. The Association for Computing Machinery, a professional organization for computer scientists, created a code of ethics in 1992. Like the Hippocratic oath for doctors, the ACM's code admonishes computer scientists to warn the client of all risks, to seek guidance when the practitioner is unsure, and to always act in a way that brings credit to the profession.

Hacking

The term hacker means different things to different people. To some, it is always a negative term, while others use it more broadly. The broadest definition of a *hacker* would be a computer expert who is capable of clever or novel solutions to computer problems. By this definition, a person in an office who is able to automate a budget forecast spreadsheet in a way no one else thought of would be a hacker.

A narrower definition of hacker is someone who gains unauthorized access to computer systems or performs mischievous or destructive computer-related activities, such as defacing a company's Web site.

The common thread in both definitions is the exploitation of unknown or poorly documented features. Hackers of all stripes enjoy finding out more about how a program works than anyone else. The hacker with the powerful spreadsheet may be using a cell func-

tion in a way the spreadsheet program's creators never anticipated. The hacker who has changed a company's Web site may have discovered a flaw in the Web server software.

The good and bad hackers, then, have similar personalities. What separates them is their ethics. Even among hackers of the narrower type, those who try to gain unauthorized access can be divided into two camps. Some may gain access but do nothing with that access, and merely report the problem in the software they exploited to the company that developed it. Others are there to do harm. Some call the former "white-hat hackers" and the latter "black-hat hackers."

Some people say that white-hat hacking, while still illegal, performs a valuable service and should be applauded or at least accommodated within the computing community. Others argue that the ends cannot justify the means and that performing an illegal act is wrong, even if to prevent other illegal acts. An analogy can be made with "homeland security" as it relates to airports. If a person sneaks a knife on board an airplane just to expose a weakness in the screening procedure, an illegal act has taken place, but overall, is this act good or bad?

COMPUTERS IN BUSINESS

The business world has seen great change from the introduction of computers. Whole industries have arisen that were not possible before their advent.

E-Commerce

One area where computers have clearly transformed business is *e-commerce*, the sale of goods and services through the Web. Sales have reached tens of billions of dollars per year. A few years ago e-commerce meant buying books or music CDs, but now people are buying stoves, automobiles, and everything else over the Web.

Customers like e-commerce Web sites for a number of reasons. The selection of items, for instance, is not limited by what one store in the mall can carry; comparison shopping is quick and easy; and you don't have to leave your home to go shopping.

Almost every major retailer has a Web site. This thinking has gone so far that many physical stores have computers in them to allow customers to access the company Web site. This use of computers is a tacit acknowledgment that the physical store can never provide as extensive a selection of products.

Companies have found an interesting "synergy" between physical stores and e-commerce Web sites. A customer of J. Crew, a clothing retailer, may visit the www.jcrew.com site, see a good-looking pair of pants at an acceptable price, and then drive to the local J. Crew store to try the pants on. Similarly, a customer browsing the racks at the J. Crew store may find a good-looking pair of pants but need it in a petite size that the store doesn't stock, and then drive home to see if the pants in that size are on the Web site.

While e-commerce is growing every year, it's still a small part of retail sales. The U.S. Commerce Department estimates that in 2004, e-commerce accounted for only about two percent of all retail sales. Even though e-commerce is a small piece of the retail pie, though, companies are working hard to get that piece because the profit potential is so high.

Consider a traditional department store like Macy's or Sears. These stores sell just about everything, aside from groceries and gasoline: housewares, tools, clothes for every member of the family, appliances, jewelry, and so on. The stores are huge, with expensive leases, floors and fixtures that must be cleaned every night, utility bills, and an army of sales associates.

In contrast, consider the purest example of big e-commerce, Amazon (www.amazon.com). This company grew from a simple Web-only bookstore to a place where you can buy almost everything, just like a department store, including CDs, appliances, sporting goods, clothes, and computers, in addition, of course, to their staple offering of books. Amazon, however, has no stores. Instead, it has an extensive Web site and a set of "fulfillment centers," which are warehouses where employees find the items customers order on the shelves and ship them out. One can imagine that the rent on a warehouse is a fraction of the rent on a department store.

One problem with e-commerce is taxation. Courts have ruled that mail-order business cannot be subject to state sales taxes as long as the company doesn't have a physical presence in that state, and Internet retailers have operated under this rule (Figure 10.2). Products from Amazon may not be subject to the sales taxes that a purchase from www.sears.com would be because Sears has a store in every state. Some traditional retailers have complained that this unfairly makes their products more expensive to consumers. After all, Sears actually employs local people in each of its stores, providing a community benefit beyond the taxes it collects, while Amazon has no employees at all in most states. State governments, of course, are upset because they are losing tax revenue.

Figure 10.2—Todd and Marta Buy CDs

Some states have tried to introduce a "use tax," with each taxpayer expected to track his or her own Internet and mail-order purchases, compute the tax they owe the state, and then add that amount to their tax bill when it comes time to file a tax return. Predictably, this method has not been successful. It's too easy for filers to simply not pay the use tax because there's no way for the state to know how much anyone should pay. Even if a taxpayer wants to pay the tax, it would require a diligent effort to track all of one's purchases. Sales taxes work because they place the burden of tax collection on the seller instead of the buyer.

ERP

ERP stands for Enterprise Resource Planning and refers to an integrated suite of applications to manage resource data from one end of a business to the other, including manufacturing, inventory control, and sales. A broader definition of the term that is sometimes used is the integration of all company data.

ERP originally caught on because companies were buying different software applications from different vendors for each area of the business. A company's factory, for example, might have inventory control software to track the reordering of parts for the products they make. Meanwhile, back at the corporate headquarters, the profit of each good sold would be tracked using accounting software. The two applications are completely separate and have no way to communicate with each other. When the accountants need a value for the part inventory held at the factory, they may resort to an estimate based on how many parts were purchased last year. If the two applications were connected, though, the part inventory could be accounted for in a precise and up-to-the-minute manner.

Despite the name, ERP is actually a tool for resource tracking, not planning. The application merely provides the data the user needs for planning. If a new contract starts in November that will result in higher production of a certain product, then the parts that make the product will need to be ordered in larger quantities at some point. The ERP software can help determine what that point is so that the factory orders the parts at the last possible moment, rather than stockpiling extra parts, which costs the company money. Delivering parts for manufacturing when they're needed is known as *just-in-time delivery*, abbreviated as JIT. The JIT principle would be very difficult to follow without computerized tracking of inventory.

The general benefit of ERP is that all parts of a company know what the rest of the company is doing. If orders are up on one end, parts can be ordered faster on the other end. If there's a problem with a part supplier, order takers on the other end know to adjust delivery dates for the finished products.

All of this works only if all employees "buy in" to the system and use it faithfully. One of the lessons learned from the widespread adoption of ERP systems is that once people are comfortable with a system, they are reluctant to change, regardless of the supposed benefits. In companies where sales staff traditionally took orders on paper forms, the introduction of an ERP system seemed to increase the sales staff's workload without a benefit, because instead of dropping the paper forms and entering everything in the ERP system, they would use the paper form as before and then copy the data from the form to the ERP system, duplicating work. When the staff needed to reference the data, they used the forms they knew how to use, not the ERP system. Although the data they entered may have been useful to other segments of the company, it appeared to the staff that they were doing more work and getting nothing out of it.

The companies that have most successfully migrated to ERP systems seem to be those that were willing to modify their business practices to meet the design of the system, rather than trying to mitigate the changes the new system brought about. While a major change in corporate culture is uncomfortable for employees, the benefits of ERP will not be realized with halfhearted implementation.

COMPUTERS IN EDUCATION

Computers have been involved in education since the introduction of the personal computer. The original Apple computer, for example, gained widespread popularity after Apple donated large numbers of them to schools.

Interaction with Children

Twenty years ago, a computer in a classroom was a rarity, something for the teachers and students to marvel at but not a central part of the educational experience. Computers were for adults, not children. Now, computers are common in classrooms, and children regularly use them at school and at home. The National Center for Educational Statistics reports that ninety percent of children use computers either at school, at home, or both, and about half use the Internet.

One purpose of computers in education is to expose children to computer use, since it's increasingly likely they will have to use a computer at some point in their careers. Another purpose is to enhance their learning in traditional subjects, like reading and math. Children often seem to learn better when lessons are reinforced with computer-based activities. The reason for this is not entirely clear. Children may be benefiting from the direct and immediate feedback a computer program can provide, or it may simply be that learning with a computer is more fun.

A marked example of this occurs with autistic children. Autism is a disorder that starts in young children, impairing the development of communication and social skills. Depending on the severity, an autistic child may appear very shy or could be prone to outbursts when exposed to too much stimulation, as in a crowded room. Such children are difficult to educate using traditional classroom techniques. Many autistic children, though, respond very well to computers. A child with poor language skills overall may be able to log into a computer and type in the name of a favorite Web site in a browser. A child who is easily distracted by any activity in the classroom can focus on a computer program for hours.

It's not clear why autistic children do so well with computers. Some have theorized that because the computer requires their focused attention, autistic children can block out other stimuli in a way they cannot normally do.

Distance Education

One negative aspect of rapid technology advancement for some people is that the skills and knowledge they learned in school are not as important once they've been in the workforce for a decade or two. More than ever before, people are finding it necessary to leave the careers they started with, and even those who stay find themselves falling behind because of technological change. It's no longer enough for people working with technology to keep up by reading magazine articles and attending the occasional one-day seminar.

People in both groups need a formal education to ensure that they have mastered the new skills and knowledge and can apply them to future projects. In short, they need to go back to college. This presents a problem for most people in these groups, however. For "traditional" college students, those who have recently graduated from high school, the main barrier to attending a college is money. For these new types of students, the main barrier is time. The term *adult learner* refers to a student who hasn't been formally educated in a

few years but who has a host of real-world commitments that may take precedence over learning.

The most common of these commitments are work and family. Traditional students may hold jobs while attending classes, but these tend to be part-time jobs, and in fields outside their intended careers. Adult learners, though, may already have full-time jobs they can't afford to give up, and may even be working in their chosen field but need more education to keep their jobs or to climb the corporate hierarchy. They are unable to attend classes during normal working hours, which is when most college courses are offered. The other commitment is family. Adult learners often have spouses and children, which means that events like Little League games and kitchen remodeling take precedence over attending classes.

Thankfully, technology can help solve some of the problems it creates. In this case, *distance education*, a form of learning in which students do not have to physically attend classes, allows adult learners to take courses and earn degrees while still meeting all the demands of "real life."

Distance education grew out of correspondence schools, in which students received boxes of materials through the mail, worked through tests on their own time, and then delivered the completed work back to the school through the mail. While this allowed the student to avoid any predefined "class time," there was almost no interaction between the student and the school. The student often felt alone and unmotivated.

The Internet changed this, as it changed so many things. A distance education school may use postal mail to deliver some materials like textbooks, but most of the learning process is geared toward e-mail and the school's Web site. Through chat rooms and discussion boards on the site, students can meet other students, discuss problems concerning their schoolwork (and about fitting schoolwork into their lives), turn in assignments, check grades, and do everything else students do. Depending on how the program works, the student may need to log in to the school's Web site at a particular time, but even if that is required, it's not as onerous as with a traditional class, because the student remains at home.

The Internet could also facilitate the social aspects of learning for geographically diverse students. Schools might have a "pep rally" in a chat room every month, though instead of rallying for a team, it would be an excuse for students and staff to get together, swap stories, and keep each other motivated to get that next assignment turned in.

Ten years ago distance education was considered second-tier, but with many top traditional schools now offering courses in this fashion, this is no longer the case. Distance education has become a major industry, and some software now targets it directly. For example, many schools offering distance learning rely on a computer program called a *learning management system*, or LMS, which allows course instructors to easily post content into the courses, arrange class meetings, distribute the course syllabus, as well as provide a "drop box" for student assignments. The two largest companies in this area are BlackBoard and WebCT. These programs have become so popular that many textbook publishers make test banks and other supplementary materials available in compatible formats.

COMPUTERS IN ENTERTAINMENT

Early in their history, computers were seen as entertainment. The first computer game, "Spacewar," was implemented way back in 1962. Since that time, a huge industry has grown up around computer games. In addition, computers are increasingly used in filmmaking.

Computer Game Industry

Computer games are played on a personal computer, while video games are those played on a console system (like a PlayStation 2) or as a stand-alone game in an arcade. The two have grown to the point where they rival Hollywood in revenue.

A hit computer game, though, is much more profitable than a hit film because it can be created for much less money. Both a hit game or film can bring in hundreds of millions of dollars in sales, but a major film costs $50 million or even $100 million to create and promote, and the most expensive game production cycles are under $10 million.

Movies and games hire many of the same sorts of people. They both employ artists to design the images the customer sees, composers and sound engineers to orchestrate what the customer hears, writers to develop the stories, and producers to run the business end of development. Computer games, of course, also employ teams of programmers, who, although well paid, get considerably less money than movie stars, whose salaries probably account for a large part of the overall cost difference.

Some game companies, however, make money not just from selling the games. Video game console makers, like Nintendo and its GameCube, and Sony with the PlayStation 2, collect a royalty on every game sold. (They actually price their consoles at or below cost, which means they make no money from the consoles themselves.) These royalty payments contribute to the higher average cost of video games compared to computer games.

Game companies also make money licensing their technology for other games. When Epic Games released the game "Unreal Tournament," it was not only a game they could make money on, but also a showcase for the latest revision of their Unreal game engine. The engine provides not only graphics rendering (in Chapter 8 we noted that 3-D graphics renderers are hot commodities), but also provides support for sounds, music, networking (for multiplayer games played over a network), and more. The engine has been used not only for Epic Games products, but also for a host of other popular games, including "Deus Ex: Invisible War" and "Splinter Cell." Because of additional revenue from the licensing deals, Epic games can warrant spending more time and money on the engine's development than if they were using it only for their own titles.

Another emerging profit center for companies is the *MMORPG*, which stands for Massively Multiplayer On-line Role-Playing Game. These games support enormous and persistent online virtual worlds in which thousands of players at a time journey. A good example is "City of Heroes," a game in which players design superheroes, outfit them with costumes and superpowers, and then rove the streets of Paragon City dispensing justice to computer-controlled thugs and supervillains. Each player must be running the game software on his or her PC, but connects through the Internet to the virtual world, which is housed on servers run by the game's developers. Because there's no game without those servers, each player must pay fifteen dollars each month to play.

With MMORPGs, the longer you play a game, the more money the game company makes—in addition to the initial price of the game itself (which often includes a free month of play). Cryptic Studios, the developer of "City of Heroes," says that its subscriber base exceeded 180,000 after only a few months. At fifteen dollars a player, that works out to almost $3 million per month in subscriber fees, and "City of Heroes" is one of the smaller games. Other MMORPGs have much larger subscriber bases.

Films

More and more computers are used to create the worlds seen in feature films. Special effects that were once created using models, painted backdrops, and puppets now employ computer graphics. Visuals produced on a computer to be composited into a film are known as *computer-generated imagery*, or CGI. Knowledgeable filmgoers seeing a tricky shot on the screen might whisper, "Was that real, or CGI?"

Computer graphics were slow to catch on in films. Early uses of the technique, such as the stained-glass knight who figures in the climax of *Young Sherlock Holmes* (1985), were small key elements in films that otherwise relied on traditional special effects. Other films that used extensive computer graphics, like *Tron* (1982), displayed images that were intended to look artificial—most of *Tron* is a visualization of a world inside a computer.

A watershed moment come with the release of *Jurassic Park* in 1993, a film about breeding dinosaurs in the present using ancient DNA. For the film to work, the dinosaurs had to appear as real as the human players. Because director Steven Spielberg wasn't sure if computer graphics were up to the task, he commissioned both a computer graphics team and a second team to create dinosaur puppets, including an animated Tyrannosaurus rex figure that weighed over 10,000 pounds. Spielberg found himself using the computer graphics much more than he'd originally planned, including some shots that had nothing to do with dinosaurs. In one shot, the character Lex Murphy is seen from above, hanging from a tile ceiling as velociraptors approach on the floor below. The shot was performed by the character's stunt double, who inadvertently looked up into the camera. Rather than reshoot the scene, the computer animators pasted the face of actress Ariana Richards over that of the stunt double.

When the film was released, audiences saw dinosaurs they could believe in, couldn't tell when they were looking at puppets or at graphics, and had no idea it wasn't Ariana Richards hanging on for dear life from that ceiling. The movie created a new way of thinking about fantastic visuals in films. Before then, there were technical limitations on what films could show. Plenty of movies before *Jurassic Park* had included dinosaurs, but none approached that sense of realism. Now, films are limited only by their budget for computer effects and the imaginations of the artists.

It should be said that this is not entirely a good thing. A "more realistic" image is not always a "better" one. Some avid filmgoers prefer black-and-white images over color, for example, even though color is more realistic. Similarly, the yellow brick road through the woods in *The Wizard of Oz* leads to an obviously painted backdrop on a soundstage, yet its dreamlike image tends to stay in the mind after more plausible images have left. Like every other advance in film history, including sound recording and widescreen formats like Cinemascope, computer-generated imagery merely widens the possibilities. It still takes an artist to use these tools to make something special.

SUMMARY

As increasingly large stores of data develop in companies' databases, consumers are becoming more concerned about privacy. Data that was intended to be anonymous can sometimes be linked with an individual. Many people are also concerned with how the Internet allows anyone, including children, easy access to pornographic and otherwise objectionable material.

Copyright and patent protections have served authors and inventors well, but these protections are problematic when applied to software. Copyright tends to break down when it is easy to violate, as is often the case with software. Patents do not seem to have more negatives versus positives when applied to software as opposed to other inventions.

Computer science must adopt the same high standard of ethics as professionals in other fields. Computers and software are too interwoven in our lives to do otherwise.

The popularity of e-commerce, shopping for goods and services over the World Wide Web, is increasing. E-commerce allows companies to sell without the overhead costs involved with retail stores. But state and local governments are concerned over the loss of sales taxes, because e-commerce purchases are not taxed at the point of sale like those at traditional retailers.

Enterprise resource planning, or ERP, is software that allows resources involved with production to be tracked throughout a company. This level of tracking allows companies to plan well enough to avoid costly inventories.

Computers can play a vital role in education. Children often respond better to instruction when they are more in control of it, as they are with computer-based education. Distance education allows adult learners to gain new knowledge and skills without conforming to a traditional class schedule.

Computer gaming has evolved into an industry that rivals Hollywood, while Hollywood itself turns to computers both for the creation of wondrous visuals and to make alterations and corrections that otherwise would have required expensive reshooting.

GLOSSARY

abacus
A mechanical device with beads sliding on rods, which is used as a counting device.

accessibility
Ease of use for people with disabilities.

acknowledgment
A short message sent in the opposite direction of the original message on a network, to tell the sender that the original message arrived. Also called an ACK.

address
A whole number, starting from 0, that identifies the location of a word in RAM.

adult learner
A student who hasn't been formally educated in a few years but has a host of real-world commitments that may take precedence over learning.

algorithm
A series of instructions that define how to solve a problem.

alpha blending
A trick for operating systems that show menus and boxes of text that seem to "fade" into and out of existence. A value called "alpha" is used to indicate a bitmap's transparency.

alpha channel
Extra bits used for each pixel, to indicate something other than the color; for example, transparency.

alpha testing
Testing performed by members of the programming team.

ALU
Arithmetic Logic Unit. The part of the CPU that performs mathematical calculations and logical operations.

analog
Describes data with continuous values, like a dimmer switch on a lamp. The opposite of analog is digital.

anchor tag
A link in a web page to another web page or to a different place on the same page.

anti-aliasing
The use of subtle shadings of pixels to smooth out the appearance of curves and lines.

application software
Programs that provide specific services to the user. Examples of application software include programs for word processing, e-mail, computer games, financial management, spreadsheets, and image manipulation.

applications programmer
Someone who writes programs, such as Microsoft Word, directly for users.

artificial intelligence
A field in computer science that involves programming computers to perform tasks that require intelligence if humans were performing the tasks.

assembly language
Machine language written in a human-readable form.

authentication
The technique of confirming the identity of a message's sender. Public-key cryptography allows for authentication.

backbone
A major pathway in a network.

background task
A program that receives no direct user interaction. An example of a background task is a print spooler.

backup
A copy of all the data on a computer's primary storage devices, or at least all the data that cannot be easily replaced.

backward chaining
An inference method that starts with the goal and works back toward the facts.

backwards compatibility
For processors, the principle of ensuring that programs that execute on a previous version of a processor will execute on the new one. In general, the principle of ensuring that a new version of a program or hardware device works seamlessly with everything that the previous version did.

bandwidth
The amount of data that a particular network can transfer in a given time frame. Usually measured in bits per second.

batch processing
The process of having an operating system execute only one program at a time.

benchmarking
The practice of running the same program on multiple computer systems and timing the results.

best effort delivery
A network service that performs no error checking, does not track the message, and doesn't ensure that the message is delivered.

beta testing
Testing performed by users or potential users.

binary
Having two states. In the computer's case, the two states are off or on.

binary digit
A single on/off indicator, written as a 0 or 1. Also called a bit.

BIOS
Basic Input/Output System. A set of small programs that is stored in ROM. When a computer's power is turned on, the BIOS loads the operating system.

bit
A single on/off indicator, written as a 0 or 1. Short for binary digit.

bit blit
A bit-block transfer, which is the copying of one bitmap into another.

bitmap
A rectangular block of pixels that can be referenced using coordinates.

bits per sample
A measurement indicating how large a range is given to each quantized value during sampling.

black box testing
Testing in which the testers do not have any knowledge of the inner workings of the program.

blocked process
A process waiting for some event to happen.

Bluetooth
A network protocol for short-range wireless communication.

boot sector
A special location on the primary hard drive where the first part of the operating system is stored.

booting
The process by which a computer starts and executes the operating system. Short for "bootstrapping," which means to lift oneself up by one's own bootstraps.

bounce
The return of an e-mail to its sender because delivery was a failure.

bps
Bits per second. A measurement of transmission speed.

branch prediction
Logic to help a CPU guess how a numerical comparison will turn out, used in pipelined CPUs.

bridge
A node that logically divides a network into smaller subnetworks.

broadcasting
The technique of sending out a single message to multiple receivers at once.

browser
A program that displays HTML formatted documents. Also called a Web browser.

buffering
In a network, the technique of accumulating data before passing it on to the user.

bursty data
A network situation in which a sender transmits a lot more data than its average rate.

bus
An electrical path that connects the CPU, main memory, and all the other devices.

byte
A group of eight bits.

cable modem
A gateway that communicates between two different LAN protocols so that a home user's computer can communicate over the cable television line to make an Internet connection. Despite the name, a cable modem is not actually a modem.

cache
Fast-access memory that is used for faster retrieval than is possible from main memory.

capacitor
A device that stores a small electrical charge. In a computer, each capacitor stores one bit. If the capacitor is mostly charged, it's considered a 1 bit, and if it's close to empty, it's a 0.

case
The box that contains the circuitry of the actual computer, along with some devices and connections for others.

CAT scan
Computerized Axial Tomography scan. A method that produces a three-dimensional view using X rays.

CD-ROM
An optical disc used for storing computer data.

CD-ROM drive
A CD reader in a computer system.

CD-RW drive
An optical drive that can read discs and create discs using specially made blanks.

character
Any letter, digit, or other symbol that can be displayed by typing on a keyboard.

chat
Any application that allows a group of people to type text messages that are seen by everyone in the group.

chip
The CPU and other packaged circuits inside computers, so-named because of its small size and flat, square shape.

CISC
Complex Instruction Set Computer. A CPU with large numbers of powerful instructions.

client
A computer that uses a server for some service.

client side scripting
The technique of embedding small pieces of programming code in a web page, which is run on a user's machine in response to user interaction.

clock speed
The number of CPU cycles per second, given in Hertz (Hz), which is cycles per second.

coaxial cable
A network medium in which one wire is placed inside the other. This is the same cable used in cable television.

collision
In Ethernet, an incident in which two nodes try to send at the same time, the result being garbled data.

collision domain
In Ethernet, the maximum distance of wire between two nodes, so that the beginning of a message from one node reaches the other before the end of the message is sent.

COM
Component Object Model. Microsoft's solution for interoperability, which allows the building of applications using components from different developers.

compilation
The process of translating a high-level language into a machine language.

components
Programs that conform to some standard interface to facilitate interoperability.

compression
The technique of reducing the size of stored data.

computer
An electronic device for performing logical and mathematical operations based on the programs.

computer engineering
An extension of electrical engineering covering the design and analysis of computer hardware.

computer forensics
The study of breaking through security to retrieve partially deleted files for the purpose of obtaining and analyzing evidence to be used in a court trial.

computer game
A program that allows a user to play a game on a computer.

computer-generated imagery
Visuals that are produced on a computer to be composited into a film. Abbreviated CGI.

computer graphics
The generation of images through computers. This area ranges from simple text displays to images that appear to be in three dimensions.

computer science
The systematic study of computing processes. Computer scientists work primarily in the development of software, either at the practical level (improving the speed at which a web page performs a search) or the theoretical (exploring the limits of computers' recognition of human speech).

computer security
The study of how to protect data from unauthorized access.

computer vision
The technique of having a computer recognize real-world objects in still and moving images.

computer visualization
The pictorial display of data in a way that is most understandable for the user.

conditional execution
The process of executing a program instruction based on a condition tested when the instruction is reached.

control flow
The order in which program instructions are executed.

control structures
Elements of programming languages that determine control flow.

copy protection
Any technique that prevents unauthorized duplication of software or renders unauthorized duplicates useless.

copyright
The legal right to produce and sell a "work," such as a book or program.

CORBA
Common Object Request Broker Architecture. An open standard, which means it is supported by a nonprofit organization (in this case, the OMG, or Object Management Group) that any programmer or company may join.

CPU
Central Processing Unit. The device that actually performs the computing tasks. In a sense, the CPU is the computer.

cracking
The practice of modifying a program to remove its copy protection features.

crash
Incident in which a program halts prematurely.

crosstalk
A phenomenon that occurs when two network connections interfere with each other.

CRT
A cathode ray tube monitor, which works like a television.

cryptography
The study and practice of encrypting and decrypting messages.

CU
Control Unit. A device that controls the movement of data inside the CPU.

data link
The direct connection between two nodes in a network.

data mining
The practice of extracting hidden knowledge from the relationships among data.

data warehousing
A method of aggregating low-level data from multiple sources for further analysis.

database
In general usage, a machine-readable collection of facts, organized for easy retrieval and modification. In computer usage, organized collection of data that is stored in a computer-readable form.

decompression
The technique of returning compressed data to its original state.

defragmenter
A program that carefully shuffles the file fragments on a hard drive to get the files contiguous again, improving performance.

design
The phase of software development that creates the blueprint for the software's creation.

device
In computer science, any hardware component.

device driver
Software that acts as a middleman between the operating system and a device.

digital
Describes data stored in binary form. All digital data is discrete. The opposite of digital is analog.

digital camera
A camera that uses optical sensors to capture a photo directly in digital form.

Digital Millennium Copyright Act
A law passed in 1998 that added a number of provisions, some of them controversial, to copyright law as it applies to technology. Abbreviated DMCA.

discrete
Describes data with distinct values, like a lamp that is either on or off.

display adapter
A specialized device that produces the images for the computer monitor. Also called a "graphics card."

display buffer
A block of memory in a computer that stores the data for each pixel in the display.

distance education
A form of learning in which students do not have to physically attend classes.

domain name
A unique name given to Internet nodes so users do not have to memorize IP addresses.

domain name server
A computer on the Internet that can return the IP address for a given domain name. Abbreviated DNS.

dongle
A device that plugs into a computer port (like a printer or USB port), which must be present for a particular program to execute.

dot pitch
The distance between phosphors of the same color on a CRT monitor.

dot-matrix printer
A printer that works by pressing an inked ribbon against the paper with a set of pins.

double-buffering
A technique in which all the graphics are drawn to an off-screen bitmap, which then becomes the display buffer.

downstream
Describes the direction of data flow from the Internet to the user's computer.

DSL
Digital Subscriber Line. A method of connecting to the Internet that transmits data digitally over normal phone lines.

dual-core processor
The combination of two logically independent processors on the same chip.

DVD
An optical disc of much greater capacity than a CD-ROM. The name DVD originally stood for Digital Video Disc because it was developed to store movies digitally, but it was later changed to Digital Versatile Disc because any kind of data can be stored on a DVD, just like a CD.

DVD drive
A device in a computer system for reading DVDs.

dye sublimation printer
A printer that works by heating a ribbon so that the solid ink inside turns into a gas and then seeps into the paper.

dynamic memory allocation
A request for main memory that occurs during a program's execution.

dynamic RAM
Memory that uses capacitors that must be recharged periodically. Slower but cheaper than static RAM.

dynamic web page
A web page that is generated when the user requests it, rather than being created once and simply copied to the user.

e-commerce
The sale of goods and services through the Web.

EIDE
Enhanced Integrated Drive Electronics. An improved version of IDE, which allows for faster data transmission and larger hard drives.

e-mail
Messages, most often text, sent across a network from one user to one or more users.

e-mail client
A program that allows a user to receive electronic messages. Called a "client" because it interacts with a server to send and retrieve e-mail.

embedded system
A computer and program in one self-contained package; for example, a "smart appliance" such as a DVD player.

encryption
The technique of encoding a message so it can only be read by the intended receiver.

ERP
Enterprise Resource Planning. An integrated suite of applications to manage resource data from one end of a business to the other, including manufacturing, inventory control, and sales.

error correction
A scheme in some network protocols that allows an original message to be recovered even with some corruption of bits.

error detection
Rules in a protocol that help identify whether some bits in a message have been changed during transmission.

Ethernet
A set of popular LAN protocols that use different media and have different capacities.

event
A specific action that produces a reaction in some program. For example, mouse clicks and keystrokes are user-initiated events.

executable
A program in the form of a machine language. Also called "machine code."

expert system
A program with a knowledge base derived from a human expert and which is used to make decisions in that expert's area.

extreme programming
A software development paradigm emphasizing team programming and code modules that can test themselves.

file
A collection of data on a storage device.

file management
The ability to read and modify files on storage devices and to create and delete files. A responsibility of the operating system.

financial software
A program that tracks a user's financial accounts or prepares finance-related paperwork, such as tax forms.

Firewire
A high-speed serial bus intended for connecting computers with video devices like camcorders and digital cameras.

flag day
A change that is not backwards compatible, requiring all users to implement the change on the same day.

floppy disk
A flexible circle of plastic that stores data magnetically (like a tape drive). Today's floppy disks are stored in rigid shells, but it's the disk inside that's "floppy," not the casing.

floppy drive
A device to read and write floppy disks.

flow control
A method in network protocols for allowing the receiver to control how often messages are sent by the sender.

font
A set of styles for each possible character, including letters, numbers, and punctuation.

forward chaining
An inference method that starts from the base facts and tries to progress toward the goal.

fragmentation
A situation with hard drives in which files have been split up into small pieces across the disk.

frame
A complete drawing cycle in a computer-generated animation.

frame rate
In a computer-generated animation, the number of buffer switches a program performs in a second.

Frame Relay
A high speed network protocol used for connecting LANs to make a WAN.

FTP
File Transfer Protocol. A mechanism for transferring files across the Internet.

full-duplex
A transmission involving two computers sending to each other across a network at the same time.

fuser
A set of very hot rollers inside a laser printer that melt the ink into the paper.

fuzzy set
A set that offers partial membership. In a "rich" fuzzy set, Bill Gates could be a 100 percent member, while someone with $100,000 in the bank could be a twenty percent member.

gamepad
An input device specialized for controlling games.

gateway
A node that connects two different kinds of networks.

GIF file
Graphics Interchange Format file. A file that uses lossless compression to store an image with a maximum of 256 different colors.

Gopher
A mechanism for publishing both files and menus on the Internet.

GPU
Graphics Processing Unit. A processor specialized for rendering 3-D scenes.

graphical user interface
A method of computer use, mostly visual with little text. Chief features are windows on the screen and a mouse.

graphics card
A specialized device that produces the images for the computer monitor. Also called a "display adapter."

graphics primitives
Shapes like points, lines, curves, rectangles, and circles that can be drawn on the monitor.

hacker
Broadly, a computer expert who is capable of clever or novel solutions to computer problems. More narrowly, someone who gains unauthorized access to computer systems or performs mischievous or destructive computer-related activities.

half-duplex
A transmission involving two computers sending to each other across a network, but only one can be sending at a time.

hard drive
A device that stores data on a rigid magnetized disk or set of disks.

hardware
The physical devices that make up a computer system, both those inside the computer "case" and those outside the case, like monitors, keyboards, and mice.

head
A small electromagnet that produces or retrieves signals from magnetic media. Also called a "read/write head."

heatsink
A metal block with fins that draws away heat from the CPU.

Hertz
Cycles per second. Abbreviated Hz.

hidden line removal
In a 3-D scene, the removal of parts of triangles that are obscured by others.

hop-count
The number of network nodes a message must pass through to reach a particular computer.

hot-swapping
A feature that allows safe plugging or unplugging of devices while the computer is running.

HTML
HyperText Markup Language. A combination of plain text and specially formatted instructions that indicate how the text should appear.

hybrid language
A programming language that does not enforce a single programming paradigm.

hypertext
A document containing embedded links to other documents.

icon
A very small bitmap.

IDE
Integrated Drive Electronics. A standard interface for connecting hard drives and optical drives.

illustration program
A program that imitates an artist's traditional tools.

image manipulation
The technique of altering images using software, such as Adobe's Photoshop.

implementation
The phase of software development in which the program is actually written.

index
A database table that relates a single item back to the records in which that item is found and that is designed to be quickly searched.

inference
The process of reaching a conclusion through logical rules.

inference engine
A program that uses inference to answer questions about a knowledge base.

information hiding
The practice of placing data out of direct reach. Information hiding is a key principle of object-oriented programming.

information systems
The study of how computing technology is used in business.

information technology
The design, development, and implementation of computer hardware and software.

ink-jet printer
A printer that works by spraying ink at the paper.

input device
A device used to give data to the computer.

installation
A process in which software is copied onto the hard drive and registration steps are taken to connect the software to the operating system, including making the new software appear in the operating system's "list of programs."

instant messaging
An application similar to chat, in which two users can exchange text messages and have the messages arrive immediately.

interface
A particular device's method of communication with the rest of the computer.

Internet
The worldwide internetwork that developed out of the NSFNET project.

Internet Service Provider
A company that provides connections to the Internet. Abbreviated ISP.

Internet2
A consortium of universities and government agencies working to develop the next version of the Internet. The current network created by Internet2 is called "Abilene."

internetwork
A network of networks. Also called an internet.

interoperability
The ability of different pieces of hardware and software to communicate with each other.

IP address
A numerical address that identifies a node on the Internet.

IRC
Internet Relay Chat. An Internet-based protocol for chatting.

join
A database operation that matches rows in two different database tables based on a specified column they both share.

JPEG file
Joint Photography Experts Group file. A file that uses lossy compression to store images of any color range. The JPEG format was designed to store photographs digitally.

just-in-time delivery
The practice of delivering parts for manufacturing just when they are needed.

kerning
An indication of how characters should be spaced relative to one another.

killer app
An application of a new technology that convinces people to buy the technology.

knowledge base
Facts and rules organized into a repository for use by artificial intelligence techniques.

laptop
A compact personal computer with all the devices shrunk into one container to make the computer easily portable.

laser printer
A printer that works using electrostatic principles to transfer the ink to the paper.

LCD
A liquid crystal display. In computers, a monitor that uses a liquid crystal display.

learning management system
A program used by distance educators that allows instructors to post content into courses, arrange class meetings, and distribute the course syllabus, as well as provide a "drop box" for student assignments. Abbreviated LMS.

level of abstraction
The distance between a particular view of a situation and the concrete reality. In general, the term describes whether someone has a "big picture" view or is focused on details.

local area network
A network that connects computers in a single building, or in adjacent buildings. Abbreviated LAN.

local loop
A pair of wires leading from a home or office to a building known as a central office, or CO.

logic circuit
A particular way to connect a group of transistors.

logical tag
A tag like <em>, which describes how HTML text relates to the document, rather than how it actually appears.

looping
The process of executing the same program instructions more than once. Also called "repetitive execution."

lossless compression
Compression that returns the data to its exact original form.

lossy compression
Compression that loses some part of the original data so that when the data is decompressed it is a little different than it was originally.

machine code
A program in the form of a machine language. Also called "an executable."

machine language
The format of computer instructions specific to a particular model of CPU.

main memory
The internal component of the computer where programs and data are stored while it is on.

mainframe
A powerful computer that is shared by multiple users at one time.

maintenance
Support and additional development of a program after it has been released to the users.

malware
Short for "malicious software." All the programs that users don't want on their systems, including viruses, Trojan horses, and spyware.

media
The plural of medium.

medium
The physical connection a message in a network crosses to get from sender to receiver.

memory leak
A block of memory that is allocated but unused, the result of a program neglecting to deallocate dynamic memory it no longer needs.

memory management
Services associated with the allocation of main memory.

message
Data transmitted across a network.

meta tag
A tag in an HTML document that provides information about the page's content. Meta tags are useful for indexing the pages and may also aid browsers in displaying the page properly.

minicomputer
A computer powerful enough to be used by multiple people but not powerful enough to be considered a mainframe. This term is fading from use.

MMORPG
Massively Multiplayer On-line Role-Playing Game. A computer game that supports an enormous, persistent online virtual world through which thousands of players at a time journey.

modem
A device that can convert a digital signal to an analog signal, and vice versa. A modem is used in a dial-up connection to the Internet.

modulation
The opposite of sampling, this process takes numbers and converts them back into continuous analog signals.

monitor
A computer display screen.

motherboard
A large circuit board that contains the components inside a computer, including the CPU, RAM, and connections for other devices, like the hard drive and CD-ROM drive.

mouse
A device that moves a cursor (a small arrow or other "pointing" shape) on the screen as it is moved.

mouse pad
A square of specially designed material, smooth enough so a mouse ball doesn't "skip" but not so smooth that the ball slides without turning.

MS-DOS
Microsoft Disk Operating System. The operating system software for the original IBM PC computer.

multiprocessing
The use of multiple CPUs in the same computer.

multitasking
The process of having several programs running at once.

multitier database
An application that is broken into three layers: a data storage layer, a business logic layer, and an interface layer.

negative acknowledgment
A short message sent in the opposite direction of the original message on a network, to let the sender know the original message was garbled in transmission. Also called a "NACK."

network
A set of computers connected so they can share data.

network manager
Someone who keeps a network operational, connects new computers to a network as new employees are hired, upgrades the networking technology as needs change, and does other network tasks.

node
A computer connected to a network.

nonpreemptive multitasking
Multitasking in which the applications are responsible for giving up the CPU when their time slice is over.

normalization
The process of refining data tables into the form best suited for a database.

object-oriented programming
A programming paradigm in which instructions are grouped together with the data they operate on.

OLAP
On-Line Analytical Processing. A methodology that allows efficient data mining.

open-source
Describes a product that no one company owns or controls. Anyone can look at how the product works and even make suggestions on how to improve it.

operating system
The core program that allows the computer to function. When you turn on a computer, the program that starts to run before you touch the keyboard or the mouse is the operating system.

optical drive
A storage device that reads data using a laser and light sensor. CDs and DVDs are read by optical drives.

optical fiber
A network medium that transmits data as light along a thin glass or plastic filament.

optical mouse
A mouse that tracks the mouse position using an optical sensor, not a rolling ball.

output device
A device that transmits data from the computer back to the user.

page fault
A process request for a virtual memory range that is not currently in main memory.

pages
The blocks of physical memory that the operating system hands out.

parallel transmission
The transmission of bits in groups by having a wire for each bit that is sent.

parameter
A placeholder for an actual value in a procedure. The parameter's value is specified when the procedure is used.

parity
An error detection scheme in which the sender counts the 1's in the message and attaches a 1 to the end of the message if the count is odd and 0 if it is even. This means that in the final message that is sent, the number of 1 bits is always even.

patent
A property right that grants an inventor the ability to limit who produces or sells the invention.

performance
As applied to networks, the principle of ensuring that the message arrives at the receiver on time.

personal computer
A computer designed for use by one person at a time.

phosphor
One of the countless red, green, or blue dots from which images are created on a CRT monitor.

piconet
A small, ad hoc wireless network created under the Bluetooth protocol.

pipe
In Unix, a mechanism for setting the output of one program as the input of another program.

pipelining
The technique of breaking up instructions into smaller pieces so that their execution can overlap.

pixel
Short for "picture element," the smallest logical element of a computer's display.

platform-independent
The practice of producing programs that can be executed on different processors and operating systems.

PNG file
A file that uses lossless compression to store images. Unlike GIF files, PNG supports true color, including an alpha channel.

point-to-point connection
A network that connects just two computers.

POP3
The third version of a protocol called POP, or Post Office Protocol, which is used by an e-mail program that receives a message.

portable document format
Format developed by the Adobe Corporation to provide document designers with the kind of control unavailable in HTML. Abbreviated PDF.

preemptive multitasking
Multitasking in which CPU control automatically returns to the operating system after an application's time slice is up.

principle of locality
The idea that when a particular address in memory is accessed, it's likely that nearby addresses will be accessed soon.

printer
A device that outputs text or images to paper.

private-key cryptography
Cryptography in which the encryption key is the same as the decryption key.

procedural programming
A programming paradigm that defines the control flow necessary to solve a task, using procedures to divide the source code into functional units.

procedure
A named block of program instructions that, when referenced, results in execution of those instructions.

process management
The methods of keeping all the programs and background tasks executing in a multitasking computer. A responsibility of the operating system.

processor
A device that performs computing tasks. Includes CPUs, although processors can be used outside of the "central" role of a computer.

program
A series of steps to accomplish a given task. In general usage, a program is written in everyday English, such as instructions to register for a university class or to change a tire. In computer science, a program refers to a series of steps given to a computer.

programmer
Someone who creates programs.

proprietary
Describes a product owned or controlled by one company, which means that no one outside of that company knows exactly how the product works.

protocol
The set rules defining a network's function.

prototype
A rough version of a program, quickly created, that approximates the appearance of the final program but without all the final program's functions.

public-key cryptography
Cryptography in which the encryption key and decryption key are different.

punch card
A card that encodes data with holes in specific locations.

quantization
The process of converting an analog measurement to a number.

quantization error
The difference between analog data and its discrete representation.

query
A request made to a database for a subset of its data.

RAM
Random Access Memory. RAM is made of capacitors, which are devices that store small electrical charges. Main memory in a computer is made of RAM. The data in the memory can be accessed in any order.

random access device
A storage device that can jump to any point without going through the previous points first. Also called "direct access."

rapid prototyping paradigm
A software development plan in which the programming team creates a prototype as early in the process as possible.

ray tracing
A rendering technique that plots the progress of individual rays of light emanating from each light source in the scene.

read/write head
A small electromagnet that produces or retrieves signals from magnetic media. Also called a "head."

ready process
A process waiting for its turn to execute on the CPU.

real-time animation
Animation in which frames are generated as the user watches them.

receiver
A computer to which a message is transmitted across a network.

record
A row in a database table.

recordset
A set of records returned by a database as the result of a query.

refresh rate
The number of times per second the phosphors in a CRT are lit, given in Hertz, which is cycles per second.

register
A temporary storage location inside a CPU.

reidentification
The process of linking anonymous data to the actual identity of an individual.

relational database
A set of one or more tables of data with specifically defined relationships between the columns in one table and the columns in another.

reliability
As applied to networks, the principle of ensuring that the message that arrives to the receiver is the same message that left the sender.

removable media
A storage device that can be easily taken out of the computer and taken elsewhere. A floppy disk is removable media.

renderer
A program that performs the task of rendering.

rendering
The process of transforming the 3-D description of a scene into a 2-D bitmap for display.

repeater
A network device that reads a signal on one wire and reproduces it on another.

repetitive execution
The process of executing the same program instructions more than once. Also called "looping."

resolution
The number of pixel rows and columns a monitor is displaying.

RISC
Reduced Instruction Set Computers. A CPU with a small set of fast-executing instructions.

robot
A machine with moving parts controlled by a computer.

ROM
Storage space that can be read but not altered.

router
A node that forwards packets toward their destination.

routing
The process of determining the path a message in a network will take from the sender to the receiver.

run-length encoding
A compression method in which repetitions of the same number are replaced with a special notation.

running process
A process currently executing on the CPU.

sample rate
The number of measurements taken per second during sampling.

sampling
The process of taking analog measurements at intervals and then quantizing each measurement.

scanner
A device that converts printed images into computer images.

scatternet
In a Bluetooth network, multiple piconets linked together, with the master of one piconet playing the role of slave in another.

scripting language
A language in which the source code is processed by a program called an "interpreter," rather than compiled. Scripting languages are used for smaller tasks than compiled languages.

SCSI
Small Computer System Interface (pronounced "scuzzy"). A standard interface for hard drives and optical drives.

search engine
An application that allows users to find particular records or files from a large collection.

seek time
The length of time needed to move the heads over a specified track.

select statement
A query made using SQL, so-named because it starts with the word "select."

sender
A computer that transmits a message across a network.

sequential access device
A storage device in which data must be accessed in order. There's no easy way to jump immediately to a specific piece of data.

sequential execution
The process of executing program instructions in the order listed in the program.

serial transmission
The transmission of bits one at a time along the same wire.

server
A computer on a network that provides a service to other computers.

server side scripting
Programming performed on a Web server using a scripting language.

set
A group of items that share some quality.

shell
The part of the operating system that can be seen and interacted with.

shielded twisted pair
A twisted pair covered with a metal mesh that tends to reduce interference. Abbreviated STP.

simplex
A network connection of two computers in which only one computer can send messages.

sliding window
A method of flow control in which the sender and receiver agree to a set number of unacknowledged messages that can be in transit at any time.

SMTP
Simple Mail Transfer Protocol. The protocol used to transmit e-mail through the Internet.

sneakernet
A humorous term for putting files on disk and walking them from one user to another.

software
The programs the computer executes; for example, Microsoft Word, the computer game "Half-Life," or a program that displays on the cell phone to allow the owner to select a new ring-tone.

software engineer
A person involved in all stages of software development, from the initial meeting with prospective clients to installing updates to a program years after it is first developed.

software engineering
The branch of computer science that attempts to improve the process of making software.

software piracy
The practice of installing software without remuneration to the copyright holder.

sorting
The process of putting items in some order, like alphabetizing a list of student records by last name.

sound card
A device that produces the audio in a computer.

source code
A program in the form of a high-level language.

spam
E-mail messages that are commercial in nature, unsolicited, and usually sent in bulk to multiple addresses.

specification
The first step in a software development project that determines exactly what abilities the finished software will have.

spider
A program that "crawls" through references on Internet sites to find new sites and material.

spiral paradigm
A software development plan in which the phases of development are repeated over and over.

spreadsheet software
A program that provides a matrix of cells, in which each cell can be a number, a line of text, or a calculation involving the values in other cells.

spyware
Hidden software that tracks user activity and reports back to the program's developer.

SQL
Structured Query Language. The standard way to query a relational database. (Pronounced "sequel.")

static RAM
Memory that uses capacitors that hold their charge indefinitely. Faster but more expensive than dynamic RAM.

stop-and-wait
A method of flow control in which the sender sends a single message and does not send another until the first message's ACK is returned.

storage device
A device that keeps data for later use.

stored program concept
The idea of storing programs in the same memory as data.

stylesheet
A document that an HTML document can reference to determine how its text is displayed.

subpixel font rendering
An anti-aliasing technique developed for improving text display on LCD monitors.

suite
A set of applications sold as one package.

supercomputer
A computer that is among the fastest of current computers. Systems that were considered supercomputers ten years ago are ordinary in their abilities today.

swap file
Used in virtual memory, a special area on the hard drive used for the temporary storage of pages.

system manager
A person responsible for maintaining an existing computer system.

system software
All the programs necessary to run a computer. Chief among these programs is the operating system.

systems analyst
A person who makes decisions when whole systems must be introduced, upgraded, or replaced.

systems programmer
Someone who writes programs that operate computers behind the scenes. For example, a systems programmer would create the software that directs traffic around the Internet.

T1 line
A specific T-line service that is usually a twisted pair and provides a bandwidth of about 1.5 megabits per second.

T3 line
A bundle of T1 lines that provides a bandwidth of about 44 megabits per second.

tag
An instruction in an HTML document that tells a browser how to format the text.

tape drive
A storage device that records information on tape the same way an audio- or videocassette does—by creating a pattern of magnetic impulses on it.

task switching
The technique of pausing one process and starting another.

TCP
Transmission Control Protocol. A higher-level protocol for the Internet used alongside IP, TCP provides for message tracking, retransmitting, and error checking.

tearing
A visual artifact occurring in animation when part of an old frame is shown with part of the new.

terminal
A keyboard and screen combination used to access a mainframe or other powerful computer.

testing
The phase of software development that determines if the software meets the specifications and the design.

texture mapping
A technique in 3-D rendering in which a bitmap picture is applied to an object in the scene.

thrashing
A situation with virtual memory in which the main memory is so small versus the number of active processes that the computer spends most of its time swapping pages.

3-D graphics
Descriptive graphics that, unlike 2-D graphics, use three coordinates instead of two.

TIFF
Tagged Image Format File. A file that supports both lossy and lossless compression. The TIFF format is intended as a kind of universal format that can use the types of compression in GIF, PNG, or JPEG files.

time-slicing
A technique for multitasking on a single CPU in which the operating system runs a process for a short period of time (a fraction of a second), then sets it aside and runs another process for a while, and so on.

T-line
A line leased from a service provider to connect a business network to the Internet, and which comes in different levels for different bandwidth needs.

toner
A powder form of ink that has been given an electrostatic charge for use inside a laser printer.

tower
A computer case that is taller than it is wide and sits on the floor.

transaction
A set of commands issued to a database that must be executed in a block.

transistor
A device that allows one flow of current to control another. This is the basic bit manipulation control that allows computers to function.

Trojan horse
A program that masquerades as a legitimate piece of software but has a sinister ulterior function.

twisted pair
A network medium consisting of two copper wires braided together.

2-D graphics
A graphics system in which a coordinate pair (row and column) is used to reference a pixel.

unique key
A value that identifies a single record in a table in a database.

unshielded twisted pair
A twisted pair without any additional covering to reduce interference. Abbreviated UTP.

upstream
Describes the direction of data flow from the user's computer to the Internet.

USB
Universal Serial Bus. An interface for external components, like a mouse, keyboard, and printer.

user
A person who uses a software program or computer.

user authentication
The process of positively identifying a user, usually through a user name and password.

vacuum tube
A device that resembles a lightbulb through which one electrical current can control another.

virtual memory
A technique in which a larger main memory is simulated through the use of storage on the hard drive.

virtual reality
Through all-encompassing computer graphics and sensory feedback, an experience in which the outside world is temporarily blocked from our senses.

virus
A short piece of programming code that attaches itself to a legitimate program and attempts to replicate by copying itself to other programs.

von Neumann architecture
Another term for the stored program concept. However, John von Neumann did not invent the concept.

von Neumann bottleneck
A situation in which the speed of a computer is limited by the speed of main memory access.

waterfall paradigm
A software development plan in which the development phases are performed in order.

Web browser
A program that displays HTML formatted documents. Also just called a "browser."

web page
A single text document written in a special format called HTML for the Web.

Web site
A group of web pages stored under the same Internet domain.

white box testing
Testing in which the programmer uses his or her knowledge of the program to pinpoint locations of possible failure.

wide area network
A network that connects computers that are widely separated, either in different parts of a city or in different countries. Abbreviated WAN.

wireless
The transmission of data via electromagnetic waves through the air.

word
A cell in RAM, which may be a single byte (eight bits) or multiple bytes. Each word's location in RAM is specified by a unique address.

word processor
A program that allows a user to create, edit, and format textual documents.

workstation
A computer designed for use by one person at a time that is connected to a network.

World Wide Web
The entire collection of interrelated hypertext documents on the Internet. Also called WWW, or "the Web."

worm
A type of virus that spreads not only to other programs on the computer it has infected, but also across network links.

REFERENCES

Apple Computers, Apple Macintosh commercial, 1984. http://www.uriah.com/apple-qt/1984.html.

Association for Computing Machinery, "ACM Code of Ethics and Professional Conduct," 1992. http://www.acm.org/constitution/code.html.

Bell, Eona, and David Potter, "Computer Applications for People with Autism," 2001. http://www.nas.org.uk/nas/jsp/polopoly.jsp?d=303a=3276.

Bellis, Mary, "The History of the IBM PC," (n.d.). http://inventors.about.com/library/weekly/aa031599.htm.

Brain, Marshall, "How computer mice work," 2004. http://www.howstuffworks.com/mouse.htm.

Business Software Alliance, "Global Software Piracy Study," 2004. http://www.bsa.org/globalstudy.

Calore, Michael, "Internet2 and You," Webmonkey (The Web Developer's Resource), 2003. http://webmonkey.wired.com/webmonkey/03/08/index4a.html.

Da Cruz, Frank, "Herman Hollerith," 2004. http://www.columbia.edu/acis/history/hollerith.html.

Department of Computer Science and Engineering, Washington University in St. Louis, 2004. CSE. http://www.cse.seas.wustl.edu.

Dowler, Mike, "Beginners Guides: Legally Copying Software and Music," PC Stats, 2003. http://www.pcstats.com/articleview.cfm?articleid=868.

Fernandes, Luis, "A Brief History of the Abacus," 2003. http://www.ee.ryerson.ca:8080/~elf/abacus/history.html.

Fog, Agner, "Branch Prediction in the Pentium Family," *Dr. Dobb's Journal*, 2004. http://www.x86.org/articles/branch/branchprediction.htm.

Foley, James D., Andries van Dam, Steven K. Feiner, and John F. Hughes. *Computer Graphics: Principles and Practice* (2nd ed.). Boston: Addison-Wesley, 1991.

Forouzan, Behrouz A. *Data Communications and Networking* (4th ed.). New York: McGraw-Hill, 2004.

Friedrich, Otto, "Machine of the Year: The Computer Moves In," *Time*, January 3, 1983.

Gibson, Steve, "How Sub-pixel Font Rendering Works," 2003. http://grc.com/ctwhat.htm.

Great Idea Finder, The, "Invention of the Jacquard Loom," 2002. http://www.ideafinder.com/history/inventions/jacquard.htm.

Honda Corporation, ASIMO history, 2004. http://world.honda.com/ASIMO.

Howe, Walt, "A Brief History of the Internet," 2004. http://www.walthowe.com/navnet/history.html.

Hynes, Daniel W., "State Taxation of Internet Sales," The Taxpayers' Federation of Illinois, 2000. http://www.taxpayfedil.org/internet.htm.

Iowa State University, "John Vincent Atanasoff and the Birth of the Digital Computer," (n.d.). http://www.cs.iastate.edu/jva/jva-archive.shtml.

Irlam, Gordon, "Examples of Software Patents," (n.d.). http://www.base.com/software-patents/examples.html.

Koch, Christopher, "The ABCs of ERP," 2002. http://www.cio.com/research/erp/edit/erpbasics.html.

Leurs, L., "Decimal, Binary, Hexadecimal, and ASCII Table," 2001. http://www.prepressure.com/library/binhex.htm.

MacMillian, Robert, "Primer: Children, the Internet and Pornography," *Washington Post*, June 29, 2004.

Microsoft Corporation, "An Introduction to Professional Photo Printers," 2004. http://www.microsoft.com/windowsxp/using/digitalphotography/expert/proprinters.mspx.

Microsoft Corporation, "Windows Products and Technologies History," 2003. http://www.microsoft.com/windows/WinHistoryDesktop.mspx.

Moore, Gordon E., "Cramming More Components onto Integrated Circuits," *Electronics*, April 19, 1965.

NASA, "Mars Exploration Rover Mission," 2004. http://marsrovers.jpl.nasa.gov.

Object Management Group, "CORBA Basics," 2004. http://www.omg.org/gettingstarted/corbafaq.htm.

O'Connor, J. J., and E. F. Robertson, "Charles Babbage," 1998. http://www-gap.dcs.st-and.ac.uk/~history/ Mathematicians/Babbage.html.

O'Connor, J. J., and E. F. Robertson, "Donald Ervin Knuth," 1998. http://www-gap.dcs.st-and.ac.uk/ ~history/Mathematicians/Knuth.html.

Platt, John, "Optimal Filtering for Patterned Displays," *IEEE Signal Processing Letters* 7 (7), 2000: 179–80.

Professional Marketing Services, Inc., "How Dye Sublimation Printing Works," 2002. http://www.promarketinc. com/technical/dye_sub_process.html.

Quittner, Joseph, "Biography of Jeff Bezos," *Time*, January 4, 1999.

Russell, Stuart, and Peter Norvig. *Artificial Intelligence: A Modern Approach* (2nd ed.). New York: Prentice Hall, 2002.

Sebesta, Robert W. *Concepts of Programming Languages* (6th ed.). Boston: Addison Wesley, 2004.

Silberschatz, Abraham, Peter Baer Galvin, and Greg Gagne. *Operating System Concepts* (6th ed.). New York: John Wiley & Sons, 2001.

Stallman, Richard, "Software Patents—Obstacles to Software Development," speech given at University of Cambridge, February 25, 2002. Transcript available at http://www.cl.cam.ac.uk/~mgk25/ stallman-patents. html.

Taylor, Philip, "Pixel Shaders, Part 1: An Introduction," 2001. http://msdn.microsoft.com/library/default.asp?url=/ library/en-us/dndrive/html/directx09172001.asp.

Tuck, Mike, "The Real History of the GUI. Sitepoint," 2001. http://www.sitepoint.com/article/real-history-gui.

Turley, Jim, "Silicon 101," 2004. http://www. embedded.com/showArticle.jhtml? articleID=17501489.

Ullman, Jeffrey D. *Principles of Database and Knowledge-base Systems*. New York: W. H. Freeman, 1990.

Vogel, Harold R. *Entertainment Industry Economics*. Cambridge: Cambridge University Press, 2001.

Warford, J. Stanley. *Computer Systems* (2nd ed.). Sudbury, Massachusetts: Jones and Bartlett, 2002.

Weik, Martin H., "The ENIAC Story," *The Journal of the American Ordnance Association*. 1961.

Wong, Wylie, "Microsoft to Add 5,000 New Workers," CNet News, 2002. http://news.com.com/ 2100-1001-946300.html.

INDEX

NOTES